# Cohabiting Earth

# Cohabiting Earth

## Seeking a Bright Future for All Life

Edited by

**JOE GRAY AND EILEEN CRIST**

Published by State University of New York Press, Albany

© 2024 State University of New York

All rights reserved

Printed in the United States of America

No part of this book may be used or reproduced in any manner whatsoever without written permission. No part of this book may be stored in a retrieval system or transmitted in any form or by any means including electronic, electrostatic, magnetic tape, mechanical, photocopying, recording, or otherwise without the prior permission in writing of the publisher.

Links to third-party websites are provided as a convenience and for informational purposes only. They do not constitute an endorsement or an approval of any of the products, services, or opinions of the organization, companies, or individuals. SUNY Press bears no responsibility for the accuracy, legality, or content of a URL, the external website, or for that of subsequent websites.

For information, contact State University of New York Press, Albany, NY
www.sunypress.edu

### Library of Congress Cataloging-in-Publication Data

Name: Gray, Joe (Natural historian), editor. | Crist, Eileen, 1961– editor.
Title: Cohabiting Earth : seeking a bright future for all life / edited by Joe Gray and Eileen Crist.
Description: Albany : State University of New York Press, [2024] | Includes bibliographical references and index.
Identifiers: LCCN 2024010905 | ISBN 9781438499970 (hardcover : alk. paper) | ISBN 9781438499987 (ebook) | ISBN 9781438499963 (pbk. : alk. paper)
Subjects: LCSH: Social ecology. | Human ecology. | Nature—Effect of human beings on.
Classification: LCC HM861 .C64 2024 | DDC 304.2—dc23/eng/20240814
LC record available at https://lccn.loc.gov/2024010905

# Contents

Acknowledgments ix

Foreword xi
    *Stephanie Mills*

Introduction: Undoing Earth's Humanization 1
    *Eileen Crist and Joe Gray*

## Section One: Restraint

1. Restoring Balance through Procreative Responsibility 21
    *Nandita Bajaj and Kirsten Stade*

2. Restraint in Consumption 35
    *Luke Philip Plotica*

3. Technologies Fit for an Ecological Future 49
    *John Michael Greer*

4. Social Ecological Transformation of Economies: Where the Environmental Movement Went Wrong and What Is Needed 63
    *Clive L. Spash*

5. Artful Descent: An Aesthetics of Existence 79
    *Samuel Alexander*

## Section Two: Respect

6. Is It the Call of the Wild . . . or of Deep Law?
What Is the Moral Heart of Conservation? 97
*Freya Mathews*

7. Protecting, Restoring, and Rewilding Ecosystems 113
*Reed F. Noss*

8. Coexisting with Africa's Carnivores 129
*Tarik Bodasing*

9. For the Bounteous Beauty of the Living Seas 143
*Eileen Crist*

10. The Future of Food Production 163
*Ryan D. Andrews*

11. Human Identity, Oppression, and the Rigors of Hope 177
*Chelsea Batavia*

12. Respecting Nonhuman Life: The Guide for a Better Pathway
in Outdoor Recreation 193
*Joe Gray and Ian Whyte*

## Section Three: Reverence

13. Enchantment, Modernity, and Reverence for Nature 209
*Patrick Curry*

14. There Are Gods Here Too: For an Inhumanist
Animal Aesthetics 221
*Matthew Calarco*

15. Rediscovering Tree Sentience and Our Reverence for Life 235
*Simon Leadbeater and Helen Kopnina*

16. Seeking Ecosocial Cultural Change: Boldly Going beyond
Nature Deficit Disorder 251
*Sean Blenkinsop*

| | |
|---|---|
| 17. Gratitude Is a Way of Life<br>*Kathleen Dean Moore* | 267 |
| List of Contributors | 281 |
| Index | 287 |

# Acknowledgments

Chapter 4 is adapted from an article that first appeared in the *Ecological Citizen* (vol. 4, no. 1, 2020). Chapter 5 draws on work that is being undertaken for a book the author is writing, called *S M P L C T Y: Ecological Civilisation and the Will to Art*. Some early passages in chapter 6 are adapted from Mathews (2021a; 2021b; 2022). Chapter 9 is revised and updated from an article that first appeared in the *Ecological Citizen* (vol. 3, suppl. A 2019).

## References

Mathews, F. (2021a). From wilderness preservation to the fight for Lawlands. In R. Bartel, M. Branagan, F. Utley, & S. Harris (Eds.), *Rethinking Wilderness and the Wild: Conflict, Conservation and Co-existence* (pp. 254–73). Routledge.

Mathews, F. (2021b). Law in the Living Cosmos: The "ought" that is core to the "is." In J. Farris & B. P. Gocke (Eds.), *Routledge Handbook on Idealism and Immaterialism* (pp. 481–95). Routledge.

Mathews, F. (2022). Conservation needs to include a "story about feeling." *Biological Conservation, 272*, 109668. https://doi.org/10.1016/j.biocon.2022.109668

# Foreword

### Stephanie Mills

The manuscript of *Cohabiting Earth* arrived in early May 2023, just after I'd returned to Northern Michigan from three weeks as a tourist in Japan. I came home to the fresh marvel of a Northwoods spring, and a proposal by neighbors down the road to stage regular enduro motorcycle races on their land. Thus my state of mind as I read the book spun among worldviews, from Buddhist-Shinto decorousness and urban modernism to innocent exurban Mad Max motorheadism. Then the gathering of thinkers in this good book with their erudite, heartfelt biocentrism spun me back to a realm of ideas, practices, and philosophies that could lead to a bright future on Earth for all life, not just my kind. It's the sort of book that can cause you not just to think about what people are doing but to think about the thinking that drives the doing as well.

Reconnecting with this place, I resumed my evening walks and tacit practice, in meeting with more-than-human-nature, of greeting the Beloved. Spring hereabouts elicits many such greetings. Ambling down the road, away from the potential motorcycle course, off the pavement and along some scraps of woodland, I rejoiced to see that the blue cohosh were still around, and flowering. Bellwort with its yellow blossoms was gaudily everywhere in company with other, less showy ephemerals such as Dutchman's-breeches and meadow rue. After exotic travel, just to be walking by myself, breathing new-made oxygen and fugitive fragrances, seeing countless maple sprouts, was a mingled happiness. My silent salutation: "Gratitude to all you Beloveds for your beauty and example, your generosity, and for keeping faith with life." Reflecting on the gist of *Cohabiting Earth*, I got that appreciation of self-willed nature is not noblesse oblige but humble, indebted reverence.

The book enjoins the need for fundamental shifts in perception: knowing that life on Earth is not a human domain here for our pleasure and exploitation but a dynamic, near-infinite realm of sovereign beings with intrinsic rights to existence and evolutionary destinies. That said, owing to human agency, ash, beech, and hemlock are succumbing to invasive insects, and fungi and are vanishing from those nearby scraps of forest, indeed from most of their ranges. Woodlands everywhere are under all manner of assault. In them, every tree species hosts its own interdependent universes of birds, mammals, and insects, also perishing—swathes of life gone. As the absences compound, the imbalances grow grave. Countless local instances of deliberate and collateral habitat destruction are causing the extinction crisis. Confronting its systemic causes is among the aims of *Cohabiting Earth*. What's remarkable is that such deep engagement with the planetary plight somehow doesn't end in apocalypticism or technofantasy.

Walking on in the here and now I see that the one great hemlock still stands near the road in full foliage, a fallen ash tree lodged on an upper limb. Those tattered woods still hold life, Darwin's "endless forms most beautiful and most wonderful." They attest that Earth's ecosystems, some living, some dying, some beautiful, and some ravaged, still have the vital elements of resurgence. *Cohabiting Earth* is a project of finding fitting ways for humanity to forgo its civilizational errors and maladaptations, to abide within life's bounds and patterns and participate in that resurgence. Restraint, respect, and reverence—the three major themes of *Cohabiting Earth*—will be key.

The authors in this collection are kin to those doughty spring ephemerals, or the myriad maple seedlings, or the few warblers that returned this year. Despite countervailing forces, like those diverse more-than-human beings, they ally with life. Through their work they raise the glimmering possibility of a wilder world of equity and just proportion, of a renewed flourishing of all beings, including humans.

Neither an eco-apocalypse book nor a nature panegyric, *Cohabiting Earth* is a far cry from the *Hundred Simple Things You Can Do to Save the Earth* of yore, or even from today's latest climate disaster headlines. Although this wide-ranging collection of essays can serve as a trenchant introduction to the planetary crises of our time, it is not primarily concerned with what Thomas Berry once called "the human pathos."

There's much that's original and interesting in chapters on human overpopulation, consumerism, appropriate technologies, agriculture, economics, aesthetics, outdoor recreation, and the law of nature; on ecosystem protection, restoration, and rewilding; on the ghastly state of the industrially fished oceans; on coexisting with African carnivores, questions of dualisms, sentience, and human identity; on enchantment with the living world; on reverence for animals in their inhuman beauty; on tree sentience; on educating children with nature; and on gratitude. Not only are the authors generally brilliant, they are gutsy in questioning the "crackpot realism" of secular modernity.

*Cohabiting Earth* is an altogether thought-provoking encounter with the nexus of ecocide. It explores ideas to found an ecological civilization, proposing necessarily epochal moves to avert ecocide: ending industrial agriculture, forestry, and fishing. Ideologies of dominance, reductionism, objectification, rationalization, and anthropocentrism sanction our alienation from more-than-human nature, whereas a biocentric worldview might transform our species' role, per Aldo Leopold, from despot to "plain member and citizen" of the biotic community. For a bright future for *all* life, as called for in the book's subtitle, something's got to give. What's got to give way is human hegemony.

The inconvenient reality that the shift to an ecological civilization will require a humane, deliberate, and steady decline in human numbers recurs through many of the chapters. The implications—degrowth of our grossly overshot globalized industrial economy, relinquishing our violent, delusional technological hubris in favor of what one author calls *retrovation*, and a strategic enlargement, reconnection, and rewilding of Earth's self-willed terrains—are momentous. The ways and means of these great changes would be impossible to detail in full, but there are stars to steer by in *Cohabiting Earth*: clarity of reason, purpose, and intention.

The intellectual endeavor of developing serious ideas is hard work. With rigor and style, these authors are reclaiming the discourse from vaguenesses like "sustainability," "resilience," and "renewable." Some of the authors reckon with the many intellectual and linguistic structures of domination, keenly, and without cant. Others critically assess the politics of environmentalism and the history of conservation. There are careful parsings of terms such as *nature* and *wild*. The book abounds in liberatory views, gems of insight, and lapidary writing that repays close reading. Work like this, the opposite of tweets, will change the vernacular and advance ecocentric thought and practice.

Restraint, respect, and reverence—those major themes of *Cohabiting Earth*—are antitheses of today's degrading consumerist free-for-all. In this hoped-for and honorable lifeway, human cultures will abide by more-than-human nature's existential claims also to be and will rejoice in a resurgence of the wild not just as a source of rare orchids for possible cancer drugs or as a spectacle but as matrix. Humanity's evolutionary worthiness is never in question, but anthropocentrism absolutely is.

In a 1969 graduation speech on overpopulation and ecological destruction, in which I vowed to refrain from childbearing, I referred to humanity as a "great unthinking, unfeeling cancer." I've since had misgivings about that stark misanthropy (although seldom about the personal decision not to procreate). Crude as it is, in an age of extinctions, the humans-as-cancer metaphor is hard to avoid. But loathing our species leads to despair. These authors aim to prompt needful change, not quash spirits. Compassion and skill ground their work. By the means that come to their hands—philosophy, teaching, research, and work in the field—they show wisdom and care in their articulation of revolutionary ideas with tremendous implications.

With flashes of passion and luminous writing, through philosophical analysis, careful argument, surveys of recent scholarship, accounts of current conditions, and case studies, they outline the sociocultural, spiritual, and economic transformation that the moment requires.

The upshot will be quite another worldview and metaphysic than the one that won the West, modernized the East, and deracinated indigeneity. We have so much to unlearn—the many unconscious, unquestioned, or comfortable assumptions propelling this ecocidal civilization—and so much to learn, relearn, or imagine of genuine human dignity and purpose, of cohabitation with more-than-human nature. To seek such profound spiritual and civilizational change may seem impossibly visionary. Visionary it may be, yet the call itself gives reason to hope.

# Introduction

## Undoing Earth's Humanization

EILEEN CRIST AND JOE GRAY

> In the course of history, there comes a time when humanity is called to shift to a new level of consciousness, to reach a higher moral ground. A time when we have to shed our fear and give hope to each other. That time is now.
>
> —Wangari Maathai (2004)

The existential catastrophes that we are witnessing today—from pollution, depletion of fresh water, and degradation of soils, to extinctions, paroxysms of forest fires, and climate breakdown—clearly demonstrate that human well-being is in lockstep with that of nature's broader whole. For just as humanity's planetary overreach is devastating nonhuman populations everywhere, it is also gravely jeopardizing the prospects of a human future worth living. There is no "humans versus nature" trade-off: the thriving and malaise of both are inseparably entwined. It follows that the only effective solutions to the dire predicament shared by Earth's living communities will be those that strive for harmony between human presence and the rest of nature. At this moment in our history, though, we are badly off track, as evidenced, not least, in the expanding technosphere and the unfolding mass extinction event (Ceballos & Ehrlich, 2018; Elhacham et al., 2020).

In recent work, Sean Maxwell and colleagues reveal that the two key drivers of the extinction crisis are the killing of wild beings and agricultural expansion (Maxwell et al., 2016). Through the fatal impacts of these activities on habitats, species, and individuals, coupled with other formidable drivers such as infrastructural expansion, mass toxification, and anthropogenic changes in weather and seasonal patterns, we have forced life on Earth into a death spiral. The toppling of exploitation as modern humanity's modus operandi is long overdue. We must step down from our position of domination and begin to thrive alongside the countless others with whom we share the planet. In order to do so, we need nothing short of a new view of Earth and a new human identity that will enable us to cohabit Earth with grace and generosity. If we fail in this goal, then all is lost sooner or later.

Certain indicative Earth system trends warrant rehearsing. Some 80 to 90 percent of big fish have been destroyed. An average of nearly 70 percent of wild animal populations have been extinguished. Since 1870, half of the live coral reef cover has disappeared. With a 2°C warming above preindustrial levels, scientists estimate that coral reefs may decline to one percent of their former cover and the majority of terrestrial species will see their ranges shrink dramatically. Human plus domestic animal biomass now comprise 96 percent of the global vertebrate biomass, leaving a mere four percent for the wild ones. Yearly, 300 to 400 million tons of industrial toxic waste are dumped into Earth's waters (IPBES, 2019).

These catastrophic trends, among others, are not even static catastrophes, since humanity's demand for food, water, farm animal feed, energy, timber, metals, and other materials is expected to increase substantially over the coming decades, as are anthropogenic waste and pollution output. As unprecedented and foreboding as the facts confronting us are, however, they remain mostly unheeded by governments and policymakers. Relatedly, it is fair to say as a general statement that these dire trends are only vaguely (if at all) perceived by the public. Many people worldwide continue to ignore the precipitous decline of the planet's living systems and wild beings. The reasons for the disconnect include, but go well beyond, urbanization and ecological illiteracy: much of humanity inhabits today's catastrophic trends as the *reality* of Earth's humanization; and Earth's humanization is starkly displayed in the expansion of the technosphere.

The technosphere today has become the planetary sea, while what remains of wild and free nature—that is, of the autonomous and self-governed nonhuman domain—resembles islands. Further, these islands are shrinking and becoming evermore degraded. Meanwhile the modern technosphere, especially since the turn of the 20th century, has been expanding in leaps and bounds. The technosphere is defined as the totality of the human-built environment and objects. It includes everything manmade, such as houses, airports, highways, ships, cars, paper, pavement, kitchenware, factories, the electric grid, clothing, electronic devices, and so on and so forth. Nothing delivers more formidably and viscerally the reality of Earth's humanization as the technosphere's nonstop, sprawling march.

A 2020 *Nature* publication took the world by storm in its sobering quantification of technospheric growth. In 1900, the mass of the technosphere was three percent of Earth's biomass. By 2020, the technosphere exceeded the weight of all living beings. Buildings and infrastructure now outweigh all the trees and shrubs of the world, while the total amount of plastic weighs twice as much as all terrestrial and marine animals combined. Today, the amount of stuff made *each week* is roughly equivalent to the weight of the entire human population. Looking toward the near future, present trends continuing, the mass of human stuff will grow to three times the planet's biomass by 2040 (Elhacham et al., 2020). Briefly stated, the industrial technosphere of modern humanity, composed of some eight billion people connected within a global consumer capitalist system, trading prodigiously, is driving planetwide humanization.

The humanization of the planet means the modern human remaking of the world as the dominant ontology. Technospheric takeover fills the world with human structures, objects, and traces. Human representations, perhaps most especially every kind of mapping and signposting under the sun, further consolidate the technosphere's restructuring of the world as "reality." The mass of manmade physical and symbolic trappings absorb and rivet human attention. Technosphere-dominated reality comes to appear as "natural" reality, and human beings soon lose the capacity to imagine human life and inhabitation differently than in the modality of dominance—that is, as a center (human) to periphery (nonhuman) relationship. Modern humanity, ensnared by what seems like an uncontrollably sprawling technosphere, finds itself within an impoverished and receding *biosphere* (the latter term meaning the living portion of the planet). Humanity itself thus becomes swallowed up within a human-colonized world of its own making. What's more, the emerging facts of a looming mass extinction, rapid climate change, and global-scale toxification speak volumes: it is not going to be the hoped-for "good Anthropocene" (Asafu-Adjaye et al., 2015).

Humanization has many layers. The coarsest involves the takeover and conversion of land and seas for settlements, agriculture, industrial fishing, production and consumption centers (like factories and malls), highways (and dirt) roads, airports and seaports, cables and pipelines, and so on. Correspondingly, all the waste—virtually all of the technosphere turns into waste—is extravagant and unassimilable by Earth: trash, pesticide and nitrogen pollution, e-waste, plastic and lost industrial fishing gear in the ocean, greenhouse gases and industrial effluents, and assorted toxins (such as pharmaceuticals). As the technosphere marches on, the humanized world becomes foregrounded and thereby inescapable to human attention. By the same token, the natural world becomes backgrounded, appearing subliminally as the stage for the technosphere's exhibition and advances. Attempts by people to escape into the receding wild biosphere, to find some respite from the human buzz, are increasingly met with the experience of trash, signs, infrastructure, and mechanical or other human noise. Father of modernity Francis Bacon is often credited with coining the expression "human empire." Yet we fail equally often to acknowledge that Bacon's dream is coming to fruition and his estate—though bound to be fleeting—is imminent.

A political ecology is taking shape "under the radar" of the modern human producing it. Geographical space appears de facto as human property. The nonhuman wild and free world recedes, declines, and disappears often without note or record; such ecological vanishing acts are variously described in science as the declining ecological baseline, empty landscape syndrome, defaunation, critical endangerment, and extinction. "Reality" increasingly presents itself as the ontological province of the human, in conversation with itself. Simultaneously, the nonhuman domain appears, and is linguistically coded, as resource and service provider. All of these political ecology dimensions, as cognitions and lived experiences, *befall* the human. They are not choices that humanity as a whole has consciously made but rather supervene from humanity's ontological entrapment within a human-supremacist Earth regime. To call it a regime is no mere metaphor: human supremacy is a regimented status quo, entrenched on the ground of human–nonhuman unequal power, codified in language, law, and "common sense," which robs nonhuman places and beings of their autonomy and imposes upon them an existence regime over which they have no choice.

At a biological level, humanization produces *deep monoculture.* The nonhumans who survive in abundance do so at the beck and call of human demands and allowances. Among the abundant nonhuman animals are the so-called livestock (now over 60 percent of the aforementioned

96 percent of human plus domestic animal biomass). Among the abundant plants are (genetically) modified crops that "feed the world" from croplands globally occupying an area the extent of Africa and South America combined. The livestock are being bred to endure the torments and feed the coffers of factory farms. While many people object to describing those industrial animal agriculture production sites as "concentration camps," the analogy suggests itself. Meanwhile, the expanding croplands sponsor the poisoning of the world: hundreds of millions of tons of glyphosate, for example, are dumped yearly into the world. Insect populations—so critical to everything—are suffering annihilation from glyphosate and a galaxy of other agrichemicals. Annihilation is also suffered by estuaries, rivers, streams, lakes, and wetlands.

The wild nonhumans who are able to persist in a humanized world are the ones who can prowl in the shadowy edges or parasitize upon humans, species that tend to be generalist, versatile, cunning, and swift in reproduction. All other wild beings are squeezed into smaller and smaller spaces, dwindled to minimal numbers, managed with a heavy hand, hunted, poached, fished, subjected to extermination programs, evicted out of their habitats, or extinguished outright. For example, the fish have suffered catastrophic declines and destruction of their habitats. Even recreational fishing, now motorized and technologically equipped, contributes handily to the destruction. Ancient forests are still falling to agriculture, logging, and mining. Wild places and wild creatures are constantly subject to the collateral damage of pollution, climate change, roadkill, and sprawl.

Humanization, in brief, is the monoculture of modern humans plus nonhuman beings who survive *for* them and *despite* them. The diversity of the natural world that scientists call biodiversity—meaning the variety of beings, places, and relations that planet Earth creates—is vanishing, and along with it are disappearing all the strands of meaning that weave the planet we inhabit into a cosmos of interdependent coexistence. This irremediable undoing is the meaning and reality of the Sixth Mass Extinction.

The humanization of Earth produces a false consciousness of Earth and humanity. The supremacist human gone global temporarily shapes an ontology of Earth as ostensibly human-owned, which subsequently is experienced and lived by humanity as reality. In parallel to the entrenched normal of Earth ownership—wherein all beings and places are tagged as subject to human action—the human-supremacist identity that forges all this itself becomes objectified. The planet conqueror appears as "the natural human." The double danger for humanity is to find itself engulfed in the false consciousness of Earth and of itself: to blithely bequeath a mass extinction event to all posterity, while becoming lost in an anthropological hall of mirrors and a constructed world of increasing scarcity of "resources." In this world, inevitably, *as we are seeing*, militarism and militarist ventures dangerously multiply, spurred by nationalisms and profiteering and legitimated by the fear and aggression that humanization-produced scarcity brews.

Humanization (now bearing the geological label "Anthropocene") yields empty world syndrome. Grimly enough, it used to be that the world was full of wild animals, indigenous peoples, pristine streams and lakes, rivers with more fish than water, living coastal waters and estuaries, and unbounded ecologies. That life-filled world was perceived by colonial settlers (human supremacists) as *empty*. The code "empty" signified "ripe for the takeover." In the bitterest of ironies, after nature's takeover the world *actually* becomes empty of its biospheric exuberances: it becomes empty of wild animal abundances and diversities, divested of their meaning-*full* manifestations such as tracks, dens, nests, burrows, spectacles, songs, and cries. The world becomes empty of indigenous human ways and their nonmodern modes of knowledge, cognition, worldview, stories, and languages; such modes fall into extinction. The world becomes empty of ecologies, such as expanses of grasslands, continental shelves, and forests, as well as of lush ecotones, those biodiversity crossroads where ecologies flow unhindered into one another, such as in estuaries, coastal forests, riparian zones, and wetlands. In other words, Earth becomes bereft of the rich ways it makes itself and is divested of life's abundances, diversity, complexity, biodisparity, and intricate coexistence. And yet, we may still lean into the memory of life's fullness, and that leaning will open the path. We cannot bring back the Holocene. But we can choose to give this *in potentio* fullness-of-world its freedom to remake itself richly and diversely again.

Through the technosphere's engulfment of the face of Earth, humanity loses a cosmic view, the understanding that we inhabit a planet within a vast and inhospitable universe, a lovely planet with a onetime treasure of Earth's remaining biodiversity. Humans, in their supremacist identity of reigning over all, lose the capacity to participate in the web of life, to be wide awake to its preciousness, fragility, and self-being. The Indian mythological concept of "Indra's net," which imagines creation as uncountable jewels strewn connectedly on an infinite web, has no semiotic hold on modern humanity, which cannot see itself as one jewel among countless others but behaves instead with insolence and arrogance, as if it were the net itself. What is lost, and subsequently manifests as cascades of hollow words, is the sacredness of existence and the intrinsic value of every life form and every being. From mere words, we may lift such existential and ethical presentiments into our calling. We may ask ourselves, truly, What does this vibrant, without-a-second living world entreat of us and inspire us to become?

In the chapters presented in this book, we offer a way to voice the living world's entreaty and inspiration: that we may discover *the beauty way* of inhabiting Earth with restraint, respect, and reverence, and through this learn, or *re*learn, that we are one jewel in the web of existence, and not the net. Otherwise, humanity forfeits the reality and still-extant possibility of preserving a pristine and beautiful biosphere within which we can be contained and life-supported. A world where we forfeit the restless and entitled modality of treating the ecosphere as "frontier" to encroach upon, extract from, and conquer.

Are these unrealistic aspirations? Should we not just throw in the towel now? The answer to both questions is a resounding *no*. Erazim Kohák, in *The Embers and the Stars* (Kohák, 1984: 91), observes, "If, in the course of the last three centuries, we have become increasingly marauders on the face of the earth rather than dwellers therein, it is not because we have become more distinctively human, more distinctively cultured, but rather because we have become less so." Furthering this, David Abram, in the *Spell of the Sensuous*, refutes the notion that "a generally exploitative relation to the rest of nature is part and parcel of being human" (Abram, 2017: 93). Indigenous cultures, he notes, have derived the sustenance that they need over long periods of time without overwhelming their local ecologies. Furthermore, he adds, native peoples often show a profound solidarity with their lands, while practicing restraint, respect, and reverence for the other species who inhabit them. There is a pressing need, in the words of Ngozi Unuigbe, "to learn from the wisdom of the world's indigenous people, accumulated over millennia of living sustainably within ecosystems" (Unuigbe, 2023: 5).

In this way, it needs to become better and widely understood that the modern human monoculture will not endure for long, because monoculture is not nature's way. We can still make the turning toward another human identity and inhabitation, undoing human monoculture as our free choice grounded in consciously favoring the beauty way. Then we have a chance to avert the suffering of the accruing penalties of humanization's totalitarianism, and the boomeranging of this on humanity with equally devastating force.

The route to a new identity for our species will comprise fundamental changes across the gamut of human existence, as shown through the diverse contributions to the present book. Arranged thematically into three broad sections—restraint, respect, and reverence—the chapters are summarized below.

## Restraint

To reweave ourselves equitably within the web of life demands from us restraint in our relations with the more-than-human world. This motivation for the sake of all-species justice will support us to downscale our presence and activities, thus freeing the natural world expansively to take over the reins of Earth system variables (such as biochemical cycles, biodiversity, and climate) once again.

At this pivotal historical moment, we can choose to exercise reproductive restraint in order to end ecologically devastating human population growth and gradually reduce our numbers. Nandita Bajaj and Kirsten Stade approach the population question by deconstructing the pervasive pronatalist forces that, subtly or forcefully, coerce reproductive behavior and drive continued population growth. Dismantling the pronatalist bias—globally prevalent in the arenas of culture, politics, business, and religious institutions—will achieve genuine human reproductive autonomy and authentic choice regarding the question of parenthood. Bajaj and Stade argue that we must supersede the inculcated view of childbearing as "biological destiny," and as the default life choice for women and men, both for the sake of realizing human freedom at a deep level and for reversing the mindless, disrespectful, and catastrophic growth of the global population.

Luke Philip Plotica tackles the issue of restraint in consumption by piercing through the mirage of "green consumerism" as solution to the ecological crisis, urging us instead to reduce our overall consumption and to question consumerism as a way of life. As a general rule, we are conditioned to think of restraint as deprivation, as rescinding human freedom and potential. On the contrary, Plotica argues, restraint and critical thinking around consumption can infuse new existential meaning and fulfillment into human life. Bending the imagination in favor of restraint lets us encounter the latter as freedom from clutter and the compulsions of consumerism, opening a new direction toward reenchanting our lives and elevating our well-being without the acquisition or mediation of commodities. Turning away from habitual consuming, and toward the primacy of simply being, promises humanity being reborn into an elegant yet simple material culture, by means of mindfully "identifying our needs and scrutinizing our wants," while seeking enduring satisfaction in relationships with Earth's beings, places, and one another.

John Michael Greer explores the theme of restraint in the realm of technology. He starts with an indisputable premise: that a future of hypercomplicated technologies and limitless energy will not manifest. The fact that "fantasies of progress take precedence over sober analysis," in his words, only delays dealing with the moment of reckoning at the end of cheap abundant energy. In alignment with the other contributors, Greer submits that the restraint called for—as humanity "powers down" at the end of dense fossil-fuel energy and its sundry catastrophes—does not have to be a future of deprivation and sacrifice. The necessary closing of the fossil-fuel era can be welcomed as an opportunity to reimagine human life in slower rhythms and simpler built surroundings, while rethinking technological development as nature-harmonious ecotechnics and ingenious forms of "retrovation." Moving beyond the overproduction, consumerism, and waste excesses that fossil fuels have bankrolled, we can look toward higher aspirations, such as a global culture of high-level literacy and of fundamental human services supported by a robust ecological world. In such a future, the failures of "the civil religion of progress" give way to the return of enchantment in the emergence of new forms of human inhabitation and ecological renewal.

The chapters by Clive Spash and Samuel Alexander focus more concertedly on economic life. Spash methodically deconstructs mainstream attempts to build a sustainable global society by reforming capitalist market forces—the very forces that have unraveled planetary integrity. This approach, he argues, is an exercise in oxymoronic reasoning, hypocritical or at best self-defeating policy, and loss of precious time. Earth and humanity's fragile situation demand the courage and clarity to pursue, without further delay, the one pathway that can make a real difference and avert a myriad of catastrophes: We need to shrink the production of stuff, ramp down the technosphere, lower our consumerist demands, and—pursuant of these economic goals—decelerate and reverse population growth. Alexander extends the exploration of human economic life by querying meaning. He contends that consumerism—even if hypothetically achievable by billions of people without ecological collapse—is a false vision of prosperity and a sure path to meaninglessness in human life. He ventures the argument that aesthetics—meaning a human life devoted to beauty and immersion in the beauties of nature—is the ground of fulfilling our existence. The thrust of this passionate perspective, which he sums up in the acronym S M P L C T Y, is that global humanity can create an elegant, sufficient, nonconsumerist, beautiful material culture wherein human life, through the practice of consciously embraced simplicity, can find authentic existential meaning. The economy of an ecological civilization chooses to retain and mirror the beauty of diverse and abundant life on Earth.

## Respect

In an anthropocentric world, respect appears as a value created by humans to ethically regulate relationships, but in an Earth-centered context respect emerges in a new and deeper light. Respect organically *arises*, for it resides in what Freya Mathews calls "the normative logic" of ecological relations. In her chapter, Mathews finds the essential origin and work of respect within self-renewing ecological systems where organisms, and by extension species, in obeisance to life's imperatives to survive and grow, follow the ways of "accommodation" and "least resistance" toward one another. Living beings—contrary to a still prevailing social Darwinist view—*avoid* unnecessary competition and conflict with one another, thus circumventing a squandering of their life force in confrontations. In an ecological reality of *interdependence*—the hallmark of life's resilience over eons—ecocompositional designs emerge and consolidate wherein living beings sustain each other's existence through nutrient flows and an attending etiquette of coexistence. Breaking through the stale Western notion of a supposed gulf between the "is" and the "ought," Mathews points out that life's very design contains an inherent "ought." Indigenous people understood well this normative dimension of ontological relations and followed nature's command (Law) by means of intimate attunement with their surroundings and through elaborating worldviews and stories that recognize the inherent standing and contributions of all life. Following the native wisdom way, we contemporaries are called to recover this vision of nature's moral law, which is natural relations manifesting as mutual accommodations and reciprocities expressed as tolerance, easefulness, and avoidance of competition. Such is nature's etiquette, summed and summoned through the word "respect" in human language. Through this flow of coexistence, as nature's way, we may seek to reestablish focus toward the more-than-human world as well as toward one another.

For Reed Noss, respect inheres in the recognition that the land—in Aldo Leopold's sense of the living world and the creatures who compose it—is an intrinsic good and a community within which we belong. This understanding aligns with the conservation imperative, and its cornerstone components of protected areas, ecological restoration, and rewilding. To counter the forces of humanization, which as deep monoculture runs the logic of nature aground and constitutes a big show of disrespect, we must create sanctuaries where nonhuman species and communities may continue to exist. How much nature protection does our current distorted reality demand? According to Noss that depends on the ecoregion in question, but the general-level response is between 25 and 75 percent of all representative ecosystems. Spatially generous landscape (and seascape) protection will ensure that extant ecologies continue to thrive, and that large carnivores will have the expansive areas they need to persist. Yet nature protection, as well as ecological restoration and rewilding, will be effective only if we simultaneously address the ultimate threats to nature, which, as Noss points out, are overconsumption, overpopulation, and anthropocentric blindness to the goodness of a biodiverse world. In protecting the world as the world demands, and simultaneously downscaling our own presence and activities, we practice respect for the world that birthed us and holds us. Through the renunciation of constant encroachment and killing, we also find our own dignity and self-respect.

Tarik Bodasing carries this line of reasoning forward with a special focus on Africa, particularly the desperate predicament of the continent's carnivores. Consumerism displays its toxic face in the practices of trophy hunting, wet markets, and wildlife poaching that have become a reign of terror and a form of nonhuman "cleansing" for our animal brothers and sisters in Africa and globally. The lack of respect for the being of the world itself echoes in human depravity and human inequity. The preservation and recovery of Africa's (and the whole world's) expanses of grasslands, shrublands, and forests demands a revolution of heart: the end of wet markets and demand for animal parts in urban centers, within and outside

Africa; the necessity of contracting the livestock population worldwide; the need to address rapid population growth, seeing its incompatibility with conserving Africa's exquisite nature; and the expansion of protected areas to save the continent's natural heritage and beauty.

Eileen Crist's chapter focuses on the state of the global ocean and the profound reparative work it is due. She details ecological knowledge of former abundances of marine biodiversity and its bludgeoning by industrial fishing. Ocean-wide pollution, acidification, and above all marine life destitution call for work on several levels. Most important is large-scale marine protection: we must start with full protection of the high seas stitched to an interconnected network of protected areas along coasts, estuaries, islands, and continental shelves. In parallel, the consumer world, which bears the brunt of responsibility for marine life devastation, must end subsidizing industrial fishing and trading fish so recklessly, while its citizens can choose to stop consuming seafood or eat it sparingly. Industrial fishing, an egregiously extractivist and ecologically disrespectful activity, must be abolished in favor of the reinstatement of the ecotechnics of artisanal fishing, which is equitable, artful, and respectful of the seas in its modest ecological impact. The most important precondition for heeding these reparative actions and policies is the human recognition of the inherent majesty of the living ocean, which alone can awaken the desire to reinstate and protect it.

The modern food system is devastating Earth's living systems—most especially biodiversity, climate, fresh water, and soils—and violates all decency in the treatment of farm animals, wild beings, and disempowered people whose lands have been stolen and are left with low-quality, contaminated food. Ryan Andrews looks to a future of sustainable and ethical food production. The collective well-being of Earth and all her residents, he argues, hinges on how we approach food in the coming decades. There is much to be changed in the status quo of food production, including shifting away from materials- and energy-intensive food processing, packaging, and trading. Andrews structures his chapter around three key ideas for transformation: one, that eaters will emphasize a variety of minimally processed plant-based foods; two, that farming will be built around agroecological regenerative systems; and, three, that food will be valued and not wasted. A mostly plant-based, whole-food diet, where practicable, will nourish human beings, and will also allow the lowering of the global numbers of farm animals, who, returned to farms, can live in synergy with cultivated plants, soil, food scraps, and other dimensions of farm life. Embracing agroecology means modeling agricultural systems on ecological principles, including diversification, nutrient cycling, animal–plant beneficent feedback loops, soil building, and sensitivity to local and regional biogeography. Food grown with deep respect for the land—from its ground of soil to the needs of its wildlife—can be received as sacred nourishment by human beings in gratitude for Earth's fertility.

In her chapter, Chelsea Batavia centers on the idea that humanness, per se, is not the root of environmental destruction, and that eradicating its influence over the more-than-human world, therefore, is not a proper focus for conservationists' energies. She argues that conservationists should instead focus more intently on exposing and dismantling systems of oppression, through which dominant human groups undermine, repress, exploit, and often destroy other human and nonhuman beings. The work of overturning oppression presents undeniably daunting challenges. Conservationists can be heartened and invigorated, however, in finding solidarity between their work and the work of related movements promoting justice for marginalized groups, be they nonhuman or human.

The chapter by Joe Gray and Ian Whyte focuses on outdoor recreation, starting out by observing the conflict between the deep value of human experiences in wild nature and the negative impacts these can have on nonhuman life. They identify respect for the more-than-human world as the guiding lights to lead us through this thorny territory, and explore existing codes for outdoor pursuits, including Leave No Trace and Conscious Impact Living. Gray and Whyte also explore how respect can translate into mindful choices, including restricting ourselves both spatially and temporally in the outdoors activities in which we engage. They propose that through such intentional decisions we can learn to connect with wild nature without undermining its flourishing. Finally, Gray and Whyte offer some questions that we might ask ourselves, from an ecocentric perspective, before or during recreational activities. In alignment with other contributors, Gray and Whyte show that the virtues of restraint and respect elevate, as opposed to constrict, human beings, by cultivating more nuanced appreciation of recreational impacts, attuning humans to the needs of nonhumans, exploring alternative ways of recreating if called for, and self-reflecting from the perspective of others. Thus, the authors' recommendations reveal that respect serves both the needs of the more-than-human world and the elevation of human consciousness.

## Reverence

Reverence heightens the felt experience of respect for Earth and her beings by enfolding the element of awe before the natural world—indeed, before a natural world that *calls awe forth*. The chapters clustered under this heading emphasize, each in their own way, that reverence is not a human-originated value, much less a culturally specific one, projected onto nature, but rather an attitude that nature's magnificent physical and numinous presence elicits within an attentive and humble human being. The very experience of reverence, and its conceptual distillation into a word, arose within the human mind through encountering the very nature of the world that humans emerged within and inhabit.

Patrick Curry traces the modern loss of capacity for reverence in the Western intellectual tradition he characterizes as a "philosophy of death," the elaboration of a necrophilic life-hatred that paved the way to ecocidal modernity and its condemnation of the natural world into a domain of "servitude, if not outright slavery." Only by superseding the anthropocentric profanation of nature and loss of relationship with belittled "others" (banalized and turned into resources), may we rediscover enchantment—meaning sheer wonder before existence. When we open up to nature's inherent experience, Curry writes, we find that "reverence is the appropriate response." According to Curry, enchantment always entails a relational and situated receptivity to nature's intrinsic being. Enchantment expresses an awakening to reality, an experience that arises when we have learned "to love nature for its own sake." It is surely due humanity to rediscover enchantment, as we slog through the ecocidal culmination of a philosophy of death that has produced arid, devastated inner and outer landscapes in the wake of "the disenchantment of the world."

Certainly enchantment has deep ties with beauty. Matthew Calarco makes the case for an "aesthetic turn" in discourse and activism centered on the more-than-human world, one with an orientation that is fundamentally "inhumanist." Pursuing a line of thought opened up by Aristotle, and further developed by contemporary philosophers and poets such as Pierre Hadot and Robinson Jeffers, Calarco argues that attention to the wonders and beauties of the natural world, especially animals, serves as the ground for a properly inhumanist aesthetics. Such an aesthetics offers an alternative vision of the ethico-political task that faces us today, one in which our response to the contemporary diminishment and degradation of animal life is viewed less through a lens of reparative duty and more through one of preserving beauty.

Moving from animals to plants, the chapter by Simon Leadbeater and Helen Kopnina links the plight of the world's forests today to the development of Western thinking, constituting them as quasi-inanimate resources for extraction. They explore the human behavioral changes that are called for in response to increasing scientific evidence for plant sentience, particularly that of trees. In their discourse, Leadbeater and Kopnina draw on ancient and indigenous epistemologies surrounding the plant kingdom that mesh with recent scientific findings, offering hope for a renewal of our reverence for all nature.

Sean Blenkinsop presents a deeply honest appraisal of a long-term project, in collaboration with his colleagues, to "ecologize" public education and counter nature deficit disorder in British Columbia. In this project, substantial transformations have been wrought in the mode and setting of schooling, with a key goal of creating space for students to discover and respond to the cultural limits of imaginative play. Through a series of vignettes, Blenkinsop unpacks crucial student-initiated themes that have emerged from this work, including nature as coteacher, nature as colonized, and nature as supporting cultural change. The stories give us a window through which to see the educational journey of these researchers and to help us understand Blenkinsop's contention that in order to help overcome nature deficit disorder, even at the level of the individual, educators must think at the broader level of community and culture.

Finally, in her chapter, Kathleen Dean Moore offers a fitting conclusion to the section on reverence, and the book as a whole, with her poetic exploration of gratitude as a way of life. Starting out with a portrait of life around her cabin in Alaska, she explores questions about the essence of nature's gifts and what they ask of us—namely, profound gratitude built on attentiveness, gladness, and reciprocity. Moore delves into the role of humility and restraint in an ecological life and refutes the notion that we should act to oppose Earth's wounding only if we are confident of success.

## Concluding Thoughts

While humanity can *seemingly* defer accountability to the ecological and ethical demands that Earth places upon us, and continue postponing a genuine response by avoiding "the Earth question," that question will not go away. We are inescapably accountable to the devastation of nonhumans and their homes. Acquiescing to Earth's humanization—the default decision so far of modern culture at large—means consenting to the irreversible disappearance of innumerable and unique forms of beauty, knowledge, complexity, wellness, consciousness, and experience. By the same token, "destination Anthropocene" guarantees widespread human desolation and anguish, and a human identity crisis for all. Life gone missing everywhere, from the sheer momentum of entitlement and a refusal to limit the expansionism of the human enterprise, haunts Earth's landscapes and seascapes. As far as humans are concerned, the penalties are not only widespread physical suffering but also psychic pain, increasingly visible in epidemics of depression and other forms of sociopsychological malaise, and in the grieving of more and more people for Earth's integrity and our fellow Earthlings.

In this time called the Anthropocene by many, we have indeed come to "meet the enemy," but it is not us: it is not the human species or human nature. The enemy of the natural world, and of our own survival and potential as a unique lifeform, is an expansionist way of life premised on unrestraint, disrespect, and profound loss of reverence. Yet this way of life is not biologically ordained but historically contingent and inherited, ossified in political, economic, and educational institutions, and ongoingly inculcated into the social collective. The process of humanizing the planet is violent, and its endpoint unwholesome and moribund. Ours is the historical moment to awaken to the gift of belonging with a living planet and to become joyful participants who inhabit Earth with gratitude and grace.

## References

Abram, D. (2017). *The Spell of the Sensuous*. Vintage Books.
Asafu-Adjaye, J., Blomqvist, L., Brand, S., et al. (2015). *An Ecomodernist Manifesto*. http://www.ecomodernism.org/
Ceballos, G., & Ehrlich, P. R. (2018) The misunderstood sixth mass extinction. *Science*, 360, 1080–81. https://doi.org/10.1126/science.aau0191
Elhacham, E., Ben-Uri, L., Grozovski, J., et al. (2020). Global human-made mass exceeds all living biomass. *Nature*, 588, 442–44. https://doi.org/10.1038/s41586-020-3010-5
IPBES (2019). *The Global Assessment Report on Biodiversity and Ecosystem Services: Summary for Policymakers*. https://ipbes.net/sites/default/files/inline/files/ipbes_global_assessment_report_summary_for_policymakers.pdf

Kohák, E. (1984). *The Embers and the Stars*. University of Chicago Press.
Maathai, W. (2004). Lecture on being awarded the 2004 Nobel Peace Laureate. https://www.nobelprize.org/prizes/peace/2004/maathai/lecture/
Maxwell, S. L., Fuller, R. A., Brooks, T. M., & Watson, J. E. M. (2016). The ravages of guns, nets and bulldozers. *Nature*, 536, 143–45. http://doi.org/10.1038/536143a
Unuigbe, N. (2023). What can we learn from indigenous ecological knowledge? *The Ecological Citizen*, 6, epub-089.

Section One

# Restraint

1

# Restoring Balance through Procreative Responsibility

NANDITA BAJAJ AND KIRSTEN STADE

As a concept, restraint is not one that holds much appeal to the human psyche. Our destiny, we are told, is dominion over Earth and all its species, and expansion into its farthest reaches with our society and our technology.

Human supremacy is a worldview held by most at a more or less conscious level, and it tells us that we alone possess intrinsic value and that the more-than-human world—nature and nonhumans—hold value only in their ability to serve us. It also tells us that humans, alone among species, are exempt from any constraints imposed by the carrying capacity of our global ecosystem. Yet our ecological predicament tells us otherwise. The climate crisis, the extinction crisis, dwindling freshwater supplies, and expanding desertification tell us that while we have so far managed to escape these constraints on our population and expansion, we have done so only at tremendous cost to other species and to the ecological support systems upon which we depend. Such is the nature of overshoot: we can ignore carrying capacity, but only by transferring the costs of its transgression onto other creatures and future generations.

Overshoot, defined as human demands that exceed Earth's regenerative capacity, has left us in a state in which we are consuming 75 percent more than Earth can provide sustainably (Global Footprint Network, 2022). Because overshoot allows us to avoid, at least for the time being, experiencing the full ecological costs of our expansion, we are able to devote ourselves wholeheartedly to it—to exploiting or extracting every substance on Earth of any conceivable value to us. We are enabled in this dominion by our large cerebral cortex, our ability to use tools, our capacity for abstraction and complex social organization, and especially the large-scale exploitation of fossil fuels that began a couple of centuries ago. These taken together have allowed our societies, cities, and technologies to encircle the globe, and our population to grow from a mere billion in the early 19th century to eight times that today (Heinberg, 2021).

And as our population has grown eightfold, our consumption of the "resources" upon which we depend—the animals, the topsoil, the freshwater, and wood and minerals that we use to fuel our societies and feed our growing numbers—has exploded by a factor of 100 (Rees, 2019). Of course, human beings are not alone among species in this tendency to expand to fill the ecosystems we inhabit and to use available resources. But we are alone in having the technology that enables our expansion well beyond the boundaries of those ecosystems, to the state of profound overshoot and ecological collapse in which we find ourselves today (Heinberg, 2021).

Overshoot results not only in the current state of ecological meltdown but also in widespread inequality, food insecurity, poverty, and conflict. While it stems from a combination of large populations consuming locally as well as high-consumption industrialized powers exploiting distant vulnerable populations through extraction of their "natural capital," those vulnerable populations bear most of the impacts. These impacts will only be intensified by population growth, most of which—a projected 80 million people per year in the coming decades—will occur in these countries (Rees, 2019; Bradshaw et al., 2021).

Meanwhile, the middle class, which accounts for two-thirds of global household consumption (Kharas & Hamel, 2018), is the fastest-growing segment of the global population. So while the projected expansion of the global middle class to five billion by 2030 (Crist et al., 2017) may be celebrated because of what it means for human well-being and poverty reduction, its costs for biodiversity and our planetary life support systems cannot be ignored. The addition of billions more people to the middle class means an extraordinary rise in demand on our food systems, which have already transformed 40 percent of the planet's ice-free land area and have been identified as the primary threat to 86 percent of the species at risk of extinction (Crist et al., 2017; Benton et al., 2021). It also has grim implications for animals kept and killed as "livestock," as the number of land animals slaughtered globally over the past 50 years, with the doubling of the world's population and a steep rise in meat consumption, has increased from 12 billion to 80 billion (Ritchie et al., 2017). That we are in 75 percent overshoot already should inform us that one-planet living will require fewer of us, if we are to have a comfortable standard of living for all while living in harmony with nonhuman beings (Rees, 2019).

The biodiversity and climate crises, and other symptoms of overshoot, command the attention of an ever-growing array of international conferences, at which world leaders wrangle over the technologies and funds they will throw in the direction of equalizing inequities or saving species from extinction or preventing cataclysmic climate change. Yet no leader has yet agreed to the one two-pronged intervention that might actually prevent cataclysm: substantial shrinkage of the size of our global economy and our population (Tucker, 2021). It is perhaps not surprising that there is little interest among world leaders to degrow our economy, given that economic growth benefits primarily these leaders and the wealthy elites who fund them (Vieira, 2016). It is less obvious why there should be such resistance to the notion that in order for us to thrive within the bounds of our planetary ecosystem, our population must stabilize and then shrink.

## Population Denialism

Population is a sensitive topic, and understandably so given the history of coercive campaigns targeting the fertility of traditionally marginalized people. These campaigns, including the eugenics movement in the United States and Europe, India's and Puerto Rico's forced sterilization campaigns, and China's one-child policy, stemmed from a legacy of institutional racism, ableism, sexism, classism, and nationalism.

These programs were not only gross violations of reproductive rights themselves but also had the disastrous legacy of tainting all family planning campaigns—including the majority, which have focused on liberating women—with the blemish of coercion. This association was firmly cemented at the International Conference on Population and Development (ICPD) in 1994 in Cairo, Egypt, where discourse on population was cast aside in favor of an exclusive focus on reproductive health. Since then, the tendency in both academic and policy circles has been to avoid and even silence discussion of the role of population growth in environmental degradation (Kopnina & Washington, 2016; Kuhlemann, 2019; Tucker, 2021). This trend has erased the vast majority of international family planning efforts that have supported the reproductive autonomy of women and girls and have played a dramatic role in elevating their status by affording them control over their own fertility (Sinding, 2008; Campbell & Bedford, 2009; Potts, 2014). And it has actually strengthened and legitimized the oldest and most pervasive form of reproductive coercion: pronatalism.

## Pronatalism and Overpopulation

Pronatalism refers to the extraordinary array of social and institutional pressures to have children that influence people's lives at every level. These make themselves felt through family, society, and culture; through religious messaging that celebrates large families while stigmatizing the single and child-free; through state-imposed restrictions on contraceptive use and abortion bans; and through economic messaging that catastrophizes lower fertility. Not only does pronatalism undermine reproductive autonomy, it is also at the heart of unchecked population growth (Bajaj & Stade, 2023).

Some of the most intense pronatalist pressures women encounter are those that originate within their own families and generally stem from a desire to maintain the family's genealogical legacy. In many societies, these conventional pressures result in severe consequences for women who cannot or do not fulfill this expectation, ranging from social isolation to marital neglect, abuse, and divorce to the covert use of contraceptives out of fear of domestic violence (Bajaj & Stade, 2023).

Pronatalism also exerts a powerful influence through popular media and culture. Product advertising, along with women's magazines, celebrity pregnancy announcements, and parenting blogs glorify and sentimentalize parenthood, with the effect of reinforcing the narrative that motherhood is the only complete manifestation of womanhood (Carroll, 2012). The result of this popular cultural fixation on pregnancy, motherhood, and traditional family—as defined by the presence of biological children—results in the marginalization of single adults, child-free people, LGBTQ+ people, adoptive families, and families that do not include offspring (Nandy, 2017; Latchford, 2019; Bajaj & Ware, 2022a). It has also led to extraordinary confusion and suffering for women who regret having children, and whose stories are largely erased from the cultural narrative (Donath, 2015).

Many individuals undoubtedly feel an authentic desire for children, and experience grief and loss as a result of infertility. But these feelings of inadequacy are exploited by the multi-billion-dollar fertility industry, which has been growing at an annual rate of nine percent with projected growth to a global US$41 billion industry by 2026 (Patrizio et al., 2022). While initially a medical specialty focused strictly on infertile couples, in vitro fertilization and other assisted reproductive technologies are today also marketed aggressively to a much broader population, and many of the expanded fertility services being offered are of dubious clinical validity (Patrizio et al., 2022). Through assisted reproductive technologies the medical profession expresses and reinforces society's bias for biological motherhood and pressures infertile women to endure great expense and physical discomfort in favor of fertility treatments over adoption, which was once considered the obvious solution (Nandy, 2017; Latchford, 2019). Meanwhile the challenges that women experience in locating doctors willing to perform voluntary sterilization is yet another manifestation of medical pronatalism (Lalonde, 2018).

The notion of the "biological clock" adds to a sense of pressure surrounding motherhood. While based on the biological fact of diminished fertility as women age, the term has become a convenient trope that allows avoidance of earnest exploration of a woman's true desires by means of invoking an urgent, time-sensitive biological imperative. Yet there is no evidence of such an imperative, otherwise fertility rates all over the world would be consistent and high, and rates of child-free adults would not have climbed in recent decades in countries where women have some freedom of reproductive choice (Carroll, 2012; Gimenez, 2019). The longing for meaning that many women—and men—feel around midlife is attributed by a pronatalist society to the "biological clock," when, in fact, many other experiences besides childbirth can provide the sense of meaning and purpose that is sought (Stade, 2022).

Religious leaders, a source of community and connection for many families, are also one of the most powerful sources of pronatalist pressure. Most religious traditions have strongly pronatalist teachings and scriptural mandates to "be fruitful and multiply," which are further buttressed through misinformation about the health effects of contraceptives and abortion and proscriptions on their use (Carroll, 2012).

In countries and settings where religions exercise political power, pronatalist religious teachings are even more sinister. The Vatican, for example, played a role in the aforementioned derailing of international family planning activities at the ICPD in 1994, where religious actors lobbied delegates against continued support for rights-based family planning activities that had enjoyed international funding and widespread success in the preceding decades (Sinding, 2008; Kuhlemann, 2019).

Pronatalism inspired by religious sentiment has been on display on national stages worldwide. With the growing global trend toward feminism and lower fertility rates, there has been a reactionary rise in right-wing populism that has furthered the influence of religion in perpetuating pronatalist cultural norms, especially in order to fuel demographic growth of desired ethnic groups such as the Sunnis in Turkey, Hindus in India, or white people in the United States. This movement represents an insidious alliance of religion, ideology, populism, and governments to combat liberalism, gender equality, and economic empowerment of women as it seeks to marginalize groups that don't conform to standards of white, heterosexual masculinity (Gökarıksel et al., 2019; Graff et al., 2019).

This trend has fueled the rise to power of political leaders using right-wing rhetoric to justify pronatalist policy in many countries. These policies, ranging from bans on abortion or contraception to stigmatization of nontraditional families or queer communities to subsidies for assisted reproductive technologies for politically preferred ethnic groups, are on the rise in countries as diverse as Argentina, Brazil, Germany, Hungary, India, Iran, Ireland, the Philippines, Poland, Russia, Turkey, and the United States (Gökarıksel et al., 2019; Graff et al., 2019). This trend only fortifies existing exploitive pronatalist justifications, such as pressure from the military-industrial complex to maintain strong armed forces and ethnocentric or racist motivations to win a "demographic war" over a competing ethnicity or tribe (Bajaj & Stade, 2023).

Over 50 countries today have policies to increase birth rates. Indeed, the number of countries with explicitly pronatalist policies—ranging from tax incentives and baby bonuses to abortion bans—rose from ten percent in 1976 to 28 percent in 2015 (United Nations Department of Economic and Social Affairs, 2021). Where these initiatives are not justified with explicit reference to religious or ethnocentric ideologies, pronatalist calls and policy increasingly hitch demographic anxieties to economic ends. Indeed, economic arguments for pronatalist policy have become increasingly predominant since the emergence of demography as a discipline and the increased formalization of the official census in the 19th century, when birth rates became a topic of relevance to those who make policy (Hoffman, 2000).

Economists, political leaders, and corporate elites regularly argue that keeping fertility high ensures a steady supply of workers, consumers, and taxpayers, while generating a larger pool of potential inventors—although proponents of this view seem to forget the lost innovative potential of women overwhelmed by the demands of childcare (Skirbekk & Bowen, 2022). China, which attempted to downregulate women's fertility with its infamous one-child policy from 1980 to 2016, has shifted course to manipulate women into having more children with a three-child policy. Policies such as closing abortion and vasectomy clinics and subsidizing fertility clinics, as China has done in response to the contraction of its fertility rates and then its population, are transparent examples of a pronatalism that exploits women's bodies as vessels for external economic and political agendas (Zhou, 2022).

Popular media has only given cover to this regressive landscape, rather than promoting commonsense solutions to the "aging crisis" such as increasing taxation of the wealthy, removing ageist institutional barriers to older people continuing to work, or deescalating militarization in order to redirect bloated military budgets into social services (Götmark et al., 2018; Klein, 2019; Bricker & Ibbitson, 2020; Skirbekk & Bowen, 2022). The sensationalist coverage that frames fertility decline as a "collapse" or "crisis" of existential proportions misses the many positive aspects of an aging, shrinking society. These are many, and include higher wages and better working conditions; longer, healthier, more productive lives for older people; much-reduced infrastructure costs; liberation for women from the burdens of childcare; and increasing automation that replaces much of the shrinking workforce (Skirbekk & Bowen, 2022).

Pronatalism emerges in particularly complex ways in countries and communities that have been affected by past injustices, including genocide, eugenics, and colonialism. In India, China, and Puerto Rico, as well as in Israel and in Black communities of the United States, histories of reproductive coercion, slavery, eugenics, and genocide have resulted in an embrace of pronatalism as a corrective measure to injustices of the past. Though often advanced by neoliberal feminists and other progressive actors, these arguments are then handily wielded by conservative factions and religious leaders to further fortify the existing culture of coercive pronatalism (Briggs, 1998; Donath, 2015; Kerr, 2016).

Despite the convergence of religious, nationalistic, and neoliberal economic interests behind a pronatalist program to fulfill their particular agendas, the rise in education, opportunity, and contraceptive access for women has resulted in lowered birth rates across the globe. Staggering national investment in pronatalist incentives such as tax breaks and direct payments for additional children in numerous countries has proven insufficient to compel women to go back to the high fertility rates they have left behind, and, in fact, the number of adults choosing to forego parenthood altogether has been steadily rising (Skirbekk & Bowen, 2022). This suggests that as pronatalist pressures are dismantled and lose some of their potency to shape reproductive behavior, that behavior tends toward low fertility—a choice that has been described as women's "latent desire" for no or few children (Campbell & Bedford, 2009).

## Beyond Reproductive Autonomy: Reproductive Responsibility

The ubiquity of pronatalist institutions and social norms throughout the world underscores their significance in driving high fertility rates and resultant population growth; it is not coincidental that those regions of the world that have the highest population growth rates are also those in which women have the least reproductive autonomy to push back against these institutions. In an environment so shaped by pronatalism, clearly the first step toward realizing a balanced population is the neutralization of forces that pressure people into having children. Such a program might begin by eliminating the most obvious forms of coercive pronatalism, such as abortion and contraceptive bans, and removing egregious and costly incentives such as state subsidies for assisted reproductive technologies. A playing field leveled by the removal of pronatalist pressures, so that parenthood, including adoption, and nonparenthood are available as equally acceptable options would allow authentic exploration of individuals' true desires so that their reproductive decisions are rooted in their individual values, talents, and life plans (Campbell & Bedford, 2009; Carroll, 2012; Purdy, 2019).

But given our already advanced state of ecological overshoot, which will only grow more dire with each child born and with continued global economic development, a full spectrum of rights-based policies to drive down birth rates is warranted. Beyond eliminating coercive pronatalist policies, such a program would include ambitious international investment in education and the empowerment of girls and women, and family planning programs that expand access to and awareness of a greater range of contraceptive and reproductive healthcare options for all people (Campbell & Bedford, 2009).

Yet the utter saturation of cultures across the globe in deeply rooted pronatalism calls for more intensive efforts to dismantle its pervasive impacts on people's lives. Reproductive norm shifting would counter centuries' worth of cultural indoctrination as to the intrinsic and absolute benefits of large families, and could use a number of avenues to disseminate messages that enhance reproductive choice (Hickey et al., 2016). Popular television shows and radio programs, such as those currently offered by Population Media Center, encourage thorough examination of reproductive decisions and have had demonstrable success in changing cultural perceptions of family planning, increasing contraceptive use, and reducing such human rights violations as child marriage and female genital mutilation in developing countries across the world (Ryerson & Teffera, 2021; Bajaj & Ware, 2022b). These programs could be offered by governments or through partnerships among nongovernmental organizations working in concert with governments and international aid agencies.

Such a cultural program of countering pronatalism, liberating reproductive choice, and adjusting reproductive preferences would allow for individuals to make reproductive decisions reflective of autonomous desires. But for those of us in the developed world or in places that have realized a higher degree of reproductive autonomy, decisions based on individual desires are not enough. Our disproportionate impacts on global climate and landscapes through our high levels of consumption mean that our procreative decisions must be considered in light of their direct impacts on others suffering the effects of these degradations, including the most marginalized human communities, nonhuman beings, and future generations.

And while the possibility of raising the next generation to be conscious in its consumption is an argument often raised in favor of procreation by those with greater levels of autonomy, in truth we have no control over the consumptive choices made by our progeny. And even individuals born to the most conscious parents in the developed world will inevitably cause harm to the planet and its inhabitants simply by virtue of their modern lifestyles: the greenhouse gas emissions reduction of foregoing one childbirth in the developed world is 24 times that of living without a car and 71 times that of eating a plant-based diet (Wynes & Nicholas, 2017).

What is needed to realize a new ethic of reproductive responsibility is truly a transformation of how we view our reproductive potential. While the current ideal focuses on the reproductive rights of the individual—rights that are still far from realized, as consideration of the pervasiveness of pronatalism show—an ethic of restraint recognizes limitations on these rights where they respect the rights of others to a livable planet (Carroll, 2012; Purdy, 2019; Crist et al., 2022). In addition to all existing beings who have an inarguable interest in whether more humans are born to affect their habitat and livable climate, our procreative responsibility must also extend to the rights of children not yet born (Dillard, 2010). This restraint is not a sacrifice—it is a gift born of responsibility to the myriad lifeforms with whom we share this planet, and a relief from the isolation and burden of our perceived human supremacy.

For those of us who are privileged, it is also an opportunity. For those who have amassed or inherited a degree of wealth, procreation has traditionally been a means of keeping that wealth concentrated within one's lineage, thus preserving entrenched privilege across generations. This tradition ensures the perpetuation of injustice and inequality over time. And although parents may, and sometimes do decide to, leave much of their legacy to causes other than their own children, choosing not to procreate expands that potential by freeing up the tremendous material, monetary, and energetic resources usually devoted to child-rearing by parents in the developed world. Nonparents may turn over their wealth to any number of communities that have not enjoyed such privilege, including Indigenous groups and degraded ecosystems whose exploitation has generated that wealth.

## Conclusion

Ultimately, the decision to have fewer or no children is a decision that supports the shift away from our human supremacist worldview, and toward an ethic of ecocentrism. By letting go of the unrestrained perpetuation of our genealogy and of the dominion of our species, we let go of our individual participation in the myth of human supremacy that has caused such devastation to the natural world. Our choice of reproductive responsibility, along with our transition to agricultural and economic enterprise at scales that are humane and respectful of planetary boundaries, fosters a radical shift in our relationship to Earth from one of dominion to one of reverence and harmony. The practice of reproductive restraint, when viewed in this light, is a path not just to correction of ecological overshoot but also to our integration with the web of life and reparation of centuries of injustice.

## References

Bajaj, N., & Stade, K. (2023). Challenging pronatalism is key to advancing reproductive rights and a sustainable population. *Journal of Population and Sustainability*, 7, 85–108. https://doi.org/10.3197/jps.63799953906861

Bajaj, N., & Ware, A. (Hosts) (2022a, May 24). Dr. Kimya Nuru Dennis: The unique challenges of being Black and childfree [Podcast episode]. *The Overpopulation Podcast*. https://www.populationbalance.org/episode-75-the-unique-challenges-of-being-black-and-childfree

Bajaj, N., & Ware, A. (Hosts) (2022b, September 7). William Ryerson: Soap operas for social justice. [Podcast episode]. *The Overpopulation Podcast*. https://www.populationbalance.org/episode-80-william-ryerson

Benton, T. G., Bieg, C., Harwatt, H., et al. (2021, February 3). Food system impacts on biodiversity loss. *United Nations Environment Programme*. https://www.fao.org/agroecology/database/detail/en/c/1394568/

Bradshaw, C. J., Ehrlich, P. R., Beattie, A., et al. (2021). Underestimating the challenges of avoiding a ghastly future. *Frontiers in Conservation Science*, 1. https://doi.org/10.3389/fcosc.2020.615419

Bricker, D. J., & Ibbitson, J. (2020). *Empty Planet: The Shock of Global Population Decline*. Robinson.

Briggs, L. (1998). Discourses of "forced sterilization" in Puerto Rico: The problem with the speaking subaltern. *Differences*, 10(2), 30–66. https://doi.org/10.1215/10407391-10-2-30

Campbell, M., & Bedford, K. (2009). The theoretical and political framing of the population factor in development. *Philosophical Transactions of the Royal Society B: Biological Sciences*, 364(1532), 3101–13. https://doi.org/10.1098/rstb.2009.0174

Carroll, L. (2012). *The Baby Matrix: Why Freeing our Minds from Outmoded Thinking about Parenthood & Reproduction Will Create a Better World*. LiveTrue Books.

Crist, E., Mora, C., & Engelman, R. (2017). The interaction of human population, food production, and Biodiversity Protection. *Science*, 356(6335), 260–64. https://doi.org/10.1126/science.aal2011

Crist, E., Ripple, W. J., Ehrlich, P. R., et al. (2022). Scientists' warning on population. *Science of The Total Environment*, 845, 157166. https://doi.org/10.1016/j.scitotenv.2022.157166

Dillard, C. (2010) Prospective parents and the Children's Rights Convention. *American University International Law Review*, 25(3), 485–529.

Donath, O. (2015). Regretting motherhood: A sociopolitical analysis. *Signs: Journal of Women in Culture and Society*, 40(2), 343–67. https://doi.org/10.1086/678145

Gimenez, M. E. (2019). *Marx, Women, and Capitalist Social Reproduction: Marxist Feminist Essays*. Haymarket Books.

Global Footprint Network (2022, July 29). *Measure what you treasure.* https://www.footprintnetwork.org/

Gökarıksel, B., Neubert, C., & Smith, S. (2019). Demographic fever dreams: Fragile masculinity and population politics in the rise of the global right. *Signs: Journal of Women in Culture and Society, 44*(3), 561–87. https://doi.org/10.1086/701154

Götmark, F., Cafaro, P., & O'Sullivan, J. (2018). Aging human populations: Good for us, good for the earth. *Trends in Ecology & Evolution, 33*(11), 851–62. https://doi.org/10.1016/j.tree.2018.08.015

Graff, A., Kapur, R., & Walters, S. D. (2019). Introduction: Gender and the rise of the global right. *Signs: Journal of Women in Culture and Society, 44*(3), 541–60. https://doi.org/10.1086/701152

Heinberg, R. (2021). *Power: Limits and Prospects for Human Survival.* New Society Publishers.

Hickey, C., Rieder, T. N., & Earl, J. (2016). Population engineering and the fight against climate change. *Social Theory and Practice, 42*(4), 845–70. https://doi.org/10.5840/soctheorpract201642430

Hoffmann, D. L. (2000). *Mothers in the Motherland: Stalinist Pronatalism and Its Pan-European Context.* The National Council for Eurasian and East European Research.

Kerr, C. G. (2016). *How Pronatalism Became Black: The Path from Black Antinatalism to Black Pronatalism.* Amherst College.

Kharas, H., & Hamel, K. (2018, September 27). A global tipping point: Half the world is now middle class or wealthier. *The Brookings Institution.* https://www.brookings.edu/blog/future-development/2018/09/27/a-global-tipping-point-half-the-world-is-now-middle-class-or-wealthier/

Klein, N. (2019). *On Fire: The (Burning) Case for a Green New Deal.* Simon & Schuster.

Kopnina, H., & Washington, H. (2016). Discussing why population growth is still ignored or denied. *Chinese Journal of Population Resources and Environment, 14*(2), 133–43. https://doi.org/10.1080/10042857.2016.1149296

Kuhlemann, K. (2019). The elephant in the room. In N. Almiron & J. Xifra (Eds.), *Climate Change Denial and Public Relations* (pp. 74–99). Routledge. https://doi.org/10.4324/9781351121798-6

Lalonde, D. (2018). Regret, shame, and denials of women's voluntary sterilization. *Bioethics, 32*(5), 281–88. https://doi.org/10.1111/bioe.12431

Latchford, F. J. (2019). *Steeped in Blood: Adoption, Identity, and the Meaning of Family.* McGill-Queen's University Press.

Nandy, A. (2017). *Motherhood and Choice: Uncommon Mothers, Childfree Women.* Zubaan.

Patrizio, P., Albertini, D. F., Gleicher, N., & Caplan, A. (2022). The changing world of IVF: The pros and cons of new business models offering assisted reproductive technologies. *Journal of Assisted Reproduction and Genetics*, *39*(2), 305–13. https://doi.org/10.1007/s10815-022-02399-y

Potts, M. (2014). Getting family planning and population back on track. *Global Health: Science and Practice*, *2*(2), 145–51. https://doi.org/10.9745/ghsp-d-14-00012

Purdy, L. M. (2019). Pronatalism is violence against women: The role of genetics. In W. Teays (Ed.), *Analyzing Violence Against Women* (pp. 113–29). Springer. https://doi.org/10.1007/978-3-030-05989-7_9

Rees, W. E. (2019). Ecological economics for humanity's plague phase. *Ecological Economics*, *169*, 106519. https://doi.org/10.1016/j.ecolecon.2019.106519

Ritchie, H., Rosado, P., & Roser, M. (2017). Meat and dairy production. *Our World in Data*. https://ourworldindata.org/meat-production

Ryerson, W. N., & Teffera, N. (2021). The impact of Social Change Communication: Lessons learned from decades of Media Outreach. In L. B. Frank & P. Falzone (Eds.), *Entertainment-Education Behind the Scenes* (pp. 23–38). Springer. https://doi.org/10.1007/978-3-030-63614-2_3

Sinding, S. W. (2008). What has happened to family planning since Cairo and what are the prospects for the future? *Contraception*, *78*(4 Suppl), S3–S6. https://doi.org/10.1016/j.contraception.2008.03.019

Skirbekk, V., & Bowen, C. E. (2022). *Decline and Prosper! Changing Global Birth Rates and the Advantages of Fewer Children*. Palgrave Macmillan.

Stade, K. (2022, July 11). I am not a slave to the biological clock. *Ms*. https://msmagazine.com/2022/07/11/women-biological-clock-child-free-world-population-day/

Tucker, C. (2021). It's time to revisit the Cairo Consensus. *Journal of Population and Sustainability*, *5*(2), 63–73. https://doi.org/10.3197/jps.2021.5.2.63

United Nations Department of Economic and Social Affairs (2021). *World Population Policies 2021: Policies Related to Fertility*. https://www.un.org/development/desa/pd/sites/www.un.org.development.desa.pd/files/undesa_pd_2021_wpp-fertility_policies.pdf.

Vieira, P. (2016). Is overpopulation a growth? The pathology of permanent expansion. *Oxford Literary Review*, *38*(1), 67–83. https://doi.org/10.3366/olr.2016.0180

Wynes, S., & Nicholas, K. A. (2017). The climate mitigation gap: Education and government recommendations miss the most effective individual actions. *Environmental Research Letters*, *12*(7), 074024. https://doi.org/10.1088/1748-9326/aa7541

Zhou, Y. (2022, December 28). Toward a feminist re-problematization of China's low birth rate. *Georgetown Journal of International Affairs*. https://gjia.georgetown.edu/2023/01/06/toward-a-feminist-re-problematization-of-chinas-low-birth-rate/

2

# Restraint in Consumption

## Luke Philip Plotica

> On what grounds should practices of ignorance be reproached? If knowing only aims to modify our relations to ourselves without changing anything about our relations to the world we inhabit, the denunciation is pointless. It only has meaning if it obliges us to think, hesitate, and slow down.
>
> —Vinciane Despret (2016)

In the societies of the Global North (and increasingly in the Global South) mass culture, economic activities, social structures, political practices, governmental institutions, and even personal identity are mediated in profound ways by what, how, and why we consume. What is more, as nearly every anthropogenic impact on the ecosphere traces, directly or indirectly, to acts of consumption, cohabiting Earth requires us to critically examine and be willing to meaningfully alter our practices of consumption. Yet despite vast social science and humanities literatures on consumption, the topic does not often get the attention it deserves in public representations and discussions of ecological harm and crisis. This is due in no small part to the fact that consumption is often overshadowed by its sibling, production. As economic and social engagements, the two always go hand in hand. In the oft-quoted words of Adam Smith (1776), "Consumption is the sole end and purpose of all production." Grant, for the sake of argument, this strictly instrumental view of production, which artists and artisans might justifiably dispute, and the point is that although production may be *temporally* prior to consumption, the latter is *logically* prior to the former.

The two are also deeply linked from an ecological perspective. Production causes ecological harms by way of extraction (e.g., mining), the clearing of habitats (e.g., for commodity agriculture), and the generation of pollution (e.g., agricultural runoff and industrial emissions), to name some of the most widespread phenomena. Yet the ecological harms of human activity do not end with the finished good or service that is produced. Consumption leaves waste in its wake (including packaging, worn-out items, and things simply unused), unleashes its own direct ecological harms (e.g., the impacts of household chemicals or of travel and tourism), and encourages us to do ecologically harmful things in order to secure the resources that enable consumption (e.g., long-distance commuting as well as waste and pollution at our workplaces). While the ecological impacts of consumption have been recognized for decades, the effects of production often garner more attention. When we think about the causes of ecological devastation, we are more likely to picture strip mines, belching factory smokestacks, and clear-cut forests than we are to picture someone streaming music or video on a device, ordering food at a restaurant, or getting a parcel delivered to their home. What is more, when we *are* confronted by the harms wrought by human consumption, such as sea creatures snared in plastic packaging or mountainous landfills, we often arrive, sooner or later, at the question, Why do (other) people *produce* these harmful things? Here we might remember Smith's observation: these things are produced so that they may be consumed, closing the economic circle.

There are many reasons why we are often more willing to scrutinize production than consumption, and I explore several of them in this chapter. An especially powerful reason, rooted in the Enlightenment and the Industrial Revolution, but continuously renovated, is technological optimism. Late modern societies are awash in rapidly changing and "improving" technologies and are deeply oriented by faith in what can be termed "technofixes" (Haraway, 2016). To be sure, every step of technological progress causes side effects, but these can ostensibly be remedied by later steps down the path of progress. From "green" products that capitalize on growing ecological awareness and anxiety to the messianism and long-termism of Big Tech and venture capitalist culture, we are assured that production can be made less ecologically harmful and will one day even reverse ecological harm. This seems to square with common sense: if bad modes of production have caused our ecological problems, then good (or at least better) modes of production will remedy them. Replace fossil fuels with renewable energy, use more recycled materials, and phase out highly polluting chemicals in favor of less toxic alternatives. What the production technologies of the past got wrong, the production technologies of the future will get right.

The prevailing technological optimism regarding production goes hand in hand with a related optimism about consumption, a faith that consumption can be made ecologically neutral or even beneficial, that so long as we clean up the production side of things, levels of consumption can remain the same, or even increase, without any reason for concern. Electricity consumption, one might suppose, is only ecologically problematic if the *sources* of that electricity cause ecological harms. The roots of this prevailing attitude toward consumption are partly economic and partly political. In consumer societies, such as those of the Global North, economic growth is driven in large measure by consumption, and thus the most palatable and profitable ecological "solutions" are typically to be found on the production side. However, as economic inequality and corporate influence on politics have grown in recent decades, billions of people have been compensated for the erosion of their political agency as *citizens* with the expansion of their apparent economic agency as *consumers* (Bauman, 2007; Piketty, 2014).

My aim in this chapter is to argue that although production-side measures to reduce and alleviate ecological harm are indispensable, we must take consumption equally seriously. Ecological responsibility and care require a better understanding of consumption and the role it plays in ecological harm as well as a willingness earnestly to explore and embrace various forms of restraint in consumption. Again, Smith is a helpful starting point from which to begin this critical inquiry. If the purpose of production is consumption, then what is the purpose of consumption? Or, more manageably, what does our consumption tell us about ourselves and about our relationship to the ecosphere in which we consume?

## Understanding Consumption

Consumption is an essential part of contemporary human life. We must consume a wide range of things—such as food, clothing, shelter, and basic services like education and healthcare—in order to survive and to flourish in even the most rudimentary sense. However, our current practices of consumption are not inevitable facts of nature but contingent social artifacts. The rise of consumer society was made possible by industrialization and the harnessing of new modes of production both to satisfy our needs and, importantly, to expand our wants. To say that the purpose of production is consumption is not to say that production merely responds to preexisting, context-independent wants. Rather, as economist John Kenneth Galbraith (1958) observed, many of the wants that drive our consumption are themselves manufactured or amplified by profit-seeking product designers, advertisers, and marketing firms (to which we might add social media influencers). Our wants are not fixed or constant; they are continuously evolving tensions between the actual and the imagined. New promised satisfactions tend to create the desire to enjoy them. What is more, we are purposive beings whose lives consist of continually negotiating the satisfaction of our wants (whatever their object or origin may be). Hence, our practices of consumption both affect and are affected by how we understand ourselves and what we value, how we understand the world in which we live, and what we do in light of this understanding.

In a sense, our practices of consumption are mirrors in which we can view aspects of ourselves, and three prevailing characteristics are readily apparent. First, contemporary consumption tends to be *voracious*. Not only has average consumption in most countries been steadily rising, but the intensity of consumption and its potency in defining personal identity and social standing continues to grow (Dittmar, 2008). Second, we are increasingly *omnivorous* as consumers. Globalization, the Internet, and decreasing costs of travel have profoundly diversified the range of goods and services that we can (and are told that we should) consume. At the same time, diversity of tastes and experiences serves as a mark of social standing that is available to a widening range of people (Sullivan & Katz-Gerro, 2007). Third, our consumption is becoming more *rapid*. On the one hand, we live in "throwaway" societies, in which goods and services are meant to be consumed and discarded quickly, to be replaced by something newer and better (Baudrillard, 1998). On the other hand, as social theorist Hartmut Rosa (2013) has argued, we live under persistent conditions of "social acceleration" in which the prevailing cultural imperative is to pack more production, consumption, activity, and experience into each unit of time. Taken together, we are consuming more, of greater variety, and at faster rates; and this way of life is spreading.

Despite the intensification of consumption and its undeniable ecological harms, consumption is nonetheless often presented more as the solution than as a cause of the problem. The commonsense rationale, reoriented toward consumption, is that the harms of consuming bad products can be remedied by consuming good products. Electric cars and roof-top solar panels, for instance, are presented as ways of consuming better without necessarily consuming less. Here is technological optimism at work—the problem is not that we have structured our societies and lives such that many people must drive to do just about everything or that we live in houses constantly buzzing with electrical devices but that we do not have the right car or the right source of electricity. These propositions are likely true simultaneously, to varying extents, but reduced consumption is presented, if at all, as the last resort, not the first. Similarly, sociologist Andrew Szasz (2009) has documented the rise of a "mutant form of environmentalism" that he terms "inverted quarantine." Faced with demonstrated ecological harms, we are marketed and we consume products (from water and air filters to personal wellness products to housing in affluent suburbs and exurbs) that promise to help us create our own private safe spaces. Unlike the technological optimism that counsels that we each buy an electric car to fight climate change, the logic of inverted quarantine is fully compatible with, and likely encourages, devil-take-the-hindmost cynicism. Nothing that one person does will make a difference, so stay as comfortable as you can and try not to be bothered about it. When we are confronted with existentially threatening events such as climate change, mass extinction, or global pandemics, this mindset is especially appealing—we balm our feelings of uncertainty and powerlessness with consumption, whether to distract ourselves, to protect ourselves, or both.

Why, though, are we so averse to the idea of reducing our consumption and so eager to believe that the *real* solution is newer and better production to feed and ennoble our consumption? For one thing, we are deliberately sold this narrative by those who have an interest in our continued consumption, including not only business interests who profit directly but also political interests that benefit indirectly (e.g., from the political capital generated by economic growth). Yet there is a more fundamental reason. We are embodied beings living in a world of other beings, both animate and inanimate. As phenomenologists such as Edmund Husserl (1977) and Martin Heidegger (1996) argued, we do not merely "observe" or "interact" with the world, as if these activities were occasional or optional—rather, we, as it were, are immersed in it.

Everything we think, feel, and do is shaped by our unceasing experience of this material world (even if we sometimes strive to transcend it). Accordingly, our identities, personalities, cares, and hopes are neither given to us independently of the world in which we are immersed nor crafted in autonomous detachment from this world. Things shape us and we shape ourselves in part by altering our relationships with things in the world. When it is suggested that we should change our habits of consumption, we are, in effect, being told that we should become different people, even if only in relatively minor senses. Even the smallest changes leave their imprints on us, and even if we *want* to make these changes, that does not make them effortless or inconsequential. This problematic is, as I shall suggest, surmountable, but it is nonetheless real.

There are also economic and social reasons for our reluctance. Defenses of current patterns of consumption and criticisms of calls for restraint not only trade upon narrowly imagined, yet persistent, economic orthodoxies (e.g., that a specific model of consumption-driven economic growth is the only viable path forward for humanity), they also trade upon the implicit notion that consumption does for us what we expect and hope it will do. That is, if I consume X in order to experience Y, then this is what consuming X will actually accomplish—yet things are rarely this simple. As philosophers such as Jean Baudrillard and economists such as John Kenneth Galbraith have understood, acts of consumption generally do not lastingly quench the desires that motivated them, and under the current configurations of capitalism they are often not really meant to do so. Instead, as Galbraith (1958: 129) put it, our "wants are increasingly created by the process by which they are satisfied [and e]xpectation rises with attainment." Baudrillard (1998) adds that this is because we do not consume isolated objects but objects that are interrelated elements of complex systems of objects and associated meanings. Even when objects of consumption satisfy immediate, rudimentary wants (such as water satisfying thirst), they are also often building blocks of the selves we each (are supposed to) want to be or badges of membership in imagined communities or lifestyles to which we would like to belong. Indeed, this is partly what binds acts of consumption, over time, into patterns of consumer*ism* as a guiding cultural ideology.

We can also see this in contemporary understandings of affluence and poverty. In the language of economics, there are two general forms that modern poverty takes, especially in the Global North, but increasingly in parts of the Global South as well: absolute deprivation and relative deprivation. The former is the lack of resources (such as money, time, education, or legal rights) required to obtain the essentials of life, such as food and shelter. The latter, however, is the lack of resources required to achieve and sustain a lifestyle considered typical within a specific group in a specific time and place. Both absolute and relative deprivation are as old as human societies, and both are also historically and culturally contextual. While the most basic essentials of life (e.g., nutritious food and clean water) do not profoundly change over time, the conditions under which we strive for and obtain them do. Think, for instance, of the difference between a Neolithic farmer eating from the fields they labored to cultivate and a 21st century commuter getting takeaway on the evening trip back to the suburbs. Yet relative deprivation is *essentially* contextual, defined as much by what others want and have as by what one personally wants and has. Think of the same commuter feeling embarrassed and discontented on account of being the only rider in the train car without this season's new smartphone. Absolute deprivation is also bounded and can (in principle) be satisfied simply, whereas relative deprivation is potentially boundless, demanding an open-ended quest for more and more complex consumption. Thus, we are under pressure from nearly all sides not only to consume but to consume in certain ways and to satisfy our wants not only in manners that comport with the expectations of others but in ways that also align with our (ideal) senses of self (Roscoe & Isenhour, 2021). Consumption is, thus, understandably a prickly subject.

## A Case for Restraint in Consumption

Since the basic fact of anthropogenic ecological devastation is now beyond meaningful debate, making the case for restraint in consumption is not a matter of demonstrating its ecological import. Instead, it is about articulating visions of restraint that build the ecological case upon a robust understanding of the overlapping economic, social, psychological, and political dimensions of consumption. Doing this requires addressing arguments made, often by environmentalists, that the focus upon individual consumption is a distraction from more important institutional concerns, both economic and political.

As Timothy Luke (1993) has argued, since the 1970s emphasizing the ecological harms of individual or household consumption has, ironically, been a tool of "conservative ideological containment" deployed against environmental activism as well as a tool for cultivating new forms of ecologically ineffective "green consumerism." The attention that is superficially paid to the role of consumption has, he suggests, often been used to exonerate the inactivity of politicians and the profit-seeking exploitation of businesses. Again, apparent economic agency waxes while actual political agency wanes. We are left to fend for ourselves as individual consumers, often merely choosing between the products offered to us by the very same businesses that use the emphasis of individual responsibility to evade their own responsibility and regulation by government. Coupled with Szasz's analysis, this illustrates how calls to change our individual habits of consumption may be co-opted in numerous ways, at the very least by enabling government and business interests to avoid ecological accountability and by providing a ready, anxious market for new "green(washed)" products and lifestyle ideals.

None of this, however, means that restraining our individual consumption is ecologically inconsequential. If an act of consumption causes an ecological harm, then choosing not to engage in that act of consumption averts that harm. Even if another person might still consume what I chose not to, that is not the same as both of us consuming. Nor do we face a choice between mutually exclusive options: *either* a collective political response *or* an individual ethical response. Ecological responsibility and care transcend this distinction—thus, we need *both* collective political *and* individual ethical action (Plotica, 2020). The enervation of political action described by Luke, Szasz, and others is instructive, but it is not inevitable. What is more, a narrow focus upon the collective, institutional level is problematic in its own ways, two of which I will note here.

First, while current political and economic institutions are undoubtedly ecologically problematic, a deeper change in these institutional arrangements would not, by itself, be adequate. Despite their differences, capitalism and socialism (the two realistic ends of the spectrum for present purposes) have both a fundamental enemy and an ultimate goal in common. The enemy is scarcity; the goal is abundance. While they differ over how to overcome the former and achieve the latter, both seek to maximize production to enable consumption. Thus, consumption and consumerism are not phenomena generated only by one political or economic ideology, which would be remedied as a matter of course by another. Whatever the political and economic institutions under which our patterns of consumption developed, these patterns are now entrenched phenomena that provide the background against which political and economic ideologies struggle against one another. Consumption, thus, must be addressed directly.

Second, privileging the institutional level over the individual tends to encourage the very same kind of passivity and inaction that critics such as Luke and Szasz attribute to the focus upon individual consumption. Much as the practices and mindsets of green consumerism and inverted quarantine encourage individuals to passively await a menu of ecologically responsible consumer choices to be offered to them by the market, the politics-or-nothing mindset encourages individuals to passively await parties, candidates, or policies to offer and enact the solutions. Especially at a time when the pathologies of politics and governance (and their entrenched connections to economic interests) are on such conspicuous display around the world, the suggestion that the only meaningful actions to redress ecological harm are political or institutional appears tantamount to surrender. What is more, the narrow focus on political (and economic) institutions tends to rest upon an implicit, ahistorical notion about these institutions, namely, that they are crafted ex nihilo according to some comprehensive design. Most institutions are chimeras cobbled together over time in response to many different problems, plans, contingencies, and choices. They are reflections of both deliberate designs and largely unreflective cultural habits, with the former always being shaped in some way by the latter. It may sound unrealistic to expect small acts of restraint in consumption to have significant ecological impacts. It is far less realistic, however, to expect people to have the will to mobilize politically for the sake of values that they do not embrace, and are even told are ineffectual, in their daily lives. The ecological failures of green consumerism and inverted quarantine merely illustrate the point. Both approaches promise that consuming better will avert the need to consume less, working hand in glove with political and economic actors who are motivated by short-term, ecologically indifferent interests, and who benefit handsomely from a passive, consumerist public.

## Enacting Restraint

Perhaps the strongest headwind faced by advocates of restraint in consumption is that, in comparison to the promises of endless novelty and plenty that are the heart of consumer culture, "restraint" sounds almost synonymous with "deprivation," "disappointment," and "self-denial." However, consumption and restraint are relative notions, and the forms that restraint might take are no fewer or less varied than the forms consumption might. Consumption and restraint therein are also highly contextual, and thus there is no fixed list of rules to follow, only intimations to consider and explore where we find ourselves. What I describe here are several general possibilities of how one might envision or cultivate restraint, whatever day-to-day, ground-level forms it might take.

Much like Smith before him, Henry David Thoreau (1992) recognized that modern economic life is characterized by the division of labor. In search of efficiency and productivity we break activities into smaller and smaller steps, and many of us perform narrow ranges of tasks in order to get the money to purchase and consume the fruits of what we have left it to others to do for us. Both Smith and Thoreau were troubled by the effects that division of labor had upon the people who performed it, but Thoreau was especially prescient regarding how the division of labor fed both the drive to consume and the willingness to exploit the ecosphere. It is entirely unrealistic to suppose that billions of people would or could go completely DIY, but there are many ways in which we might partly heal the division of labor. Nonetheless, the return of crafts, the satisfaction of making and doing things ourselves, and the connections to both living and nonliving things that such activities help to cultivate might all lessen our dependence on consumption by helping us to find meaning in the experience of our own production and to dampen the cultural drives toward voracious, omnivorous, and rapid consumption (Sennett, 2008).

The prospects of enacting restraint also become better the more connected we feel to the more-than-human world around us. Rather than placing our hopes in technofixes, Haraway (2016) advocates practices of "making kin," building senses of connection to nonhuman and even nonliving beings. How exactly one might do this is limited only by one's imagination, but a useful starting point is recognition of the fact that on this planet, upon whose ecosystems we are entirely dependent, *every* species is our companion species. Every day is full of encounters with beings in the world whom we may recognize as our kin, for whose sake we might enact restraint. Making kin might help us to reassess our consumption by helping to dismantle the logic of inverted quarantine and the instrumentalist, anthropocentric worldview upon which it is implicitly built. Cohabiting Earth, for both individuals and societies, requires that we stop trying to keep the nonhuman world at a violently maintained distance and accept the abiding truth that the entire ecosphere is our home, shared with all other beings in it.

Making kin is just one vitally important example of something larger. Modern science, economics, and politics have gradually disenchanted the nonhuman world and our relationship to it, leaving little more than an instrumentalized heap of resources to exploit (Gerth & Mills, 1958). Consumption and consumerism thrive because, in a world thus understood, their costs appear worth their benefits and there appear to be few other ways to find meaning and fulfilment. Restraining our consumption is more likely as well as less onerous if we find ways to (re)discover and cultivate a sense of (re)enchantment with the ecosphere (and also, perhaps ironically, with the objects we so readily consume and discard). There are many paths to such re-enchantment, some secular, others religious, some individual, others communal, some episodic, others ongoing, but insofar as we develop senses of meaning, respect, and reverence toward the ecosphere, restraining our consumption likewise becomes more meaningful and sustainable.

Much as consumer culture conditions us to view restraint as deprivation, it instills a false sense of necessity. However, and for whatever reason we may do it, enacting restraint requires knowing what really matters to us and knowing what we do and do not really need. As philosophers from Jean-Jacques Rousseau (1987) to Hannah Arendt (1958) have recognized, what enters into regular contact with our lives becomes, sooner or later, a condition of our existence, interwoven with our senses of self, of meaning, of value, and of possibility. Yet the things that over time become conditions of our lives are not conditions without which our continued existence is impossible; nor are they conditions of our survival or even flourishing (as many things upon which we become dependent undermine our flourishing, as individuals and collectively, in countless ways). They become conditions of our continued comfort, things without which we (think we) would not be as happy or secure, or without which we would simply not know what to do with ourselves. Not only does consumer culture manufacture wants, it assures us that wants *are* needs and that we *deserve* to satisfy them, despite their costs or harms. There is no simple, self-evident list of necessities, but most of our dependencies are clearly no more than mere wants. It is necessary that we sleep, but not that we have a tablet or smartphone to watch in bed. It is necessary that we eat, but not that we eat animal products. Taking honest stock of our lives—identifying our needs and scrutinizing our wants—is by no means easy. Yet doing so is part and parcel of healing the division of labor, finding enchantment in the ecosphere, and making kin with fellow beings (Thoreau, 1992).

There is, ultimately, no single, ideal model of restraint in consumption to follow. The sites and forms of consumption are many, and so too are the sites and forms of possible change. The task is one of habituating ourselves to ways of living that both make a tangible ecological difference (as restraint in consumption certainly can) and cultivate in us a sense of attachment to the ecosphere. Consumption will remain an unavoidable aspect of human existence. We shall always require food, shelter, and other things that, under contemporary conditions, come from outside of ourselves. Few of us will ever provide for all of our own needs, whether as individuals, households, or small communities. Hence, the question is how to consume less and more responsibly, more thoughtfully, and more meaningfully. At the same time, we must recognize that modern societies are so complex, and their parts so variously interconnected, that if we change or eliminate one element, others that we do not wish to change will also be affected. Our patterns of consumption are not superficial blemishes that can be simply brushed away, leaving no trace behind. We have built so much upon consumption that we must be deliberate and careful in how we go about restraining it. In short, our choice is not between the good and the bad, let alone between the perfect and imperfect, but between the better and the worse, which really means between different, complex configurations of imperfections. Here Thoreau's (1992) exhortation seems appropriate: "In the long run men hit only what they aim at. Therefore, though they should fail immediately, they had better aim at something high."

## References

Arendt, H. (1958). *The Human Condition*. University of Chicago Press.
Baudrillard, J. (1998). *The Consumer Society: Myths and Structures* (transl. C. Turner). Sage Press.
Bauman, Z. (2007). *Consuming Life*. Polity Press.
Despret, V. (2016). *What Would Animals Say If We Asked the Right Questions?* University of Minnesota Press.
Dittmar, H. (2008). *Consumer Culture, Identity, and Well-Being: The Search for the "Good Life" and the "Body Perfect."* Routledge.
Galbraith, J. K. (1958). *The Affluent Society*. Houghton Mifflin.
Gerth, H. H., & Mills, C. W. (Eds.) (1958). *From Max Weber: Essays in Sociology*. Oxford University Press.

Haraway, D. J. (2016). *Staying with the Trouble: Making Kin in the Cthulucene*. Duke University Press.
Heidegger, M. (1996). *Being and Time* (transl. J. Stambaugh). State University of New York Press.
Husserl, E. (1977). *Cartesian Meditations* (transl. D. Cairns). Martinus Nijhoff.
Luke, T. W. (1993). Green consumerism: Ecology and the ruse of recycling. In J. Bennett & W. Chaloupka (Eds.), *In the Nature of Things* (pp. 154–72). University of Minnesota Press.
Piketty, T. (2014). *Capital in the Twenty-First Century* (transl. A. Goldhammer). Harvard University Press.
Plotica, L. P. (2020). Politics is not enough: Individual action and the limits of institutions. *The Ecological Citizen*, 4(1), 37–43.
Rosa, H. (2013). *Social Acceleration: A New Theory of Modernity* (transl. J. Trejo-Mathys). Columbia University Press.
Roscoe, P., & Isenhour, C. (Eds.) (2021). *Consumption, Status, and Sustainability: Ecological and Anthropological Perspectives*. Cambridge University Press.
Rousseau, J. J. (1987) Discourse on the origin and foundations of inequality among men (transl. D. Cress). In D. Cress (Ed.), *The Basic Political Writings* (pp. 28–120). Hackett.
Sennett, R. (2008). *The Craftsman*. Penguin Books.
Smith, A. (1776). *An Inquiry into the Nature and Causes of the Wealth of Nations*. Methuen & Co.
Sullivan, O., & Katz-Gerro, T. (2007). The omnivore thesis revisited: Voracious cultural consumers. *European Sociological Review*, 23(2), 123–37. https://doi.org/10.1093/esr/jcl024
Szasz, A. (2009). *Shopping Our Way to Safety: How We Changed from Protecting the Environment to Protecting Ourselves*. University of Minnesota Press.
Thoreau, H.D. (1992). Walden. In W. Rossi (Ed.), *Walden and Resistance to Civil Government* (2nd ed.; pp. 1–223). W. W. Norton & Company.

3

# Technologies Fit for an Ecological Future

JOHN MICHAEL GREER

From an ecological standpoint, modern industrial society can best be described as an ingenious way to waste as much of the natural wealth of the planet as fast as possible. While that approach to life on Earth has certain short-term benefits, the drawbacks are considerably greater. Practical as well as ethical concerns demand a saner way of life in which human societies and nonhuman nature exist in sustainable balance with one another.

Serious technical challenges stand in the way of such a project. Yet these problems are arguably less significant than the cognitive barriers closing off that set of potential futures. The most important of these barriers is the conviction that we all already know what the future must be like. Throughout modern industrial societies, the images that saturate the collective imagination of our time portray a future defined by hypercomplex technologies, supported by limitless access to energy and material resources.

This is exactly the kind of future we will not get. Half a century of analyses, beginning with the epochal study *Limits to Growth*, has shown that our civilization's misguided pursuit of limitless economic expansion on a finite planet guarantees that the human societies of the near and far future will have to cope with significantly less access to concentrated energy and nonrenewable materials (Meadows et al., 1972). Building on these analyses, most realistic attempts to make sense of our species' trajectory through time envision the industrial age as a unique and self-terminating interval of extravagant consumption and waste, followed by a permanent return to lower levels of resource and energy use (Catton, 1980; Duncan, 1993).

The only model for such a descent that the conventional wisdom of our time offers is the overfamiliar image of apocalyptic collapse. It should be immediately obvious that this is far from the only option. History provides many examples of civilizations thriving on per capita energy and resource inputs that are tiny fractions of those consumed by modern industrial societies. Consider East Asia in the early modern era: a region of thriving, complex societies in which basic health care was more readily available to the laboring classes than it is in today's United States, and in which literature and the arts flourished to a degree that makes modern industrial societies look embarrassingly backward (Brook, 1998; Naquin, 2000). In Japan during this period, to cite only one relevant detail, the three largest cities collectively had no fewer than 1,500 bookstores (Hanley, 1991).

A future that can sustain high levels of literacy, culture, and basic human services, along with robust ecological communities and the preservation or expansion of Earth's remaining biodiversity, is a goal worth pursuing. Reaching that goal requires an attitude toward technology that is deeply unfashionable in today's industrial nations. The evolution of technology is by and large presented to the public via the ideology of progress, which claims that newer technologies replace older ones because the former are objectively superior to the latter. Absent from this ideology is any recognition of the role of human agency in choosing or rejecting technologies.

As John Ellis pointed out trenchantly in *The Social History of the Machine Gun*, pretending that technology evolves by itself and human beings are merely passive recipients of the results is merely a convenient way to mask the promotion by influential groups of technologies that further their own economic or political advantage (Ellis, 1975). A strong case can be made that belief in progress functions as a civil religion—an ideology that justifies existing habits on no stronger basis than that of blind faith (Greer, 2015). The dogmatic insistence that progress is as inevitable as it is irreversible, and that current technological arrangements can be replaced only by even more complex ways of doing the same things, might best be described as the most widely accepted folk mythology of our time.

It is crucial to understand that the technologies that dominate today's industrial societies did not achieve that status by some up-to-date equivalent of the divine right of kings. They rose to dominance because in a world awash with cheap abundant fossil fuels and ample material resources, they were more successful in meeting the needs of influential sectors of society than rival technologies were. Now that fossil fuels are neither cheap nor abundant and access to material resources is becoming problematic, many of those technologies are obsolete. The attitude that insists that they are the inevitable product of progress thus stands in the way of the changes that will be needed to retool society for the future.

Regional and national electrical grids are a useful example. During the era of cheap abundant fossil fuels, it made economic sense to burn gargantuan amounts of coal, oil, and natural gas so that every home and business across large geographical areas could have as much electricity as might be desired at any time of day or night. In the process of converting heat into electricity, conveying the electricity across long distances, and converting it back into heat or mechanical energy, most primary energy derived from the fuels was lost to entropy—in the United States today, for example, 68 percent of the energy used for electricity generation is lost to entropy (US Energy Information Administration, 2022). The sheer abundance of fossil fuels makes that level of waste economically irrelevant.

Now that fossil fuels are quickly depleting, large-scale electrical grids arguably no longer make economic sense. While electrical grids on a smaller scale in densely populated areas might be a viable option, other, less wasteful ways of handling energy distribution in rural regions are worth exploring. Only the pervasive folk belief in the inevitability and irreversibility of progress bars the way to a realistic assessment of the best ways to manage energy use in the future.

## Thermodynamic Limits

In recent decades, due to the mental blocks imposed by the civil mythology of progress, nearly all attempts to harness renewable resources have been forced into the Procrustean bed of existing technological commitments. Consider solar power. The sun has impressive advantages as an energy source. To begin with, its fuel supply is assured for the next billion years or so. Technologies designed to put solar energy to work meeting human needs have been in regular use for well over 2,000 years (Butti and Perlin, 1980), providing an impressive knowledge base for further developments. Despite its advantages, solar energy is poorly suited to provide electrical current for grid power on Earth's surface: night and weather make access to it intermittent, and the 93 million miles separating the sun from Earth make solar energy highly diffuse by the time it reaches us.

It must be remembered in this context that the laws of thermodynamics impose sharp limits on which technologies will be able to function in a future of more constrained energy and material resources. Two of the implications of thermodynamic limits should be given special attention. The first is *energy concentration*. Compare a ray of sunlight to the flames rising from burning gasoline; it should not be necessary to hold a hand in each of them to notice the difference in energy concentration! The more concentrated an energy source is, the more work it can do. Crucially, however, it takes energy to concentrate energy. The energy in petroleum was concentrated by millions of years of heat and pressure deep within the earth. Sunlight falling onto the earth at this moment does not benefit from the hidden subsidies of geology, and so much more energy must be invested in order to concentrate it, if a concentrated form of it is necessary.

Sustainable uses of solar power should thus arguably focus on gathering heat from sunlight directly for such purposes as water heating, space heating, food preparation, and the many industrial processes that require heat below 200°C. None of these require solar energy to be converted into a more concentrated form: the ordinary diffuse heat of sunlight in the natural state is entirely adequate for the work. Yet the great majority of investment in solar energy in the last quarter of a century has been directed to ways to turn sunlight into electricity to provide grid power—a process that requires a great deal of concentration. The results have been equivocal at best. The same investment directed into technologies that use less concentrated forms of sunlight would arguably have contributed much more to the task of building a sustainable future.

Alongside energy concentration is the closely related feature of *resource footprint*. Today's industrial technologies rely on global supply chains extracting a galaxy of raw materials from sources around the planet, and subjecting them to complex and intensive refining and manufacturing processes. None of the activities involved in transforming these materials from substances in nature to manufactured items ready to use in energy technology happen by themselves. All of them have their own energy and resource requirements, which must be factored into any assessment of the sustainability of the resulting technology. Additionally, the destructive impact of all the extraction, processing, and manufacturing for energy technology, on Earth's more-than-human world, must be taken fully into account and made a central concern in evaluating technological sustainability.

Once again, solar energy provides a good example. Photovoltaic (PV) cells, the keynote technology of most recent attempts to exploit solar power, are complex devices, and the subsidiary technologies that are required to make and use them are at least as complex. The supply chain needed to construct, maintain, and dispose of a complete solar PV system is very large. Assessing the true energy output of a PV system requires adding up all the energy consumed by this supply chain, and subtracting that from the lifetime energy yield of the PV facility under real-world conditions (not its theoretical yield, which is many times higher). Analyses of this sort are difficult due to the sheer number of factors that must be taken into account, but those studies done so far suggest that the energy costs needed to install and run a solar PV system account for a very large fraction of the energy it will produce in its working life (Prieto and Hall, 2015).

By contrast, other uses of solar energy have much smaller resource footprints. Solar water heating is a good example (Kachadorian, 2006; Ramlow and Nusz, 2010). Solar water heaters can be made locally from ordinary plumbing components, lumber, and window glass. The supply chain of the technology is much smaller and, in a pinch, can be filled out with salvage from derelict structures. Since it requires much less concentrated energy and relies on a smaller resource footprint, solar water heating is thus a far more sustainable technology than solar PV—and this also means, of course, that it is less disruptive to nonhuman ecosystems. Reliable access to hot water has played a very significant role in improving public health in the industrial world over the last two centuries. Preserving those gains using heat from the sun as a renewable energy source is obviously a worthwhile project, but it has received little attention from sustainability advocates over the last few decades.

## Innovation and Retrovation

The folk mythology of progress makes another unhelpful contribution to the challenges ahead. Most people nowadays, when they think about a challenge of the sort faced by modern industrial societies, think at once of "innovation" as the only strategy that can meet it. There is of course much value in pursuing innovation in this context. If a small portion of the enthusiasm and technical skill that has gone into making apps for smartphones, say, were to be put instead into creating sustainable technologies, the world would be in much better shape than it is today. Encouraging innovation in the widest possible range of energy technologies, especially those that can be developed and put to the test on a small scale, would be a valuable policy move, and something that sustainability advocates might consider making a priority.

At least three potential pitfalls face an innovation-centered strategy for the development of sustainable technologies, however. The first is that by many measures, the rate of innovation in modern times has been declining steadily for well over a century (Huebner, 2005). In science and technology, as in most other fields of human activity, the law of diminishing returns is a factor that has to be kept in mind. The discoveries of 19th century physics that revolutionized the world were made with equipment that would be considered inadequate for a middle school science class today: the research program into aerodynamics that created the first working airplane was carried out by two men who had never graduated from high school, using such hours and funds they could spare from their day jobs as bicycle technicians. The low-hanging fruit of innovation has long since been harvested, and what remains to be picked may not be sufficient to meet the needs of an industrial civilization in crisis.

The second potential pitfall is that even if a new technology is envisioned and research teams set out to develop it, no one can know in advance whether that technology will turn out to be viable, or even possible. Research into perpetual motion machines, for example, began in the Middle Ages and continued for centuries thereafter, because the goal—a device that would need no energy input to yield useful work—was so obviously worth pursuing (Ord-Hume, 1976). Not until the 19th century did the physical sciences advance far enough to show that perpetual motion was impossible. Until then, all anyone knew was that no previous attempt had succeeded. Compare this to the current state of fusion power research, for example, and the similarities are hard to miss. Whether or not some law of nature not yet known makes sustained nuclear fusion impossible on a scale smaller than a star, it remains the case that billions of dollars and euros of investment in fusion research have yet to yield a single watt of grid power. Nor does the impressive cost of fusion research facilities offer much hope that fusion power, even if it does become possible, will produce electricity at a price any society can afford.

This shades over into the third pitfall for sustainability innovation, which is the tendency already mentioned for fantasies of progress to take precedence over sober analysis when future technologies come up for consideration. Fusion power is again a good example. If not for the widespread faith-based assumption that fusion must be part of the future, the entire fusion research project worldwide would have been shut down decades ago, and the vast sums of money and the trained minds that have worked on it might have found something more useful to do with their time. Yet the attitude science journalist Charles Seife describes as "the science of wishful thinking" retains its grip on the collective imagination of our time, and prevents a more pragmatic attitude toward technology from having its say (Seife, 2008).

Innovation is certainly necessary as we confront the challenges of the future. It needs, however, to be paired with another approach to solutions: the systematic harvesting of viable technologies from the past, which I have termed *retrovation* (Greer, 2017). Older technologies have advantages that newly innovated technologies do not: they have already been proven to work; their costs, requirements, and side effects can generally be determined without too much difficulty from historical records; and their impact on nature is generally speaking gentler and easier to remediate. Retrovation thus sharply reduces the uncertainties involved in replacing unsustainable technologies with sustainable substitutes while also contributing to the protection of nature.

An example may be useful here. In the 18th and early 19th centuries, many regions in Europe and eastern North America built transport canal systems to provide cheap, efficient middle- and long-distance inland transport for bulk commodities and industrial products. Many of the resulting canals are still available for use today—Great Britain, for example, currently has 4,700 miles (6,700 km) of canals in working condition. The conventional wisdom defines the canal system as a pretty anachronism, useful solely for recreational purposes. Here, again, the mental blockages caused by the ideology of progress make constructive responses to the challenges of our time more difficult than they have to be.

What makes canal systems potentially valuable to a sustainable future is that canal transport is extraordinarily energy efficient as a way of transporting large cargoes: canalboats carrying tons of cargo were traditionally drawn along their routes by the muscular strength of a single mule plodding along the towpath. The technologies needed to build and operate canals and canalboats require equally modest inputs of energy and resources. In almost any conceivable future, canal transport will therefore be a viable way of moving cargoes to inland destinations. In those areas that still have viable canal systems, furthermore, canalboats can be put to work immediately in crisis conditions—for example, in the event of fuel shortages that interfere with truck and rail transport. This could provide a great deal of potential resilience in emergencies, as well as a framework for transport into the far future. The goal of reshaping society to work more harmoniously with nature becomes, in this way, a matter of making use of familiar options, rather than a leap into the unknown. This will be all the more the case in an ecological society, where consumption has been substantially downscaled.

## Technological Suites

The concept of technology itself deserves a closer look than it usually receives. While contemporary rhetoric very often uses the word "technology" in the singular, and equates it with the current assortment of technologies in use by industrial nations, it is more useful to think of technologies in the plural—or, more precisely, of *technological suites*. A technological suite is a set of technologies that work together directly or indirectly to meet some human need. The portion of the suite that is put to work by the end user rarely if ever accounts for the largest share of the suite to which it belongs.

Consider a standard bicycle with a steel frame and rubber tires. The frame and other metal parts are machined from steel, which is made from iron ore and carbon using a considerable amount of energy and complex technical processes. The tires are made either from synthetic rubber, requiring the mastery of certain branches of organic chemistry, or of natural rubber, requiring the mastery of rubber tree silviculture and latex preparation. Lubricants also have to be provided, requiring more chemical knowledge, and the overall design requires certain kinds of engineering such as gear design. All these things belong to the technological suite that yields bicycles.

Some technological suites allow considerable substitution. The suite that produces bicycles is one of them. Aluminum, wood, and bamboo, among other materials, have been used successfully to produce bicycle frames and parts, and rubber tires are not strictly speaking necessary—handmade bicycles in the Global South routinely do without them. Other technological suites have far more exacting requirements and allow far less substitution. Although there are exceptions, it is usually the case that the more complex and energy-intensive a technology is, the less substitution in its technological suite is possible.

The difference between these two ends of the spectrum of technological suites has little economic importance now, while fossil fuels and exotic raw materials (such as rare earths) are still available; their significance in terms of human impact on the nonhuman world is considerable, of course, but that has had little impact on public decision making so far. In the future it will no longer be possible to ignore these differences. For a technological suite to be sustainable, every part of the suite must be available within the limits of the material resources and energy supplies that our descendants will be able to provide. If even one element of the suite fails this test, the entire suite will become unavailable unless something else can be substituted for the missing piece.

Any human need, furthermore, can be met by any of several different technological suites. Even so basic a task as providing food, for example, can be carried out by hunting and gathering, village horticulture, nomadic pastoralism, mixed agriculture, or large-scale monoculture of the type practiced by Roman latifundia or modern corporate chemical-input-dependent farms. Over the last few centuries, in food production as in every other aspect of human life, the industrial world has adopted a set of technological suites that use extravagant amounts of concentrated energy and raw materials, and cause equally extravagant damage to the nonhuman world. The ideology of progress insists that these suites are better than any other in some absolute sense.

In point of fact, however, the suites that were adopted simply represent the options that provided the greatest political and economic advantages to decision-makers and elites in the dominant industrial nations of the time. As conditions change due to the rapid depletion of fossil fuels and other resources, many of those suites are proving to be very poorly suited for a world in which such extravagances are no longer affordable, and a large number of them may no longer be possible to maintain at all. The question that must be answered at this point is what alternative suites might be better suited to new conditions.

The technology of canal transport offers a glimpse at the answer. Canal systems are not suited to every region on Earth, since they require level topography and abundant water sources. Nor are canal systems the best available response to every human need, or even the best form of transportation for all purposes. They represent one technological suite that can be applied in certain circumstances to meet certain needs, while other suites may be more appropriate to different circumstances and different needs. Another glimpse comes from the movement to return to local and diversified modes of food production, which are more sustainable and ecologically friendly than the systems of today that depend so heavily on fossil fuels and cause massive pollution and destruction to the natural world.

Industrial technology has embraced the monoculture model, and not merely in agriculture. Implicit in the ideology of progress is the belief that one and only one collection of technological suites is superior to all others and should be imposed everywhere on Earth, until some even better collection can be found to replace it. This one-size-fits-all approach to technology has not worked especially well even during the age of extravagance now coming to an end around us. Discarding it and turning instead to technological suites better suited to local conditions is a better approach, even when those suites differ significantly from one another—and from the suites that industrial nations rely on today.

Yet this involves certain choices that many people nowadays will find unwelcome. While there are exceptions, it is true far more often than not that sustainable technologies are less convenient to use than unsustainable ones. Canal transport is an energy-efficient way to move cargoes from place to place, but it is slow. In the same way, a well-stocked public library can provide readers with an ample supply of books in an energy- and resource-efficient manner, but patrons have to go there; downloading books onto an e-reader from the Internet is much less trouble. In an ecological future, human beings might well desire to return to slower rhythms of life, leaving behind the frenetic tempos and "instant gratification" of modernity. We have not yet arrived at such a future, however, and the changes under discussion here may need to happen before so sweeping a change in attitudes has arrived.

As energy and resource depletion take a rising toll from the global economy, the more energy- and resource-efficient options will eventually be the only options still available. Until that point is reached, however, current technologies will likely retain their popularity, at least among those social classes that can afford to use them. Those products of innovation and retrovation that require long lead times for deployment may become temporarily or permanently unavailable as industrial civilization moves deeper into crisis. Thus it is worth discussing how to encourage the adoption of sustainable technological suites while time and resources make that process easier than it will become.

## Strategies for Adoption

It is one thing to propose guidelines for future technologies. It is quite another to take those guidelines out of the realm of might-have-beens and turn them into a practical program that has any chance of being put in place. The appropriate technology movement of the 1970s developed a considerable toolkit of technological suites that could have reduced the industrial world's carbon footprint and dependence on nonrenewable resources considerably had it been heeded (Todd, 1977; Olkowski et al., 1979). The movement's attempts to win widespread adoption of that toolkit failed to gain any traction, and even such basic energy-saving measures as adequate insulation in homes and commercial spaces dropped out of widespread use.

High prices for fossil fuel products during the energy crises of the 1970s helped spur the development of energy- and resource-saving technologies, just as the steep decline in energy costs in the 1980s helped bring about their abandonment. As fossil fuel depletion drives the cost of energy up again, a renewal of interest in energy conservation can be expected. Waiting until this happens, however, risks losing time that could be critical in helping industrial societies make the transition to more ecologically stable lifeways without traumatic dislocations affecting individuals, societies, and the biosphere as a whole.

The prospects for a general change in attitudes toward the environment among people in the world's industrial societies are discussed elsewhere in this book. For the purposes of this chapter, however, it may be worth assuming that no such general change takes place, and that sustainable technologies will have to find niches in local, regional, and global economies in other ways. I suggest three ways to facilitate their adoption.

First, technological suites suited to meeting human needs on a sustainable basis need be chosen on a regional and national basis. What might be useful in one area—for example, expanding cargo traffic on the canal system in Great Britain—will be useless in areas with different histories and environmental conditions. People interested in taking an active role in developing ecologically sound technologies might be well advised to focus their attention on the regions where they live, since their chances of identifying resources and limits there are arguably better than if they attempt to do so for places where they lack the benefit of firsthand experience.

Second, technological suites well suited to a given area should be promoted using any available means, whether or not this relates to environmental advocacy. The canal system in Great Britain, to return to the same example, will be just as useful as a transport network for our descendants whether or not it is preserved out of respect for the environment. When concern for environmental issues have become associated with one side of a bitter political and cultural divide, as in the United States today, finding some other set of ideas with which to encourage adoption of sustainable technological suites may well be a more effective option than linking those suites with ideological stances that are rejected by much of the population.

Third, since personal example is the most effective means of advocacy, those who are concerned with ecological issues should consider becoming early adopters of sustainable technologies themselves. This is partly a matter of smart politics. One of the most dangerous arguments deployed by opponents of environmental legislation is the claim that environmental activists want others to use less energy and fewer raw materials so that they themselves can continue to live energy- and resource-extravagant lifestyles. That argument has been effective precisely because so many celebrity environmentalists cling to wildly unsustainable lifestyles. So long as advocates for environmental causes fail to walk their talk by using less energy and fewer nonrenewable resources than the majority, it will see further use.

Yet there is another dimension to personal example. Every significant technological innovation catches on first with a small minority and expands from there to become more widely popular: Consider the very small number of automobiles in industrial nations in the first decades of the 20th century, or the equally small number of personal computers in the early days of the microcomputer revolution. If sustainable technological suites are to find their footing before the sheer pressure of necessity forces their adoption, small groups of enthusiasts are among the most likely ways to make this happen.

The sooner such ventures become a significant part of the lifestyles of environmental advocates, the better. Through personal example, backed by a clear understanding of the scientific, economic, ecological, and ethical dimensions of the transition ahead, those who are truly committed to making a world in which human societies are in harmony with nature can contribute much to that process of change.

## References

Brook, T. (1998). *The Confusions of Pleasure: Commerce and Culture in Ming China*. University of California Press.
Butti, K., & Perlin, J. (1980). *A Golden Thread: 2,500 Years of Solar Architecture and Technology*. Van Nostrand Reinhold.
Catton, W. R., Jr. (1980). *Overshoot: The Ecological Basis of Revolutionary Change*. University of Illinois Press.
Duncan, R. C. (1993). The life-expectancy of industrial civilization: The decline to global equilibrium. *Population and Environment, 14*(4), 325–57. https://doi.org/10.1007/BF01270915
Ellis, J. (1975). *The Social History of the Machine Gun*. Pantheon Books.
Greer, J. M. (2015). *After Progress: Reason and Religion at the End of the Industrial Age*. New Society.
Greer, J. M. (2017). *The Retro Future: Looking to the Past to Reinvent the Future*. New Society.
Hanley, S. B. (1991). Tokugawa society: Material culture, standard of living, and life-styles. In J. W. Hall (Ed.), *The Cambridge History of Japan—Volume 4: Early Modern Japan* (pp. 660–705). Cambridge University Press.
Huebner, J. (2005). A possible declining trend for worldwide innovation. *Technological Forecasting & Social Change, 72*, 980–86. https://doi.org/10.1016/j.techfore.2005.01.003
Kachadorian, J. (2006). *The Passive Solar House*. Chelsea Green.
Meadows, D., Meadows, D., Randers, J., & Behrens, W. W. III (1972). *The Limits to Growth*. Universe.
Naquin, S. (2000). *Peking: Temples and City Life, 1400–1900*. University of California Press.
Olkowski, H., Olkowski, B., Javits, T., & the Farallones Institute staff (1979). *The Integral Urban House: Self-Reliant Living in the City*. Sierra Club Books.
Ord-Hume, A. W. J. G. (1976). *Perpetual Motion: The History of an Obsession*. St. Martins.
Prieto, P., & Hall, C. A. S. (2015). *Spain's Photovoltaic Revolution: The Energy Return on Investment*. Springer Publishing.
Ramlow, B., & Nusz, B. (2010). *Solar Water Heating: A Comprehensive Guide to Solar Water and Space Heating Systems*. New Society.
Seife, C. (2008). *Sun in a Bottle: The Strange History of Fusion and the Science of Wishful Thinking*. Penguin.
Todd, N. (Ed.) (1977). *The Book of the New Alchemists*. E. P. Dutton.
US Energy Information Administration (2022). *EIA Monthly Energy Review*. https://www.eia.gov/totalenergy/data/flow-graphs/electricity.php

# 4

# Social Ecological Transformation of Economies
## Where the Environmental Movement Went Wrong and What Is Needed

CLIVE L. SPASH

People who suffer environmental injustice—people of colour, indigenous communities, and people who live on top of toxic waste dumps, or next to polluting factories, busy roads, noisy airports, and toxic rivers—have long hoped the environmental movement would do something about it. Some 40 or 50 years ago, the movement was radical, progressive, and ecologically inspired—indeed, being too radical and too progressive for both the productivist State and capitalist enterprise, environmentalism had to be tamed and mainstreamed. After the 1987 Bruntland Report, later published as *Our Common Future* (World Commission on Environment and Development, 1991), the idea of limits on the economy was converted to "sustainable development" and "green growth."

Modern environmental NGOs (ENGOs) talk only indirectly, if at all, of the systemic problems behind environmental degradation. They avoid discussing capitalism, corporations, the military–industrial complex, and economic growth. The preferred positive "framing" of things is in general terms of greening and sustaining, with metaphors of spaceship Earth, ecological footprints, and economic doughnuts. Environmentalists speak the weak words of apologetic conservative reformers who fear scaring people.

For example, the World Wide Fund (WWF), an organization formerly concerned with wildlife, now states "we love cities," supporting urban lifestyles and treating nature as capital (Spash, 2015a). ENGOs turned away from protest and towards green marketing, creating their own corporate identities with logos to match and T-shirts to sell. In the neoliberal era of consumerism, environmental messages had to be sold to people in friendly packaging. Environmentalists should not mention being anticapitalist, in favour of degrowth, or wanting population stabilized, pollution stopped, and resources kept in the ground, but nice positive things like saving furry animals such as pandas. Harsh realities should be made soft.

From the 1980s onwards the rise of neoliberalism saw the environmental movement changing. Large ENGOs increasingly concluded that communicating environmental concerns required adopting the dominant form of power discourse in society—money. Ecologists adopted the language of economics, referring to ecosystems as goods and services, nature as capital, pollution as an "externality" beyond the responsibility of economic agents, and getting the prices right as "the solution." In line with mainstream economists, everything was to be weighed-up in order to determine the most "efficient" level at which to pollute others, both human and nonhuman, and the "optimal" rate at which species should become extinct. Selling the environment to preserve it became the accepted credo. By the early 2000s this "new environmental pragmatism" was ready to dominate policy on climate change, biodiversity, and global sustainability (Spash, 2009).

## Human-Induced Climate Change Is Good for Growth

In 2006, Nicholas Stern, an ex–chief economist of the World Bank, and his 22 colleagues, produced a report heralded as the first "rational" approach to human-induced climatic change (Stern et al., 2006). It predicted a 20 percent loss in GDP, the common measure of a modern nation's success at expanding the wealth of its economy, and was widely quoted by environmentalists. Unusually for a government economic report, it talked of ethics, distributional inequity, and catastrophic events, but the bottom line was the monetary assessment of optimal and economically efficient action (Spash, 2007). Stern was honoured, becoming a professor and being appointed to the British House of Lords.

Key to Stern's success was describing greenhouse gas (GHG) control as an opportunity for (rather than a constraint on) economic growth. Financial organizations could make big money by trading government-issued allowances to pollute. GHG traders, renewable energy suppliers, and other entrepreneurs quick off the mark could profit. The headline hustlers immediately posted: "Tackling climate change is the pro-growth strategy." The environmental pragmatists joined the chorus line. The environmental crisis was an investment opportunity. Stern's cost–benefit analysis showed climate change was a good investment with positive returns, a profitable macroeconomic enterprise, and then added market-based emissions trading and new energy markets. Rather than asking why humanity should expect a positive rate of return on climatic disaster prevention, the only question became: How large is the return and where should we invest first to win the competitive market game?

The idea of a "carbon" emissions trading system (ETS)—called "cap and trade" in the United States of America—has been heavily promoted as the efficient solution to GHG mitigation. This system requires that a set of polluters within a given jurisdiction must either control their emissions directly or buy allowances held by other polluters. In 2005, in order to meet Kyoto Protocol commitments, the European Union initiated the world's largest ETS, with annual trade around 70 billion euros before the 2008 financial collapse and 50 billion euros more recently, before the latest crash. The scheme has proven susceptible to price instability, speculators, and profiteering, and large-scale fraud (Spash & Theine, 2018). Where free allowances are given to polluters to get buy-in they can make millions through trading. In general, corporate power is a major force affecting ETS operation and design (Spash, 2010a). Despite its problems, marketing GHG emissions has extended internationally and also via trading offsets.

Offsetting requires that someone (the offset provider) performs an activity that reduces GHGs in the atmosphere, for which they get a credit. They then sell the credit to a polluter who adds GHGs to the atmosphere. In theory the outcome is no net addition—the meaning behind policies called "net zero emissions." GHG offsets, or credits, can be created through investing in a variety of projects: forestry and land use, renewable energy, energy-efficiency, fuel switching, or GHG capture or destruction. Market efficiency targets the cheapest options, which means exploiting the fact that the poor sell cheaply so they should undertake GHG reduction allowing the rich to go on polluting. The Kyoto Protocol's Clean Development

Mechanism empowers industrially developed nations to offset emission with projects (such as dams, waste incinerators, wind farms, commercial forestry, and oil palm plantations) in industrially developing nations. However, these projects can just as easily increase, rather than reduce, net emissions.

Indeed, both ETS and offsets have been notoriously ineffective at controlling emissions. The main contributions to actual global GHG emissions reductions have been the collapse of the Soviet Union with the demise of industrial emissions from Russia and Eastern Europe and the economic recession due to the 2007–8 financial crisis. Similarly, the economic impacts of the COVID-19 pandemic–induced shutdown created a dramatic, but temporary, cut in emissions. That is, actual GHG reductions have required significant declines in economic growth and shrinking of industrial production and consumption and are reversed as soon as economic growth is reestablished. In sum, international climate policy has been a failure.

Besides mandatory ETS and regulated offsets, there are voluntary offsets that are unregulated traded GHG credits issued by companies (e.g., airlines) and civil society groups (Spash, 2010a; Spash & Theine, 2018). These encourage individuals to not worry about their personal, and especially consumer-related, emissions because they can pay for them. This removes moral responsibility and crowds out voluntary actions (e.g., they fly more, not less). In 2019 purchases of voluntary offsets were booming, a growth in sales attributed to the "Greta effect" after climate activist Greta Thunberg (Laville, 2019). At the 2020 annual meeting of the world's business elite in Davos, Thunberg actually countered this, stating: "We're not telling you to offset your emissions by just paying someone else [. . .] emissions have to stop [. . .] forget about net zero we need real zero" (Thunberg, 2020).

The business and banking world look at environmental crises as opportunities to make money and employ innovations in financial market instruments to do so. Both emissions trading and offset schemes distract from the need to change human behaviour, social institutions (i.e., conventions, norms, rules, and regulations), and infrastructure to avoid emissions in the first place. Their aim is to maintain a growing economy; their primary concern is to protect financial capital, not people or ecosystems.

In 2014, the Global Commission on the Economy and Climate published *Better Growth Better Climate: The New Climate Economy Report*, with Stern as lead economist (Calderon et al., 2014). Unsurprisingly, the report concludes that all countries have the opportunity to build lasting economic growth while simultaneously reducing "the immense risks of climate change." Four years later they headlined "the inclusive growth story," and argued for a "green economy" where government funds corporations, with US$90 trillion expected for energy and other transition works in coming decades (Calderon et al., 2018). This, they claim, heralds a new era of economic growth—rapid technological innovation, infrastructure investment, increased resource productivity, jobs, economic savings, improved competitiveness, and market opportunities.

The Paris Agreement was targeted by these same interests and associated neoliberal ENGOs (Spash, 2016). Nat Keohane of the Environmental Defense Fund bragged on its website how it had pushed in the corridors of Paris for "an opening for markets." An 18-country neoliberal lobby led by New Zealand had its negotiators pushing ETS. This was hidden by negotiators in the international doublespeak of the Agreement. You will not find emissions trading, markets, cap and trade, or offsets mentioned, but rather "internationally transferred mitigation outcomes" (clause 108 and article 6). After getting "carbon" markets into the Agreement, the fight to establish an international ETS became explicit and was central to the failed UN 2019 Madrid negotiations.

In the same year, over 3,000 economists endorsed a "carbon tax" because they believe substituting a price signal for cumbersome regulations would promote economic growth (see https://www.econstatement.org/). Some corporations also now prefer a carbon tax over an ETS. Why? Government officials can be lobbied to set taxes low and provide exemptions. The tax is stable, unlike ETS prices. Corporations can argue for tax revenues to be used to subsidize a "just transition"—that is, paying them to move from fossil fuels to renewable energy and related technologies. They also fear being held liable for deliberate harm of the innocent and believe accepting a tax is the price for exemptions from future damage claims and reparations. As with big tobacco or asbestos producers before them, the fossil fuel industry appears guilty of a series of acts establishing their corporate moral responsibility for knowingly creating harm over a long time frame, while having the capacity to avoid that harm (Grasso & Vladimirova, 2020). They are also culpable for denial of the truth amounting to spreading lies in their own interest, and self-enrichment by their harmful actions. The top 100 corporate polluters produced over 70 percent of global GHG emissions (1988–2015), with just 25 producing 51 percent (Spash, 2020).

## Biodiversity Loss Is a Financial Treasure Trove

In Potsdam, May 2007, the German Federal Government and the G8+5 created a UN-backed project called "The Economics of Ecosystems and Biodiversity." This was led by Pavan Sukhdev, a managing director in the Global Markets division at Deutsche Bank, with the philosophy of "you cannot manage what you cannot measure." Referencing the Stern report, the project proposed a range of mainstream economic approaches, including all-encompassing monetary valuation—reporting that the solution to our problems was placing ecosystems and biodiversity within a set of "sustainability" metrics to complement the familiar metrics of GDP growth and corporate profitability (The Economics of Ecosystems and Biodiversity, 2010). Rather than opposing this reduction of nature to money, many ecologists and conservation biologists joined with orthodox economists to promote it.

In 2008 the joint international agency Working Group on Statistics for Sustainable Development placed great emphasis on "the capital approach" and repeatedly discussed the need to be "practical" (UN Economic Commission for Europe et al., 2008). Its basic assumption is that everything can be measured on a comparable basis and added together. Implicit in this approach is the ability to trade off one thing for another: social capital (the connectivity of people), natural capital (species and ecosystems), cultural capital (both tangible and intangible), manufactured capital (machinery and buildings), and human capital (education). The claim that all values can be measured on the same basis and equated—made commensurable—is key to the whole capitalist approach to the environment.

In October 2010 the UN Environment Programme Finance Initiative published *Demystifying Materiality: Hardwiring Biodiversity and Ecosystems into Finance*, supported by Rio Tinto, Industrial Development Corporation, JP Morgan Chase & Co, Uni Credit Group, Credit Suisse, Citigroup, Barclays, Bank of America Merrill Lynch, and similar others. Rather than demonstrate that nature has measurable value, the new message was that values could be "captured." How?

Ideas like carbon emissions trading and GHG offsets could be expanded by more innovative financial market devices (Spash, 2009). In the United States of America, for example, "endangered species credits" provided companies with tradable certificates to offset their negative impacts on threatened species and habitats. They had also established wetland banking, allowing companies or individuals undertaking development or agricultural expansion to degrade or destroy wetland ecosystems by making payments, called environmental credits. The concept of "biobanking" had been pioneered by New South Wales, Australia, in 2006, allowing developers to buy credits—created by "enhancing" other land (e.g., areas previously degraded by development)—to offset negative impacts on biodiversity. The basic idea of all such schemes is to offset harmful destructive acts in one place and time by supposedly equivalent good acts in another place and time. All too often the good act is a future promise and the harm a present actuality.

There is big money in these schemes, with the market for wetland credits alone in the United States of America estimated as worth US$1.1–1.8 billion already back in 2010. No more worrying about absolute protection or annoying regulations—just opportunities to trade, create new financial instruments, and make money. This is not about biodiversity protection or conservation but seeking to remove regulation and restrictions for developers (Spash, 2015b).

## No More Heroes Anymore?

In 2019, calls for "systems change not climate change" gained ground due to Extinction Rebellion and the school strikes of FridaysForFuture fronted by Greta Thunberg. These new environmental movements return to the plain speaking of the 1960s. They emphasize that there is an imminent ecological crisis and ongoing mass species extinction, that human-induced climate change is an "emergency," and that therefore action is urgent. However, their agenda is disconnected and incomplete. As I have noted elsewhere (Spash, 2012), restrictions are necessary on both population growth and the scale of human activity, but this combined issue appears absent. Even more fundamentally, the new environmental activists have not yet substantively addressed the structure of the economic system, its consumerism and dominant corporate institutions, the political processes and politicians that maintain it, nor how such a system of political economy can realistically be transformed (Spash, 2020).

Neoliberal political leaders and the World Economic Forum, commonly known as the Davos elite, have been hosting Thunberg and promoting her speeches. This raises the question as to what they expect to achieve by doing so. She has called for a new political system without competition, a new economics, and a new way of thinking that includes living within planetary boundaries, sharing resources, and addressing inequity. In a *Rolling Stone* interview, she stated corporations are to be held responsible for knowingly perpetrating harm, which she regards as "a crime against humanity" (Aronoff, 2019). These are apparently strong calls to action. However, these statements remain generalized complaints and unspecific as to mechanisms. The danger is that environmental criticism and calls for systems change without substance and specifics are subject to manipulation and diversion from radical and revolutionary reform.

Corporations, progrowth governments, and bureaucrats have already adopted these calls for urgent action to advocate a range of environmental "deals," such as the European Commission's "Green Deal," the UN Environment Programme's "New Deal for Nature," and the UN Conference on Trade and Development's "Global Green New Deal." Ursula von der Leyen, European Commission president, stated, "Supported by investments in green technologies, sustainable solutions and new businesses [. . .] The European Green Deal is our new growth strategy. It will help us cut emissions while creating jobs" (European Commission, 2019). Typical of all these "deals" are claims of coordinating and organizing stakeholders, having civil society and government work with—or more accurately *for*—"industry," with promises of economic growth, jobs, and climate stability. Similar ideas are touted under the term "stakeholder capitalism," the theme of Davos 2020. In this "new" era of Green corporate capitalism the ENGO continues to play its passive role.

## The Corporate Green Strategy

The corporations have a well-established game plan to control potential revolutionary force from the top down. They long ago developed a strategy to address ENGOs, which can be summarized as: isolate the radicals, buy off the opportunists, cultivate the idealists, and coopt the pragmatists. Public relations firms advised them not to oppose but "work with" their opponents and employ their language—in other words, divide and conquer. ENGOs have been deliberately targeted by corporate strategists, and in several cases they have been captured at management level. Some ENGOs in the United States of America have governing boards where 60 to 70 percent of the members are current or former directors of major transnational corporations (e.g., The Nature Conservancy, Conservation International, and WWF-USA). Others, including the National Wildlife

Federation, the Sierra Club, and the Natural Resources Defense Council, suffer from corporate capture and conformity to the basic tenets of neoliberalism (Spash, 2017). The inroads into conservation by corporate interests are deep (Adams, 2017).

Foremost amongst the neoliberal ENGOs has been The Nature Conservancy, with revenues of US$1.3 billion. Its president and CEO until 2019 was Mark Tercek, previously a managing director at Goldman Sachs. Tercek worked with former Nature Conservancy vice president Peter Kareiva to promote capitalism as "natural" and berated conservation biologists for not allying with corporations. Kareiva has been key to Stanford University's flagship "natural capital" project. In a revival of social Darwinism, Kareiva and Marvier (2012) have even claimed corporations are a keystone species!

That the WWF was also captured by corporate capitalism became evident when Pavan Sukhdev became its president in 2017. In cooperation with the UN Environment Programme Finance Initiative, the WWF recently launched "the Net Zero Asset alliance" to claim that GHGs can be offset and corporations become carbon neutral and environmentally responsible. This boast was led by asset owners representing more than US$2 trillion, in a network controlling US$4 trillion (UN Environment Programme Finance Initiative, 2020). Joining Sukhdev in fronting the alliance was Christiana Figueres, former executive secretary of the UN Framework Convention on Climate Change. She had become part of the B Team, run by corporate billionaire Richard Branson of Virgin Group, an organization whose members have also included Yolanda Kakabadse, former president of the WWF.

Corporations and their billionaire owners are marketing the growth economy as green, circular, inclusive, sustainable, and smart. The think tank InfluenceMap (2019) reported that within a few years of the Paris Agreement the world's five largest oil companies have spent US$1 billion on green rebranding. This did not stop them simultaneously working to undermine environmental legislation and establish new oil supplies.

Indeed, soft policies are combined with lobbying and sponsoring politicians, media control, funding of denialism, and antienvironmental think tanks and personal attacks on scientists (Oreskes & Conway, 2010; Spash 2010b; 2014; 2018; Hoggett & Randall, 2018). The even harder line seeks cooperation of government security forces to directly target environmental protestors and activists who are subject to police harassment and brutality, surveillance, infiltration, repression, and branding as "terrorists."

In some countries, activists are even subject to assassination, especially where they oppose economic growth and "development."

The contradictions and cynicism of capitalists and financiers is rife and is evident in the US$2.66 trillion that the world's largest investment banks have funnelled into fossil fuels since the Paris Agreement (Greenfield & Makortoff, 2020). The latest rhetoric is the oxymoron of "sustainable finance" for capitalism and the growth economy. Financialization even extends to the sale of catastrophe bonds. Insurers profit from catastrophes by increasing premiums annually, spreading risk and pushing costs onto government, the ultimate insurer of last resort. For "sustainable financiers," more harm means making more money. As Hache (2020: 52) notes, "[C]limate change will enable insurers to increase their future profits through increases in the damages covered."

A prevalent claim is that "the system" can be "adjusted" to address social, ecological, and economic crises without removing corporate or capitalist structures, let alone the global imperialism they have created under the guise of "free trade" and unregulated financialization. Environmental destruction can be made into a tradable financial asset. In a strange, twisted logic, the dominance of humanity and our destruction of the environment via technology and industrialization is changed from a negative to a positive. The capital-accumulating growth economy is no longer the cause of social ecological crises but the solution!

## Social Ecological Transformation of Economies

Ecological activists must ask and answer the following question: *Under what conditions can radically alternative social ecological economies be actualized?* This requires understanding how current social and economic structures are maintained and reproduced—not just physically but also mentally. Imaginaries of the consumer society, equating economic growth to development and progress, have been forged in the minds of billions while almost all political leaders accept the orthodox economists' mantra that "growth is good, and more is better." Ideas reinforcing the economic structure include defining work as waged labour, success as financial wealth, value as money, freedom as market choice, and ethics as hedonism. Ideas of social solidarity and community are undermined by a political philosophy of individualism and limiting ethical responsibility to personal preferences expressed in the marketplace. Organizations produce social institutions that normalize these messages—reducing the potential for alternative systems to be imagined, let alone actualized.

The science upon which the environmental movement is based requires opposition to the dominant imaginary and its promoters (e.g., bankers, financiers, speculators, profiteers, billionaires, the Davos elite, multinational corporations, and international trade organizations). If the science is correct—exponential economic growth is unsustainable, dilution is not the solution to pollution, nature is not capital, global warming is human induced, and biodiversity offsetting does not prevent mass species extinction—then those who have an opposite explanation must be wrong. For example, to propound truth about human-induced climate change is to undermine the institutions of fossil fuel capitalism—something climate scientists have been slow and unwilling to recognize or act upon. In contrast to the modernist dogma of value-free science, there is no ethically or politically neutral position here. If a researcher finds that some institution causes false beliefs, then their finding is to criticize that institution and initiate its change or subversion. Social ecological transformation sets the ecological citizen against institutions making false claims for emission trading, offsetting, monetary valuation, price-making markets, decoupling, trickle-down, circular economies, and sustainable inclusive green growth. The prospect seems daunting.

However, as Bob Brown, former Australian Green Party senator, says, "Don't get depressed, get active!" Political activism is part of responding ethically to false claims. This does not necessitate joining a political party. Actions include empowering communication (art, education, media, and self-expression), organizing solidarity with the oppressed, protecting the innocent from harm (both human and nonhuman), and making silent voices heard (e.g., future generations, children, and nonhumans). Social solidarity and political acts can take many forms, extending from direct action and civil disobedience to participation in social movements and civil protest, to speaking freely and communicating with others in daily life, to leading by example through daily practices. Social ecological transformation requires simultaneously deactivating the causal mechanisms supporting the current system and activating those allowing different systems to be actualized.

Modern environmentalists use natural science to criticize government inaction but then appeal to the good will of systemically captured politicians in a world of corporate capitalism they fail to address. Society exists based on human agents acting, reproducing, and transforming social structures. Environmentalists need to be aware of the political economy within which they are operating, the role of different actors (e.g., corporations, elites, and financiers), and ideas (e.g., growthmania, productivism, and market mechanisms). If environmentalists are to reverse the losses and avoid another passive capitalist revolution in response to the latest crisis, they will need to recognize with whom their knowledge makes them politically allied and opposed. They might then begin to clearly specify detailed proposals aimed at defeating the opposition and create the necessary structural change in dominant economic systems to achieve a social ecological transformation for the better.

Social ecological economics is the study of social provisioning to meet human needs within an ethical framework of care and justice for others, both human and nonhuman. This requires envisioning concrete utopian futures that can be achieved in reality. There are more meaningful aspirations for human existence than consumerist hedonism and working to make money. An environmental ethic should be based upon promoting flourishing of the many and recognizing that individual living things and biological collectives have their own ends. This sympathy for and connection to others is constitutive of humans leading good and meaningful lives.

There is no single "solution," and certainly not a technical one. Replacing the dominant idea of "the economy" means recognizing the potential for different economies, understood as social provisioning systems, embedded in and constituted by different institutions and structures. Social ecological transformation aims for a future with a different set of values giving different meaning to human–human, human–nature, and nature–nature relations. Breaking free from existing structures means reimagining what constitutes a meaningful and worthwhile life. Exploring forms of economies involving sharing, cooperation, caring, and life without money has long been part of the aims and practices of alternative forms of social organization (e.g., ecosocial enterprises, communes, squats, protest camps, transition towns, and ecovillages). *Systemic transformation* means just that.

# References

Adams, B. (2017). Sleeping with the enemy? Biodiversity conservation, corporations and the green economy. *Journal of Political Ecology, 24*: 243–57. https://doi.org/10.2458/v24i1.20804

Aronoff, K. (2019, June 20). Don't be fooled by fossil fuel companies' green exterior. *Rolling Stone.* https://www.rollingstone.com/politics/politics-features/dont-be-fooled-by-fossil-fuel-companies-green-exterior-850285/

Calderon, F., Oppenheim, J., & Stern, N. (2014). *Better Growth Better Climate: The New Climate Economy Report.* Global Commission on the Economy and Climate.

Calderon, F., Oppenheim, J., & Stern, N. (2018) *Unlocking the Inclusive Growth Story of the 21st Century: Accelerating Climate Action in Urgent Times.* Global Commission on the Economy and Climate.

The Economics of Ecosystems and Biodiversity (2010). *The Economics of Ecosystems and Biodiversity: Mainstreaming the Economics of Nature: A Synthesis of the Approach.* UN Environment Programme.

European Commission (2019). *A European Green Deal.* https://commission.europa.eu/strategy-and-policy/priorities-2019-2024/european-green-deal_en

Grasso, M., & Vladimirova, K. (2020). A moral analysis of carbon majors' role in climate change. *Environmental Values, 29,* 175–95. https://doi.org/10.3197/096327119X15579936382626

Greenfield, P., & Makortoff, K. (2020, March 18). Study: Global banks "failing miserably" on climate crisis by funneling trillions into fossil fuels. *The Guardian.* https://www.theguardian.com/environment/2020/mar/18/global-banks-climate-crisis-finance-fossil-fuels

Hache, F. (2020). *50 Shades of Green Part III: Sustainable Finance 2.0.* Green Finance Observatory.

Hoggett, P., & Randall, R. (2018). Engaging with climate change: Comparing the cultures of science and activism. *Environmental Values, 27,* 223–43. https://doi.org/10.3197/096327118X15217309300813

InfluenceMap (2019). *Big Oil's Real Agenda on Climate Change.* https://influencemap.org/report/How-Big-Oil-Continues-to-Oppose-the-Paris-Agreement-38212275958aa21196dae3b76220bddc

Kareiva, P., & Marvier, M. (2012). What is conservation science? *BioScience, 62,* 962–69. https://doi.org/10.1525/bio.2012.62.11.5

Laville, S. (2019, November 8). "Greta Thunberg effect" driving growth in carbon offsetting. *The Guardian.* https://www.theguardian.com/environment/2019/nov/08/greta-thunberg-effect-driving-growth-in-carbon-offsetting

Oreskes, N., & Conway, E. (2010). *Merchants of Doubt: How a Handful of Scientists Obscured the Truth on Issues from Tobacco Smoke to Global Warming.* Bloomsbury Press.

O'Neill, J. F. (1992). The varieties of intrinsic value. *The Monist,* 75 (2): 119–37.

Spash, C. L. (2007). The economics of climate change impacts à la Stern: Novel and nuanced or rhetorically restricted? *Ecological Economics, 63,* 706–13. https://doi.org/10.1016/j.ecolecon.2007.05.017

Spash, C. L. (2009). The new environmental pragmatists, pluralism and sustainability. *Environmental Values*, *18*, 253–56. https://www.jstor.org/stable/30302124

Spash, C. L. (2010a). The brave new world of carbon trading. *New Political Economy*, *15*, 169–95. https://doi.org/10.1080/13563460903556049

Spash, C. L. (2010b). Censoring science in research officially. *Environmental Values*, *19*, 141–46. https://www.jstor.org/stable/30302334

Spash, C. L. (2012). New foundations for ecological economics. *Ecological Economics*, *77*, 36–47. https://doi.org/10.1016/j.ecolecon.2012.02.004

Spash, C. L. (2014). The politics of researching carbon trading in Australia. In B. Stephan & R. Lane (Eds.), *The Politics of Carbon Markets* (pp. 191–211). Routledge.

Spash, C. L. (2015a). The dying planet index: Life, death and man's domination of Nature. *Environmental Values*, *24*, 1–7. https://www.jstor.org/stable/43695206

Spash, C. L. (2015b). Bulldozing biodiversity: The economics of offsets and trading-in Nature. *Biological Conservation*, *192*, 541–51. https://doi.org/10.1016/j.biocon.2015.07.037

Spash, C. L. (2016). This changes nothing: The Paris Agreement to ignore reality. *Globalizations*, *13*, 928–33. https://doi.org/10.1080/14747731.2016.1161119

Spash, C. L. (2017). Environmentalism and democracy in the age of nationalism and corporate capitalism. *Environmental Values*, *26*, 403–12. http://dx.doi.org/10.3197/096327117X14976900137322

Spash, C. L. (2018). Facing the truth or living a lie: Conformity, radicalism and activism. *Environmental Values*, *27*, 215–22. http://dx.doi.org/10.3197/096327118X15217309300804

Spash, C. L. (2020). The revolution will not be corporatised! *Environmental Values*, *29*, 121–30. https://doi.org/10.3197/096327120X15752810323968

Spash, C. L., & Theine, H. (2018). Voluntary individual carbon trading: Friend or foe? In A. Lewis (Ed.), *Handbook of Psychology and Economic Behaviour* (pp. 595–624). Cambridge University Press.

Stern, N. H., Peters, S., Bakhshi, V. et al. (2006). *Stern Review on the Economics of Climate Change*. UK Government Economic Service, London, UK.

Stockholm Environment Institute, International Institute for Sustainable Development, Overseas Development Institute, et al. (2019). *The Production Gap*. Stockholm Environment Institute.

Thunberg, G. (2020, January 21). *Davos Forum speech transcript*. https://www.rev.com/blog/transcripts/greta-thunberg-davos-forum-speech-transcript

UN Economic Commission for Europe, Organisation for Economic Cooperation and Development, & Eurostat (2008). *Report on Measuring Sustainable Development*. UN Economic and Social Council.

UN Environment Programme Finance Initiative (2010). *Demystifying Materiality: Hardwiring Biodiversity and Ecosystem Services into Finance*. UN Environment Programme.

UN Environment Programme Finance Initiative (2020). *The Net-Zero Asset Owner Alliance*. UN Environment Programme.
World Commission on Environment and Development (1991). *Our Common Future*. www.un-documents.net/wced-ocf.htm

5

# Artful Descent

## An Aesthetics of Existence

SAMUEL ALEXANDER

What do we do now, now that we are happy?

—Estragon in Waiting for Godot

Consider this utopian thought experiment: Suppose the industrial growth economy solves the "economic problem" of poverty and manages to provide material affluence for all. Assume also—if you can imagine the impossible—that this globalization of consumer lifestyles is achieved without fatally degrading planetary ecosystems. Due to the automation of production, everyone in this society now has an abundance of stuff as well as an abundance of free time, and constitutionally protected civil liberties afford everyone an equal opportunity to shape their own life. I invite readers to imagine that this utopian society is structured according to their favorite vision of political economy (e.g., capitalism, socialism, or anarchism). In this world of universal affluence and leisure, what would we do with our lives? In what condition would we find our species?

All at once it becomes clear the permanent problem of human existence—the question of life's meaning—would remain entirely unanswered, despite the affluence and the leisure. Indeed, the problem of what to *do* with our freedom might well become more acute than ever. With the traditional purpose of life resolved (the economic struggle for existence), there might even be a risk of society-wide nervous breakdown, the onset of a profound cultural malaise (Keynes, 2010). Faced with the burden of our own freedom, we might become more unhappy than ever, choosing instead a shallow, cosmetic existence, full of "entertainments," simply to contain our anxieties and distract us from our empty condition. The following lines of verse come to mind (see Keynes [2010: 327]):

> Don't mourn for me, friends, don't weep for me never
> I'm going to do nothing for ever and ever.

It is possible, I suppose, that in this affluent society human beings might pass their time eating nice food, enjoying exotic vacations, talking about cosmetic house renovations, sleeping in the sun, watching sports, making love, and drinking fine wine. This sounds like a good life, or at least good enough, full of earthly pleasures and entertainments. Whether they are happy or not, many of the world's most affluent people spend their days like this today, even if the vast majority of the human population still suffer in material destitution. I wish to suggest, however, that for most people in this utopian society, one day a "why" would arise, and the existential problem of life's meaning would come to saturate consciousness. Like a stone in one's boot, these lingering questions could not be ignored; they would follow us around everywhere we went. An acute state of affluenza might set in as we came to realize our prepackaged, consumptive lifestyles were akin to "doing nothing for ever and ever."

One dark night of the soul we might face the source of our simmering discontent: Is consumer affluence all there is to life? Is it the proper goal of our earthly struggles? Should the pursuit of economic growth without limit define and structure our political economies? In the affluent utopia I have sketched, at some point our lives would become tinged with an unsettling existential doubt about these questions. We would begin to wonder whether we had been foolishly climbing a ladder that had been placed against the wrong wall. Staring at our diamond-studded Rolex, we might enter a state of hallucination and find the watch posing unsettling questions: Is this it? Is this the peak of civilization? Has superfluous consumption and entertainment lifted us to the heights of human achievement and capacity?

From an existential or spiritual perspective, I contend that we would come to see that material comfort was no longer "enough." It never was enough and never will be. Despite what consumer advertisements imply, human beings are not creatures that could ever be truly satisfied with "nice things," merely. At most they provide cosmetic, pleasing distractions, or ego-boosting status signals, in an otherwise difficult and often tragic existence. Material abundance is preferable to material destitution, of course, but ultimately the superfluities of consumer lifestyles are spiritually beside the point, representing a failure of imagination, a mistaken idea of wealth and freedom. Consciously or unconsciously, most of us, it seems, seek meaning in ways that market commodities simply cannot offer, even if our actions often betray this insight. In a utopian society of universal affluence, whenever we looked at our Rolexes we'd be reminded of the passing of time, the approaching specter of death, and thereby confront the question: what shall we do now, now that we are happy?

Utilitarian philosophers would have no answer to this problem, given that happiness within that paradigm is considered *fundamental*, and thus the question isn't even coherent. The most a utilitarian could say is that we should aim for *more* happiness, since happiness is the fundamental good; the ultimate value; the benchmark of success in life. We should just continue marching along the hedonic treadmill and shouldn't ask why or to what end. At some stage, however, happiness, in the sense of a comfortable life of leisure, material abundance, and sensuous pleasure, will not satisfy the inquiring mind—the spiritual seeker. If we found ourselves living in Huxley's *Brave New World*, soon enough we would start doubting—like the protagonist, John—whether a happy life induced by the drug "soma" was a satisfactory way to live. Eventually we would want to live *deeper*, and that leaves open the possibility of passing up a comfortable and happy life and choosing a meaningful life, even if that entailed increased suffering. Choosing meaning over happiness doesn't make sense within a utilitarian framework that posits happiness as the ultimate value. The best a utilitarian could do is fudge their central value, conceding that meaning is the highest good but insisting, by definitional fiat, that we must call this happiness. But that's another way of saying that utilitarian philosophy, at base, gets things wrong.

A similar challenge could be made to "rights-based" philosophers of justice who ground their political theories not in happiness but in freedom. What would we do with our lives if we managed to attain freedom? We see the problem of freedom today in the twisted faces of those lucky celebrities whom we would be wise not to envy. They, too, are still waiting for Godot. Affluence and fame seem to be inadequate, misconceived life goals. Emptiness remains, even or especially in a nice car surrounded by a crowd of adoring fans and enthusiastic photographers.

## Art and Aesthetics as the Creative Engagement with Meaning

If the dominant theories of justice in our time seek to maximize either happiness or freedom, it would seem that they have failed to ground political society on an accurate appreciation of the human situation. Those philosophers are quite right, of course, to value happiness and freedom—even if, at times, these values conflict due to their incommensurable natures. It would be a strange creature who declined or rejected freedom and happiness if they were on offer. But if we were to achieve those goals, my point is that we would still face the uncertain question of life's meaning. We would still be left waiting for Godot, who would never arrive, biding time until we were relieved of our existential predicament by death. This would be the case even if we were sitting poolside with a bittersweet cocktail.

Admittedly, human existence might be given a sense of purpose as we *struggle* for happiness and freedom, and some people achieve a genuine sense of purpose by struggling to advance the condition of others. Albert Camus, for example, in closing his essay on the myth of Sisyphus, suggests that the struggle itself is enough to fill our hearts: "One must imagine Sisyphus happy" (Camus, 2000: 111). But having attained happiness or freedom, we might discover that our struggles had been in vain, that life remains threateningly meaningless, even if everyone were happy and free.

This line of reasoning suggests that what is needed is a politics of meaning, and I believe this insight draws us necessarily into the realm of art and aesthetic experience. In a world where God is increasingly absent from people's lives, and where neither human reason nor material affluence can provide answers to life's mysteries, it seems to me that art and aesthetics are the best tools we have for negotiating the problems of human existence; the best tools for creating meaning and managing absurdity by engaging absurdity; the best tools for sublimating our primal desires and converting those psychological tensions into personally, socially, or ecologically useful, stimulating, or at least benign, creative activity. What is art if not the creative engagement with questions of meaning? What is beauty if not the definitive, albeit temporary, source of existential consolation?

Despite engaging in utopian speculation about an affluent society, it should be clear that my purposes in this chapter have been entirely practical and pragmatic, related to the here and now. These ruminations on happiness, freedom, and meaning can be taken as philosophical touchstones. I am proposing that "make art" and "contemplate art" are the best and fullest responses that human beings have to the problem of life's meaning.

One arrives at these conclusions by conceiving of human beings not as mere consumers but as artists, born of an artful universe, with an innate urge to engage in creative and aesthetic activity. As we struggle toward an ideal society, I believe we will universally become what we already are—artists—broadly defined to include not merely practitioners of the "fine arts" but also those who exercise and explore their creative imaginations and aesthetic capacities in daily living. Through our art and aesthetic experience, we would engage the eternal mysteries of our strange existence, exploring our creative potentialities, and reveling in the profound aesthetic pleasures of sharing our art and experiencing the art of our fellow human beings. The inherent and delightful ambiguities in art also serve a social purpose, as we come to engage each other in social discourse as we struggle meaningfully to understand and digest great art and our relation to it. I believe art can assist with managing an absurd universe like *nothing else can*. If there is any truth to this, then we might consider, as a social project, the goal of universalizing and maximizing opportunities for aesthetic engagement with our absurd existence, so that humanity might attain a degree of spiritual peace—or, with a nod to Freud (2004), at least convert our neuroses and misery into ordinary unhappiness.

Of course, we are not living in a world where affluence has been universalized, but the point of my thought experiment was to highlight why consumerism—the dominant conception of the good life today—is a misconceived vision of prosperity, one unable to assist with living in an absurd universe. Do not art and aesthetic experience provide more coherent ultimate values? What if these aesthetic values came to orientate and guide our lives, our economies, and our politics? This obviously wouldn't mean material provision was unimportant. It would only signify that material provision and economic growth were not considered as ends in themselves but rather as means to aesthetic ends. When material pursuits and the urge to accumulate receive too much of our life energies, we discover—as affluent society today is discovering—that "superfluous wealth can buy superfluities only," as Henry Thoreau once wrote (Thoreau, 1982: 568). There is an emptiness to affluence that simply cannot satisfy the human craving for meaning. The developed consciousness of *homo aestheticus* demands meaning, and this is both a blessing and a curse. It is the source of life's profound richness but also the cause of our unique struggles. It would be easier to be a cat.

If opportunities for art and aesthetic experience are the highest good for a species such as ours, then it follows that we should structure our social, economic, and political institutions, and shape our own lives, to support that vision. This must not be interpreted as an elitist position that holds up the "artistic genius" as being of more worth than the rest of us who are less able to capture the social imagination with our creative activity. And it doesn't look to art at the *expense* of justice but rather to *serve* social and ecological justice. Against the grain of most "aestheticist" philosophy, I am advancing an egalitarian and communitarian celebration of "human as artist." This contrasts, for example, with the aristocratic celebration of the *Übermensch* in Nietzsche's philosophy—although, to be fair, one can offer a creative reading of Nietzsche in which a communitarian ethic seems more consistent with his worldview than the admittedly elitist sounding passages in his oeuvre which dismiss "the herd." In any case, my vision seeks to "democratize the poet" by highlighting the ways in which there is genius and poetry in us all.

## Toward a Politics and Poetics of Meaning

Having outlined the problematic vision of an affluent utopia and engaged the questions to which it gave rise, one could work backward from this derivation of ultimate value to explore how humans might respond to the problem of existence today, and what implications this might have on questions of political economy. My utopian thought experiment (what do we do now, now that we are free and happy?) was designed to shed light on the human condition in ways that can guide action here and now, in a world which perhaps seems closer to dystopia than utopia. Political economy today—global capitalism—is designed to maximize growth, the planet and nonhuman life be damned. If there is a vision implicit in this economic system, it is that the rich get richer and the poorest eventually catch up. Not only is this ecocidal, but my point has been that if we ever achieved that goal, we'd discover we'd been chasing a false target. A politics of meaning, in contrast, would ensure that everyone had "enough" to explore their aesthetic potentials as artist and art lover. This vision is inconsistent with any economy focused on economic growth as a good in itself and any culture that searches for meaning in consumer goods and services.

If people were to reflect on the utopian thought experiment above and come to agree that "making and contemplating art" is a promising means of managing existential challenges, then it would follow that material affluence and high-tech industrial society are not needed to ensure these ultimate aesthetic values are attained. Material sufficiency (somehow defined) is all that is *needed* for a good life of artistic activity and aesthetic contemplation; and, furthermore, sufficiency is all that is *possible* for an ecologically viable existence on a finite planet. I certainly have not established the case herein, but I am positing the thesis that maybe art can save us from capitalism and that "[b]eauty will save the world" (Dostoyevsky, 1981: 370).

Here we see the implications of my thought experiment, for it provides grounds for a radical critique of existing society. If industrial, growth economies are trying to provide material affluence for all as a path to the good life, then our global mode of political economy is structured in ways that are neither necessary for satisfying our deepest needs (autonomous creative activity and aesthetic experience) nor sustainable (since globalizing affluence is demonstrably unsustainable). In short, industrial civilization is suppressing the creative nature of our species by grossly overvaluing material affluence while at the same time undermining the environmental foundations for universal artistic opportunity. We can, and must, do better, and I'm suggesting that art and aesthetic interventions in the world are probably the best way to achieve a sustainable, aesthetic society of artists and art lovers. Art is both the means and the end.

The vision of the political economy I am working toward—which I will call the *aesthetic state*—is ultimately one where societal structures are collaboratively designed so as to maximize the opportunities for self-governing human beings to practice and contemplate art, and immerse themselves in nature's beauty, while minimizing material and energy demands of the economy on a finite planet. This will involve considering what implications this aesthetic worldview might have on questions of distributive justice, ecological justice, sustainability, and the good life. With art being defended as the fundamental value and ultimate end point for human (and cosmological) striving, my main goal is to examine the role and importance of art and the artist in *nonutopian* societies such as our own, in which it seems not many people are happy or free, and where, under today's capitalist dispensation, it seems meaningful living is the exception rather than the rule.

We should dare to imagine better worlds and more humane and nourishing social arrangements, for both humans and nonhumans, provided these "fictions" are used to inform action rather than induce passive escapism. Imagineers are easily dismissed as utopian dreamers or escapists who lack a sense of political reality. But just as vision without politics is naive, politics without vision is dangerous. We must dream before we shape our politics, or else we will never awaken from the existing nightmare of pragmatism without principle.

## S M P L C T Y: An Ecological Civilization of Poet-Farmers

Let me now unpack some of the defining characteristics of the aesthetic form of life that I believe is a viable and desirable pathway beyond industrial civilization. What follows is neither a utopian statement nor a prediction but rather an orienting vision designed to guide prefigurative action in the here and now. I will employ the term S M P L C T Y to refer to an idealized "end state" of an ecological civilization made up of simple living poet-farmers. To live simply is to embrace an economics of sufficiency and moderation, finding harmony and balance in life by walking the middle way between too little and too much. This living strategy seeks to maximize opportunities for meaningful coexistence through artful and creative living while minimizing material and energy demands for reasons of socioecological justice and sustainability. A poet-farmer refers to an archetypal member of this envisioned civilization who identifies as a creative and artistic being (broadly conceived to include not just artists but also artisans) and who contributes to material provision, community governance, and cultural richness.

By removing the *i* from the conventional spelling of "simplicity," the neologism S M P L C T Y is intended to evoke a "less is more" philosophy—or rather, a philosophy of "just enough is plenty"—which defines the ethos of sufficiency underpinning this form of ecological civilization. The removal of the *i* is also meant to imply the achievement of a diminished egoism (or increased communitarianism) compared to the possessive individualism that has come to define globalized industrial capitalism. This transcendence of crude individualism could also be understood as a deeper communion with the Dionysian impulse or art force underpinning our shared aesthetic reality. Paradoxically, this diminished egoism will actually increase opportunities for individual self-creation.

As I conceive of it, S M P L C T Y is the desirable outcome of a voluntary process of "progressive simplification," "voluntary simplification," or "prosperous descent" (Alexander, 2015). In the broadest terms, the goal of this ecological civilization is to provide enough, for everyone, forever. I believe this is a coherent vision to embrace if humanity (as a whole) and affluent societies (in particular) are to move toward an equitable form of life that not only avoids ecosystemic collapse but ensures the flourishing of all life on Earth. This creative process of prosperous or "artful" descent—or what I have elsewhere called an "aesthetics of degrowth" (Alexander, 2017)—involves consciously transferring (both individually and socially) ever more time and attention to nonmaterialistic sources of meaning and happiness. These practices reflect a postconsumerist conception of the good life and might include nonalienated productive labor (e.g., a rejuvenation of the arts and craft movement), social and political engagement, sensuous experience, enjoyment of nature, artistic activity, and aesthetic immersion and contemplation (Alexander, 2013).

This vision is founded upon a conception of humanity that holds that our species can live its fullest existence, and with infinite diversity, while living simply on very modest yet elegantly sufficient material foundations. Thus, with the support of appropriate social and political institutions, and based on an ethic of enlightened self-interest, moderation and even austerity in our material lives will be recognized as implying no hardship or deprivation. Instead, a way of life that is "outwardly simple" and "inwardly rich" illuminates the most direct path to sustainable well-being into the deep future (Elgin, 2010), provided profound cultural changes are supplemented and supported by correlative structural changes in political economy. Art, creative activity, aesthetic experience, and the rich and beautiful surroundings of the natural world do most of the heavy lifting in justifying existence and the world as an aesthetic phenomenon.

Through this shift in emphasis from the material (or external) dimensions of life to the spiritual (or internal) dimensions, the goal is to achieve maximum flourishing for the community of life, while minimizing energy and resource demands in due respect of biophysical limits (Alexander, 2021). S M P L C T Y is, by definition, an "ideal" state that can never be fully or permanently achieved, due to the inherent tendency of civilizations to complexify as new and unforeseen societal problems arise. Civilizations based on growth and complexification eventually grow themselves into a condition of deterioration and collapse (Tainter, 1988). Voluntary simplification therefore is the *only* means of avoiding this process of growth-to-collapse, a process that has brought about the demise of all prior civilizations in history, and that is in the process of bringing down industrial civilization. My argument is that art and aesthetic experience are promising and available means of "living more with less"—of flourishing in simplicity—and thus opportunities for low-impact aesthetic practice and experience ought to be expanded as our material and energy demands contract for reasons of socioecological justice, sustainability, and well-being.

The great historian of civilizations Arnold Toynbee described the Law of Progressive Simplification as a process of "etherealization" (Toynbee, 1987: 198), whereby humanity learns to meet its deepest existential needs with declining material and energy demands. He explains that the result is "not a loss but a gain; and this gain is the outcome of a process of simplification because the process liberates forces that have been imprisoned in a more material medium and thereby sets them free to work in a more ethereal medium with greater potency" (Toynbee, 1987: 198). He adds that this involves "not merely a simplification of apparatus but a consequent transfer of energy, or shift of emphasis, from some lower sphere of being or of action to a higher" (Toynbee, 1987: 198).

Toynbee explains this process primarily in terms of efficiency improvements via "technical progress" and the "human control over physical nature" (Toynbee, 1987: 198, 199). In my view, progressive simplification ought to *include* such dematerialization or deintensification via technological innovation but refers more fundamentally to a socioethical or even spiritual approach to life that is independent of the state of technology. In other words, progressive simplification can be undertaken immediately, with or without further technological advance, and indeed, with or without biophysical pressures. We can even conceive of civilizations that embrace simplicity in advance of necessity, that is, by resisting overcomplexification as a means of *avoiding* problems, as opposed to overcomplex civilizations (such as present-day industrial civilization) that are pressured to simplify in order to *resolve* their problems.

If humanity does not learn to embrace voluntary simplification within the present iteration of (industrial) civilization, the minimally optimistic hypothesis I am positing is that humanity will *eventually* come to see that it is the only path to genuine sustainability and flourishing within a planet that retains its vibrant diversities of nonhuman life. Of course, given the profound seductions of complexity, the insecurities of the human ego, the grasping for power, and the limitations of the human intellect, it is possible and indeed likely that this lesson may not be learned until many more civilizations rise and fall as a result of the diminishing returns on complexity. Indeed, it is possible that humanity never learns this lesson.

However, the faith implicit in my vision of S M P L C T Y is that *eventually* humanity will learn that voluntary simplification is the only path to civilizational stability and flourishing. As cultures develop a historical consciousness (i.e., when they see more clearly the repeated patterns of collapse occurring over and over again), our (partially) reflective species will slowly absorb this wisdom, in a piecemeal fashion, over an indeterminate timescale. This may take centuries or even millennia, but over time the ranks who come to see this truth will expand, eventually leading to the deep transformation of human society. One way or another, there will be a Great Simplification, whether by design or disaster. Thus, as John Michael Greer (2012) declares, let's "collapse now and avoid the rush."

As opposed to a utopian fantasy or prediction, I have suggested that S M P L C T Y ought to be received as an *orienting vision* that should increasingly guide human endeavor as it becomes clearer to more people that growth-orientated alternatives will always proceed through phases of wasteful overconsumption and production before culminating in collapse. It designates a civilization in dynamic equilibrium, constantly balancing and rebalancing its societal goals in relation to its sustainable (and therefore limited) flow of energy and resources. The turn to nonmaterialistic sources of meaning and happiness does not imply a turn away from material culture, it only implies negation of practices that are unnecessarily materially and energetically consumptive (i.e., unsustainable). The questions of how much is enough, of what, and for whom, are the defining value-laden inquiries that inform the ethics and politics of S M P L C T Y.

According to this view, we are justified in being prefigurative pioneers of artful descent, even if our success or validation likely lie beyond this civilizational cycle. If we know the cause to be good, then we can take solace in the fact that we are serving a noble cause bigger than ourselves—not otherworldly but of this Earth—even if many of the rewards will accrue only to future generations. But as the Greek proverb goes, "A civilization flourishes when people plant trees under which they will never sit." When struggles are of profound existential import, patience can be a necessary virtue, and there is honor in being an underlaborer whose modest but necessary contribution will one day be forgotten.

Practicing simplicity in the here and now also has the fortunate consequence of building resilience today, preparing an individual, household, or community for potential conditions of collapse. Thus, it is an approach to life that is justifiable even if (as is very likely) the ethos of voluntary simplification does not expand sufficiently to avoid the collapse of industrial civilization. In a range of related social movements (permaculture, regenerative agriculture, voluntary simplicity, degrowth, etc.), the ranks of simplicity thinking and practice are expanding, albeit, for now, very slowly. It seems that S M P L C T Y is an idea whose time has not yet come. But that time will come, even if it takes decades or centuries.

Although the energy and resource flows are limited within this envisioned form of life, the exploration of the good life remains unlimited, in the same way that a pianist is not limited by the 88 keys of a piano. There will never be a time when all the beautiful sonatas have been written, just as there will never be a time when all possible manifestations of beautiful lives have been lived. Upon sufficient material foundations, human beings are tasked with creating as an aesthetic project the meaning of their own lives. This is the bounded infinity of human flourishing. Within biophysical limits, we are limited only by our imaginations.

The good life according to S M P L C T Y is achieved primarily through aesthetic experience, both creatively (making art) and passively (appreciating art), and this is an endless creative process of infinite diversity and stimulation. Aesthetic experience is also available through immersions within the natural world's beauties of seasons, fauna, flora, and landscape. This should be understood as a means of solving the problem of how to live an interesting and meaningful life—in ways consistent with the "less is more" strategy of voluntary simplification. Art, as I'm using the term, refers both to conventional art objects (painting, music, sculpture, literature, etc.) and the artful products created by artisans (everyday artefacts that are useful and beautiful), as well as to nature's creations which have arguably furnished the very blueprint of aesthetic appreciation. As I have explained elsewhere (Alexander, 2021: chapter 14), human beings are related to their own lives in a manner that is akin to the relationship between sculptor and clay, imposing on us the exhilarating but terrifying burden of applying our own aesthetic criteria to the spiritual practice of self-fashioning.

This aesthetic vision of the good life culminates in a mystical blurring of art and life, where human beings relate to each other neither as master and slave nor as capitalist and worker but in the reciprocal and revolving relationships of artist and art lover. This signifies an evolution from *homo economicus* (the archetype of industrial civilization) to *homo aestheticus* (the archetype of S M P L C T Y), which itself can be understood as the outcome of an underlying creative process, namely, the "Will to Art"—that mysterious creative force driving the cosmos onward, inward, and outward over time, seeking imaginative flourishes from the nodes of matter that have become conscious and creative.

The archetypal, self-governing citizen in S M P L C T Y is the poet-farmer, who lives simply in a material and energetic sense, contributes to necessary economic production and community governance in nonalienated and nonhierarchical conditions, and who otherwise explores the good life (and manages the ineliminable tragic elements of the human condition and situation) through creative activity and aesthetic experience. There will of course be artistic "geniuses" whose work captures and impresses the social imagination more than others, but the poet-farmer is an ordinary creative soul who revels in their aesthetic practices without need or expectation of social recognition. This civilization democratizes the poet. Art does not replace religion, but it answers the same (and perhaps some new) spiritual needs, such that the artist comes to replace the priest as spiritual advisor and existential provocateur. As we transfer ever more of our time and energy away from materialistic pursuits, we will turn to the spirit to satisfy our hunger for meaning.

Having undergone an artful descent, a simple-living civilization will discover that it is good and worth preserving. The fundamental structural requirement of voluntary simplification does not otherwise contain or delimit the forms of life that can be created within biophysical constraints. A diversity of aesthetic communities may arise, loosely networked for mutual support and appreciation. Call this the civilizational "pluriverse" of S M P L C T Y. This vision of creative evolution is a metanarrative whose author is aware of its narrativity—it is a cosmodicy, an aesthetic justification of existence.

Over millions of years, these aesthetico-mystical communities will live creatively and sustainably, producing and appreciating unimaginable forms of art and aesthetic experience, both human and nonhuman mediated. So many artistic geniuses will emerge that anything resembling an exhaustive "art history" will become impossible and egotistical hopes of being "remembered" will fade. There will be millions upon millions of Beethovens, Shakespeares, and Goethes to enjoy—as well as creative giants as yet unimagined. Increasingly human beings will experiment with novel ways of immersing themselves in the deep well of aesthetic resources at their disposal. Naturally, this well of resources will be so much deeper on an Earth where nonhuman life has continued to flourish, rather than being squeezed through the bottleneck of mass extinction. Thus, S M P L C T Y not only more effectively draws on but actually supports a greater wealth of beauty in our lives.

At some distant point—perhaps in hundreds of millions of years—Earth will be swallowed by a black hole, destroyed by a comet, or become uninhabitable due to the heat-death of the sun. Accordingly, the human story is, ultimately, finite. Our cosmological contribution is our art—our human stories—all of which will one day be dust, blowing in the winds of a dark, cold, silent universe. After an indeterminate duration of cosmological expansion, the universe may implode into the singularity from which it emerged or expand at the speed of light, and the mysterious cosmological process might begin again, repeating this aesthetic cycle an infinite number of times, in eternal reoccurrence. This mystery needs and allows for no primal explanation. The marvel of all marvels is that the "Will to Art" *simply is.*

To paraphrase T. S. Eliot (1941), we are the music, while the music lasts.

## References

Alexander, S. (2013). *Entropia: Life Beyond Industrial Civilisation.* Simplicity Institute.
Alexander, S. (2015). *Prosperous Descent: Crisis as Opportunity in an Age of Limits.* Simplicity Institute.
Alexander, S. (2017). *Art Against Empire: Toward an Aesthetics of Degrowth.* Simplicity Institute.
Alexander, S. (2021). *Beyond Capitalist Realism: The Politics, Energetics, and Aesthetics of Degrowth.* Simplicity Institute.
Camus, A. (2000). *The Myth of Sisyphus.* Penguin.
Dostoyevsky, F. (1981). *The Idiot.* Bantam.
Elgin, D. (2010). *Voluntary Simplicity: Toward a Way of Life That Is Outwardly Simple, Inwardly Rich* (2nd edition). Harper.
Eliot, T. S. (1941). The dry salvages. From *Four Quartets.* http://www.davidgorman.com/4quartets/3-salvages.htm
Freud, S. (2004). *Civilization and Its Discontents.* Penguin.

Greer, J. M. (2012, June 6). Collapse now and avoid the rush. *Resilience.* https://www.resilience.org/stories/2012-06-06/collapse-now-and-avoid-rush/

Keynes, J. M. (2010). Economic possibilities for our grandchildren. In J. M. Keynes, *Essays in Persuasion* (pp. 321–32). Palgrave MacMillan.

Tainter, J. (1988). *The Collapse of Complex Societies.* Cambridge University Press.

Thoreau, H. D. (1982). *Walden.* In C. Bode (Ed.), *The Portable Thoreau.* Penguin.

Toynbee, A. (1987). *A Study of History: Abridgement of Volumes I–VI.* D. C. Somervell (Ed.). Oxford University Press.

## Section Two

# Respect

6

# Is It the Call of the Wild . . . or of Deep Law?

## What Is the Moral Heart of Conservation?

FREYA MATHEWS

Is conservation currently at a crossroads? As a social movement, a sphere of policy, and a branch of science, conservation is indeed currently searching its soul (GTI Forum, 2022). Despite its undisputed legitimacy in most societies and its track record of successes, it is now manifestly losing the battle to curb the catastrophic ecological impacts of both global economic development and the sheer proliferation of human beings worldwide. Debate is therefore underway about whether and how conservation might change direction and reframe itself to achieve greater efficacy. A new direction cannot be decided, however, unless there is already agreement on what it is that conservationists are seeking to conserve—on what the object of conservation actually is. Once the object is clear, there will still be plenty of room for disagreement as to optimal means and strategies. But without some clarity about the object, it is hard to see how debate can be meaningfully engaged in at all.

## Categories of Conservation

So let us consider some of the relevant categories that have figured in the history of conservation discourse. A rich literature has grown up around each of these categories; within the space of the present chapter, it will accordingly be possible to touch on them only very briefly. But at the most obvious and popular level, conservation has perennially been characterized as *nature* conservation: it is assumed that what conservationists are seeking to conserve is nature. A moment's reflection is all it takes, however, to show that "nature" is not a category in terms of which conservation can properly define itself, for it commits the conservationist to saving either too little or too much. It commits us to too little if "nature" is understood, as it often is, as encompassing all that falls within the domain, or under the laws, of physics—all that is part of the natural, as opposed to some notional supernatural, order. So understood, nature cannot be destroyed: energy is conserved whatever we do since cycles of creation are followed by cycles of destruction unendingly, without net loss. If, however, "nature" is used, as it generally is in popular environmental contexts, to denote living things such as trees, grass, and ecosystems, and perhaps all of Earth-life exclusive of humans, then the task of conserving nature commits us to too much—to a hands-off relationship with our entire biophysical environment. Such a goal would clearly be unachievable under the conditions of civilization. To invoke "nature" then in response to the question of what it is that conservationists seek to conserve is not especially helpful.

## Wilderness

Historically speaking, conservation emerged as a mass movement when it marched under the banner of *wilderness* preservation, back in the 1970s. Though the notion of wilderness, denoting areas of land relatively undisturbed by human activity and beyond the reach of civilization, dates back to biblical times, the connotations of the term were, before the advent of the Romantic era of the late 18th and early 19th century, largely negative, signaling exile, hostility, and danger for human beings and a brutish eat-or-be-eaten existence for wildlife. In the Romantic era, the notion assumed a more positive significance: wild places afforded humans an opportunity to commune with a still-intact inner principle of nature that was also core to our own inner depths. In this way, wilderness offered escape from the strictures of civilization and from stifling forms of conventionality and domestic confinement across many spheres of social life. Such valorization of wilderness was integral to the Romantic revolt against the rationalist complacency of the Enlightenment. In the 19th century, this revolt gave rise to a new interest in preserving large areas—wildernesses—in which wildness could continue to express itself and, in turn, nourish the spirits of world-weary humans (Nash, 1967; Callicott & Nelson, 1998, 2008; Henderson, 2014).

Coming to the fore again as part of the environment movement of the 1970s–1980s, the notion of wilderness retained this positive value, though its more overtly aesthetic and spiritual Romantic associations became backgrounded to explicitly ecological meanings. Wildernesses were understood as terrains of intact ecosystem dynamics and unfolding evolutionary processes wherein all forms of life were free to follow their own ends in their own ways (Devall & Sessions, 1985: 126–29; Rolston, 1988). While it was the basic purpose of the landmark US Wilderness Act of 1964 to afford ecological protection to such terrains, the act misguidedly construed them in Eurocentric terms as lands that had never been significantly disturbed by human activity, thereby erasing centuries of careful ecological custodianship by Indigenous inhabitants (Woods, 2001).[1] Under the same misapprehension, the act categorically proscribed any kind of human occupation in designated wilderness areas.

This was a pattern followed in other parts of the world: large, ecologically intact terrains came under state control for the purpose of environmental protection, while the often key role of Indigenous practices in maintaining and enhancing the ecological integrity of such lands was overlooked. In some cases, where Indigenous communities were still actively caring for their estates, they were forcibly removed to ensure that the newly gazetted reserves would qualify as wilderness areas, which is to say, as lands unoccupied by humans (Brockington & Igoe, 2006; Callicott, 2008; Fletcher et al., 2021).

This erasure of Indigenous agency was not the only objection to wilderness as a founding category for conservation.[2] From a broader postcolonial perspective it was argued that wilderness preservation served as a pretext for wealthy colonial powers to block economic development in poorer parts of the world (Guha, 1997). Even from an avowedly ecological perspective, the soundness of construing wilderness as a basic category of conservation was challenged: areas such as remote and rugged mountain ranges, earlier designated as wildernesses on account of their outstanding scenic values, might not always be as ecologically rich and diverse as smaller, nondescript-looking remnants already affected by industrial processes (Rodman, 1983). As a result of these and many other objections, the category of wilderness began, in the late 1980s, to be quietly backgrounded in policy and scientific settings in favor of a new normative category that was emerging at that time: *biodiversity*.

## Biodiversity

"Biodiversity," unlike "wilderness," was strictly scientifically measurable and definable: it pertained to a variety of biological types found in nature, from genes and traits to species and biological communities (Faith, 2021). In the pursuit of biodiversity conservation, scientists could delineate their objects of interest and predict prospective outcomes of their interventions far more specifically than advocates of wilderness preservation had been able to do. Biodiversity conservation was also explicitly ecological in its intended meaning: no residue of Romanticism lingered in its literature. As a category then, biodiversity afforded a far higher degree of objectivity overall than did "wilderness," with its loading of aesthetic and psychospiritual connotations. It also had the crucial advantage for conservationists that it brought disturbed areas, remnant communities, and scattered populations within the ambit of conservation.

Although wilderness as a trope has continued to linger in conservation discourse, and those who favor it have adapted its meaning to meet the earlier objections (Crist, 2019: 113–36), biodiversity has historically, since the 1990s, figured as the conceptual pivot of conservation, providing the standard answer to the question, What is it that conservationists seek to conserve? In many ways, because of the respectability that this category conferred on the cause, it has served conservation well. Arguably, however, the shift from wilderness to biodiversity as the defining object of conservation also had a fatal unintended consequence. For where wilderness as a criterion mandated the setting aside of vast conservation estates, biodiversity focused attention much more on the *richness* of life forms than on how abundantly each life form was instantiated. In other words, biodiversity was geared to the saving of *types* (paradigmatically species) rather than *instances* (individual members of those species in their own right), where the saving of types was widely understood as equivalent to the prevention of extinctions. While extinction could be prevented by ensuring the maintenance of "minimum viable populations" of the species in question (Traill et al., 2007), such minimum viable populations might fall orders of magnitude below populations of the same species typically present in large wilderness areas. A simple change of framing categories thus in effect transformed the arithmetic of conservation, putting the movement on the back foot (Mathews, 2016). Its small victories were doomed to attrition in the face of ever-encroaching forces of industrial development, since while minimum population requirements might indeed be calculable for the purpose of assuring genetic viability, no such calculations can safeguard populations against unforeseeable external shocks and setbacks. Promoted under the aegis of "sustainable development," the new category of biodiversity, with its major emphasis on prevention of extinctions, helped to maximize the extent to which industrial development could be considered consistent with conservation.[3]

To question the focus on biodiversity as a founding category for conservation is not, of course, to doubt that the fostering of biodiversity is central to any plausible account of the conservation project. Diversity—of species, genotypes, and communities—is indeed a key factor in ensuring the resilience and adaptivity of life systems. But an overemphasis on biodiversity is not only likely to lead to conservation of the—inevitably attritional—biological minimum. It is also fundamentally question-begging: Why is it important to maintain minimum viable populations of all currently existing species if we are at liberty to dispense with the larger populations from which they are derived? Are we seeking to save these remnant populations merely for science, as a living typology or museum of exhibits for future generations of humans? Or is there a background value here that biodiversity-based conservation does not acknowledge?

In any case, while conservation under this new, development-friendly, scientistic biodiversity definition was well and truly purged of the Romantic "baggage" of the older wilderness concept, the scope and very meaning of conservation as a project underwent transformation in the transition. Conceptually stripped from conservation thinking now was the value of *wildness*, which had always been, even if only implicitly, core to the meaning of wilderness. It has been customary, in the philosophical literature on wilderness, to trace the etymology of the term "wild" to "will": Wild things are self-willed things, things that are free to follow their own unadulterated natures (Foreman, 2008; Van Horn, 2017). Although as etymology this now seems to be in doubt (Henderson, 2014), it points to the centrality of the notion of self-will in earlier understandings of the meaning of conservation. In valorizing wildness, the earlier movement had implicitly acknowledged the freedom of wild things and the sovereignty that their freedom implied—their entitlement to their own ways and terrains of life (Crist, 2019: 135). Wildness as a norm had touched deep chords of moral feeling—sometimes of yearning—in those who subscribed to it, for it hinted at our own lost freedom, at the price we had paid for civilization—with its amenities, yes, but also with its suppression of all that is spontaneous and original in ourselves. By defending wildness in the outer world, one might have felt that one was also affirming the very touchstone of our own nature—the essential impulse that we share with the rest of life. A Romantic sense of the redemptiveness of wildness—as expressed in Thoreau's oft-repeated dictum "in Wildness is the preservation of the World"—was thus arguably still simmering inside the wilderness movement of the 1970s and 1980s, even though the thinking of the movement had become predominantly ecological in its overt understanding and objectives.

The notion of biodiversity, by contrast, had none of these moral overtones. With its minimum viable populations, its genomic sequences, its quadrats and transects, it was entirely consistent with images of Earth-life subjugated and consigned to the fragmented interstices of human installations, of scientific surveillance and control, of counting and culling and tagging, of forced sterilization or test-tube reproduction, arguably even of DNA stored in laboratory freezers. Such legitimation of the subjugation of nature in the name of conservation also implied, at a perhaps subconscious level, the legitimacy of the subjugation of "the wild" in ourselves, under the conditions of civilization. In this way, the reliance on the scientistic category of biodiversity in the framing of conservation may have silenced the inner "cry" or "call" that gave such a depth of moral feeling to the wilderness movement.

## Rewilding

It is thus probably no coincidence that now, a generation after the relative demise of the wilderness movement, the trope of the wild has returned, via the idiom of *rewilding*. Rewilding is stirring popular passions and awakening large ambitions again, particularly in Europe and the United States, in a way rarely seen in relation to biodiversity-based conservation. In the category of rewilding, the theoretical acuity of ecological science blends with the emotional appeal of the wilderness trope. Definitions of this category are not yet settled, but at its core it consists of a protocol whereby the rewilder takes the minimum steps necessary to enable a degraded environment to recover ecological functionality for itself, in accordance with its own inner dynamics—its own intrinsic agency (Jepson & Blythe, 2020: 68; Derham, 2021). A degraded system given a chance to recover in this way is likely to end up with a species profile different from its earlier, baseline profile as its new, stabilized composition will often feature a mix of indigenous and introduced species (Jepson & Blythe 2020: 81). The minimum steps the rewilder takes to achieve this outcome might include the reintroduction of keystone species—species whose activities in the landscape generate significant opportunities for other species. The reintroduced species may be indigenous to the landscape but locally extinct or merely functionally equivalent to such locally extinct species. Keystone species include those described as ecosystem engineers—organisms that create, merely by their growth pattern, in the case of plants, or by their digging, building, or foraging activities, in the case of animals, new affordances for other species, especially habitat. Keystone too are apex predators who, via predation, limit the population size of otherwise potentially destructive, often herbivorous species. By such behaviors, keystone species establish significant interspecies reciprocities that help to balance the relations among the various elements of an ecosystem, preventing any one element from altogether outcompeting and eliminating others. Such a dynamic of reciprocity in a landscape is key to its ongoing ecological functionality.

Although rewilding thus has as its ultimate goal the restoration of ecological functionality, the nature-led means it deploys to this end—namely the reintroduction of keystone species—is also important. The kinds of interventions undertaken by traditional conservationists to restore ecosystems, such as planting, weeding, earth moving, draining, spraying, or culling, do not in themselves count as rewilding. For the rewilder, the work of repair should be performed not so much by ourselves but by nonhuman species, typically animals.

Why, we might ask, does it matter by whom functionality is restored? Isn't the real point of rewilding that it emphasizes functionality itself—that it does not look back to earlier, baseline communities as the yardstick for conservation success but focuses on the capacity of ecosystems to adapt and adjust and reinvent themselves as circumstances require? If we ourselves can help an ecosystem reach this point of regained functionality by engaging in traditional restoration activities, such as thinning, weeding, and baiting for so-called pests, why shouldn't we do so? Isn't there a tension in rewilding between the end of restored functionality and the insistence that the means to this end must be predominantly nature-led?

To unpack this tension, let us begin by examining the notion of functionality a little more closely. In the biological sciences there is, surprisingly, no agreed definition of ecosystem functionality. Biodiversity is certainly a factor in relation to it but by no reckoning is biodiversity the whole story: zoos and the "botanical gardens" beloved by old colonials are, after all, biologically diverse environments, at least at a species level, but they generally have negligible functionality as ecosystems. Based on field monitoring not only of species diversity but of population ratios and trophic relationships in particular ecosystems as well, biologists have proposed a variety of metrical indicators for ecosystem health and functionality, but these have not been widely accepted (Allesina & Bodini, 2008; Kevan, 2021). Is this perhaps because such strictly metrical approaches are too narrow to capture a notion as philosophically "thick" as ecosystem functionality, with its implied reference to a logic of self-renewal at the heart of living systems? To intuit such a logic, perhaps a different—a philosophical—approach might be helpful.

## The Normative Logic of Life

Viewing the question from a philosophical perspective then, can fundamental principles be identified that assure the ongoingness, the unending self-renewal, of living systems? I have elsewhere suggested that two such fundamental principles can indeed be identified. They are, firstly, a principle of conativity, and secondly, one of accommodation and least resistance.[4]

By *conativity* (from the Latin, *conatus*, a striving or effort), I mean, following 17th century philosopher Baruch Spinoza, the impulse of living things to preserve and increase their own existence. It is only by virtue of such an inherent drive toward self-existence that living things count as living at all. But conativity is qualified by a principle of *least resistance*: organisms that *conserve their energy* by adapting their self-constitutive ends as far as possible to the ends of the organisms surrounding them will be naturally selected over organisms that needlessly provoke resistance and competition. In other words, if, in the process of pursuing my own conative interests, I accommodate others rather than pitting myself against them—if I desire only what serves their interests in the process of serving my own—then I avoid squandering my energy unnecessarily, where this advantages me in the struggle to preserve and increase my existence. The principle of accommodation applies, however, at the level of the species rather than exclusively at the level of the individual organism: Individuals may have to accommodate the possibility of predation in order to ensure the ongoingness of their species as a whole. By adapting to predators, prey species optimize their own populations relative to nutrient supply, thereby assuring their collective future. When all members of a biotic community follow the energy-conserving logic of accommodation at both individual and species levels, the system itself will require less energy to maintain itself and will accordingly be more resilient in face of shocks and disruptions.

In such a scenario it is generally important that adaptivity should not become too narrowly specialized. The greater the range of potential reciprocities in which each member of an ecological community participates, the greater will be the likelihood that in the event of disruption, some reciprocities might persist even while others are ruptured. Equally, the community in question should not become too isolated, in terms of species composition, from the surrounding environment; there should be a degree of compositional overlap so that, again, the potential for functional adaptivity can, in the event of disruption, extend to a wider circle of species.

The behavior of most species in the biosphere has tended to follow the principle of accommodation and least resistance because this is the strategy that, being energy-conserving, logically results from natural selection. Outright conflict and competition do of course occur in nature. Where the interests of particular species or individuals cannot synchronize with those of others, conflict will result. But such conflict will always entail an energy cost for the species or individuals in question, and modes of conflict themselves will in turn be shaped by the principle of least resistance (by analogy with martial arts, in which the practitioner learns to conserve her own energy while turning the force used by opponents back against them). At the end of the day, the reciprocal imperative to desire only what also helps others to sustain their existence will be what ensures that every living thing, merely by following its own conativity, at the same time perpetuates the larger system. It is perhaps this reciprocal imperative then that drives ecosystem functionality.

The relationships of reciprocity established by the principles of conativity, accommodation, and least resistance may be described as *synergistic*. Synergy, or in this case specifically biosynergy, is not a scientific category; it is not defined by metrics or mathematical equations, though there are scientific concepts, such as symbiosis and symbiogenesis, that chime with it (Harris, 2013). Biosynergy fundamentally sets out a normative logic: If you want to persevere in your own existence, then the best way of doing so is to free-ride on what others in your environment, simply by going about their own business, incidentally provide—tailor your conativity to these local affordances. At the same time, you should minimize any opposition to those whose activities support your existence in this way, while maximizing your own contribution of affordances to them. Because this is merely a *normative* logic, you can, if you so choose, depart from it, as human communities over the last several millennia have in many instances elected to do. But the logic foretells what the consequences of this departure are likely to be.

## Biosynergy as Intimation of Indigenous Law

Intimations of this normative logic of biosynergy may be found in many preagrarian societies that relied for their livelihood on functional local ecologies: they discovered, through intimate attunement, an inherent "Ought" at the core of what was for them a living cosmos. This Ought was perceived as a logic that, being inherent in the very fabric of reality, applied as much to human affairs as to the biosphere at large. The capacity for intimate attunement that was required for its discovery, however, involved powers of feeling as well as of sensory acuity and a capacity for pattern-based inference. For this reason, to encounter the Ought at work in the world was simultaneously to feel its force and fall under its sway—to grasp it as self-evidently the existential vocation of humanity. In modern societies, however, the powers of feeling, sensory acuity, and pattern recognition required for such revelations are largely absent—industrialized ways of life foster more detached, analytical, and intellectual modes of cognition.[5]

In ancient China this Ought at the core of the living cosmos was called *Dao*. Daoism is the Indigenous tradition of China, with its deepest roots in early shamanic societies that antedate agrarianism (Kohn, 2017). According to the prime founding text of Daoism, the *Daodejing*, the cosmos owes its ongoing, unfailing self-renewal to a core principle of generativity, *Dao*. The metaphysical dynamic that internally structures Dao is that of yin–yang polarity. Among the affairs of the "Ten Thousand Things" (the individual entities that make up the observable world), yin–yang polarity is exhibited in the forces of push and pull that arise from disparate conativities. Though potentially pulling in different, sometimes opposite, directions, these conativities may, through mutual adaptation—whether at an evolutionary level or at the level of reflective choice—achieve a dynamic balance, such that no single set of interests overwhelms another. To conform to this pattern of mutual accommodation and thereby align with Dao is to follow the path of wu wei. *Wu wei*, meaning literally "no action," is a path of least resistance. Not least resistance in the sense of quietism, but least effort in the sense of biosynergy: when beings adapt their desires reciprocally to the needs of those around them, they conserve their own energy and prosper; when all beings follow this "way" (*dao*), the living cosmos is sustained.[6]

In Aboriginal Australia, the Ought at the core of the Is was known as Law. As understood throughout Aboriginal Australia, Law is not so much a human construct as a dimension of normativity inherent in reality itself: Law is already immanent in land (Watson, 2000; Black, 2011; Graham, 2019). This is why the term is capitalized here, to distinguish it from the purely conventional system of human-authored social rules that constitutes law in a European or Western sense. Life unfolding in accordance with Law is inherently regenerative: it is self-organized (in the sense of naturally selected) at every level of living systems to sustain and further beget life. Once discovered, Law serves not only as a guide to the care of the environment but also as a normative template for the social and economic organization of human communities. According to Indigenous scholar Christine Black, Law may be characterized as basically a norm of relationship. Its central aim is continually to draw competing interests and opposing forces into interdependence and hence into dynamic balance, thereby preventing any one force or set of interests from overwhelming another (Rose, 1992; Black, 2011; Graham, 2019). As such, Law bears a striking affinity to the logic of biosynergy—the logic of conativity and accommodation/least resistance. The narrative coding of Law and its translation into specific ceremonies and rules of conduct varies from one Aboriginal nation to another—Law is articulated and conveyed via locally specific Dreaming stories. But across these codings, common underlying social obligations and obligations to land remain discernible, obligations that reflect the perception that in any ongoing or enduring relationship, each party depends for its own viability on the contributions it makes to the flourishing of the other.

## Rewilding as a Protocol of Law

If we adopt the term "Law," or "Deep Law," for the logic of biosynergy, acknowledging its affinity with the normative core of many Indigenous cultures today, we might now argue that what distinguishes rewilding from earlier approaches to conservation is that it seeks to bring landscapes back into line with Law—to reinstate them as Lawlands. This is what it is to restore functionality and health to distressed ecosystems. As a normative logic, however, Law is as applicable to every aspect of human practice as it is to the functioning of ecosystems. It follows then that Law will not only appoint an end state—of ecosystem functionality—for all lands, including the lands in which as conservationists we are invested. It will also dictate the ways in which conservation itself as a human practice should be carried out: The goals of conservation, like all our other goals, should be pursued in accordance with the principle of least resistance, the path of wu wei. In other words, wherever possible we should recruit the energy of other species to do the work of conservation for us, provided that in doing so we are also affording those species opportunities to follow their own conative drives. The reintroduction of suitable apex predators and ecosystem engineers into environments pegged for ecological remediation provides, in the context of conservation, an exemplary instance of wu wei. By adopting this approach, we save ourselves the enormous expenditure of energy (and, by extension, of money) required to undertake such remediation works ourselves, the kinds of works recommended by the old-school conservation playbook—direct seeding, shooting and trapping "pest" animals, spraying weeds, and the like. At the same time, this protocol supports the species who will do the work for us. It affords them precisely what they need and want: a suitable habitat in which to express their own conative dispositions. The philosophical significance of rewilding then lies not merely in its emphasis on functionality—its goal of transforming degraded environments into self-sustaining Lawlands—but also in its insistence on bringing the conservation practitioner herself back into the fold of Lawfulness. In doing so, rewilding initiates a profound process of ecological redemption—the kind of process for which many of us long and in need of which we so manifestly stand.

As has already been noted, the logic of Lawfulness ought eventually to be applied not merely to conservation but to all areas of human praxis and politics. In pursuing our own prosperity, Law obliges us to seek out the kind of "nature-based solutions" that harness the energies of other species while reciprocally providing for their like prosperity.[7] Our ultimate goal, as Lawful persons, must be to bring all areas of praxis—including food provisioning, architecture, and manufacture, as well as, preeminently, climate change remediation—under the sway of Law (Mathews, 2023). But a natural place to begin this process of rendering civilization Lawful again is surely conservation itself. Rewilding is the first approach to conservation that has in this sense placed the person of the conservationist back inside the recursive logic of life rather than leaving her in the traditional role of manager, as an external agent of "intervention."

Rewilding then, as protocol, is, according to the present argument, very much aligned with Deep Law. But this alignment is obscured by its nomenclature, for as was noted earlier, "the wild" is, in the Western tradition, associated with freedom from constraint and captivity, from rules and indeed from everything to do with law, in the lowercase sense of "law." In the past it was this association with freedom from the strictures of civilization that imbued the wilderness movement with its characteristic depth of "call." While the same call arguably echoes through to the contemporary project of rewilding, touching chords in a younger generation, times have nonetheless changed: everywhere we look today we see cracks in the walls of modern civilization. In our new global situation of extreme precarity, wildness in the old binary, Western sense is surely no longer what we need, unless we have truly, finally, given up any hope that civilization might be redeemed. What we need instead is surely a new vision of *order*—the rediscovery of a deep, an ontological, Ought beyond the empty relativities of the modern marketplace. Such an Ought should tie us back into the living, self-renewing fabric of the cosmos. What we need, in other words, is precisely a call to Deep Law, a call not served by the nomenclature of wildness, but which rewilding, despite the avoidable ambiguity of its name, is arguably already exuberantly channeling.

## Notes

1. For the text of the US Wilderness Act, see https://wilderness.net/learn-about-wilderness/key-laws/wilderness-act/default.php.

2. For a discussion of 30 arguments for and against the idea of wilderness as a conservation category, see Nelson (2022).

3. Biodiversity was heralded as the proper object of conservation in the influential Brundtland Report of the World Commission on Environment and Development (1987).

4. For an earlier introduction to these two principles, see Mathews (2011). For a recent account, see Mathews (2023).

5. For a full discussion of this point, and the other ideas set out in this section, see Mathews (2023).

6. The interpretation of wu wei as a path of biosynergy deviates from (but is compatible with) the standard account, according to which wu wei is a path of spontaneous as opposed to premeditated action. For a full discussion of this biosynergy interpretation of wu wei, see Mathews (2023).

7. Regarding nature-based solutions, see https://www.iucn.org/our-work/nature-based-solutions and Jepson and Blythe (2020).

## References

Allesina, S., & Bodini, A. (2008). Ascendency. In S. E. Jorgensen & B. D. Fath (Eds.), *Encyclopedia of Ecology* (pp. 254–63). Elsevier Science

Black, C. F. (2011). *The Land Is the Source of the Law*. Routledge.

Brockington, D., & Igoe, J. (2006). Eviction for conservation: A global overview. *Conservation & Society*, 4(3), 424–70.

Callicott, J. B. (2008). What "wilderness" in frontier ecosystems? *Environmental Ethics*, 30(3), 235–49. https://doi.org/10.5840/enviroethics200830330

Callicott, J. B., & Nelson, M. (Eds.) (1998). *The Great New Wilderness Debate*. University of Georgia Press.

Callicott, J. B., & Nelson, M. (Eds.) (2008). *The Wilderness Debate Rages On*. University of Georgia Press.

Crist, E. (2019). *Abundant Earth: Toward an Ecological Civilization*. University of Chicago Press.

Derham, T. (2021). *The ethical and ecological principles of a novel mode of environmental restoration*. PhD thesis, University of Tasmania.

Devall, B., & Sessions, G. (1985). *Deep Ecology*. Peregrine Smith.

Faith, D. P. (2021). Biodiversity. In E. N. Zalta (Ed.), *The Stanford Encyclopedia of Philosophy*. Stanford University. https://plato.stanford.edu/archives/spr2021/entries/biodiversity/

Fletcher, M. S., Hamilton, R., Dressler, W., & Palmer, L. (2021). Indigenous knowledge and the shackles of wilderness. *PNAS*, 118(40), e2022218118. https://doi.org/10.1073/pnas.2022218118

Foreman, D. (2008). The real wilderness idea. In J. B. Callicott & M. Nelson (Eds.), *The Wilderness Debate Rages On* (pp. 378–97). University of Georgia Press.

Graham, M. (2019). A relationist ethos: Aboriginal law and ethics. *Earth Ethics*, 1, 1–6.

GTI Forum (2022). Conservation at the crossroads: Battlelines and ways forward. GTI Forum, May. https://greattransition.org/gti-forum/conservation-at-the-crossroads

Guha, R. (1997). Radical American environmentalism and wilderness preservation: A Third World critique. In R. Guha and J. Martinez-Alier (Eds.), *Varieties of Environmentalism: Essays North and South* (pp. 92–108). Routledge. https://doi.org/10.4324/9781315070766

Harris, B. (2013). Evolution's other narrative. *American Scientist, 101*(6), 410. https://doi.org/10.1511/2013.105.410

Henderson, D. (2014). American wilderness philosophy. *Internet Encyclopedia of Philosophy.* https://www.iep.utm.edu/am-wild/

Jepson, P., & Blythe, C. (2020). *Rewilding: The Radical New Science of Ecological Recovery.* Icon Books.

Kevan, P. G. (2021, September 21). Biodiversity and the functionality of ecosystems. *Open Access Government.* https://www.openaccessgovernment.org/functionality-of-ecosystems/120116/

Kohn, L. (2017). *Pristine Affluence: Daoist Roots in the Stone Age.* Three Pines.

Mathews, F. (2011). Towards a deeper philosophy of biomimicry. *Organization and Environment, 24*, 4, 364–87.

Mathews, F. (2016). From biodiversity-based conservation to an ethic of bioproportionality. *Biological Conservation, 200*, 140–48. https://doi.org/10.1016/j.biocon.2016.05.037

Mathews, F. (2021a). From wilderness preservation to the fight for Lawlands. In R. Bartel, M. Branagan, F. Utley, & S. Harris (Eds.), *Rethinking Wilderness and the Wild: Conflict, Conservation and Co-existence* (pp. 254–73). Routledge.

Mathews, F. (2021b). Law in the Living Cosmos: The "ought" that is core to the "is." In J. Farris & B. P. Gocke (Eds.), *Routledge Handbook on Idealism and Immaterialism* (pp. 481–95). Routledge.

Mathews, F. (2022). Conservation needs to include a "story about feeling." *Biological Conservation, 272*, 109668. https://doi.org/10.1016/j.biocon.2022.109668

Mathews, F. (2023). *The Dao of Civilization: A Letter to China.* Anthem Press, London.

Nash, R. (1967). *Wilderness and the American Mind.* Yale University Press.

Nelson, M. P. (2022). Wilderness. In B. Hale, A. Light, & L. Lawhon (Eds.), *Routledge Companion to Environmental Ethics.* https://doi.org/10.4324/9781315768090

Rodman, J. (1983). Four forms of ecological consciousness reconsidered. In D. Scherer & T. Attig (Eds.), *Ethics and the Environment* (pp. 82–92). Prentice-Hall.

Rolston, H. (1988). *Duties to and Values in the Natural World.* Temple University Press.

Rose, D. B. (1992). *Dingo Makes Us Human.* Cambridge University Press.

Traill, L. W., Bradshaw, J. A., & Brook, B. W. (2007). Minimum viable population size: A meta-analysis of 30 years of published estimates. *Biological Conservation, 139*(1), 159–66. https://doi.org/10.1016/j.biocon.2007.06.011

Van Horn, G. (2017). Into the wildness. In G. Van Horn and J. Hausdoerffer (Eds.), *Wildness: Relations of People and Place.* University of Chicago Press. https://doi.org/10.7208/chicago/9780226444970.003.0001

Watson, I. (2000). Kaldowinyeri Munaintya in the beginning. *Flinders Journal of Law Reform, 4*(1), 3–17.

Woods, M (2001). Wilderness. In D. Jamieson (Ed.), *A Companion to Environmental Philosophy* (pp. 349–61). Blackwell. https://doi.org/10.1002/9780470751664.ch24

World Commission on Environment and Development (1987). *Our Common Future.* www.un-documents.net/wced-ocf.htm

7

# Protecting, Restoring, and Rewilding Ecosystems

Reed F. Noss

In this chapter, I reflect on the crucial role of protected areas, ecological restoration, and rewilding—the cornerstones of ecosystem conservation—in the maintenance and recovery of native biodiversity, an endeavor that must be central to any vision for an ecological civilization. In championing ecosystem conservation, I emphasize from the start that I am not arguing against conservation of species. Every species has intrinsic value and deserves to live. Species conservation programs are needed virtually everywhere as the global extinction rate accelerates and as we learn more about the vital role that strongly interactive species (in ecologically effective populations) play in ecosystem dynamics (Soulé et al., 2005). Nevertheless, there are too many imperiled and ecologically important species to worry about how to conserve each one individually. At the very least, species of conservation concern can be grouped together by the ecosystem types they coinhabit, which has the potential to make the conservation of multiple, spatially overlapping species much more efficient and successful.

The biological status of species is usually linked quite directly to the condition of the ecosystems with which they are associated (exceptions include diseases, but even those are often triggered by habitat degradation). An ecosystem approach is more efficient than a species-by-species approach to conservation because many species with similar biological requirements and threats can be addressed by the same actions. By protecting ecosystems that are shared by multiple at-risk species, we are more likely to account for these species' individual needs, which are often poorly known, in addition to protecting many other species that are less threatened (so far) or not even known to science. In other words, ecosystem conservation can be thought of, in part, as species conservation on a bigger scale.

Ecosystems, as a higher level of biological organization, also have intrinsic value and are worthy of conservation in their own right. We have tools to inventory and map them and to figure out what factors endanger them as well as the ecological processes that keep them and their constituent species viable (Noss, 1996a). It is the ecosystem and its complete food web—including large carnivores and herbivores—that we must protect and restore to save all species within their natural (though ever-changing) ecological and evolutionary context.

My introduction to the concept of ecosystem-level conservation began when I worked as an ecologist for a couple of natural heritage programs (Ohio and Florida) in the early 1980s. The natural heritage program network was initiated by The Nature Conservancy, beginning in South Carolina in 1974, under the brilliant leadership of Robert E. Jenkins, the organization's vice president for science. In the heritage program methodology, the focus is on "elements of diversity" rather than directly on sites. As described by Jenkins (1985), "By listing, classifying, and characterizing the elements rather than the natural areas where they occur, the inventories can determine relative endangerment, track down the finest occurrence on the landscape, and identify conservation priorities in the state."

An enticing feature of the heritage programs' approach to biodiversity conservation is the application of a "fine filter" of species inventory and protection and a complementary "coarse filter" of inventorying and protecting natural communities (i.e., ecosystems). It was assumed, and has been generally observed, that the coarse filter will protect 85 to 90 percent or so of all species without having to focus on every species individually (Noss, 1987). The very rare and sensitive species that fall through the pores of the coarse filter can, in theory, be protected by the fine filter, as can species that play pivotal roles in their ecosystems and therefore deserve special attention in conservation planning (Noss & Cooperrider, 1994).

In practice, the fine filter has proven difficult to implement comprehensively at broad spatial extents. Not only are many species not yet described by science, but the status of 94 percent of known land plant species, for example, has not yet been evaluated under the International

Union for Conservation of Nature (IUCN) Red List criteria (Corlett, 2016). The coarse filter has also suffered implementation problems, with mostly small examples of ecosystem types being inventoried and protected, rather than large, spatially heterogeneous landscapes with more complete food webs. The latter are more likely to be self-sustaining.

The full potential of the coarse filter is becoming clearer with the development of well-accepted international classifications and maps of vegetation and other ecosystem types. The IUCN has developed criteria for a Red List of Ecosystems (Keith et al., 2013), and these criteria have been used to assess the status of more than 2,800 ecosystems in 100 countries (Bland et al., 2019). For example, Comer et al. (2020) assessed and mapped the extent of decline as well as the current protection status of ecosystems across the temperate and tropical Americas. From this analysis, one-third of 433 ecosystem types (classified as NatureServe ecological systems) have lost more than 50 percent of their potential distribution, which qualifies them for "vulnerable" status under IUCN Red List criteria. More than 7percent have lost more than 90 percent of their potential extent. Hence the urgent need to recognize, protect, and restore naturally functioning ecosystems.

## Protection

To maintain biodiversity, every ecoregion and every ecosystem type on every continent must be well represented in protected areas, ideally as large, intact, interconnected blocks wherever that is still possible. The goal of protecting representative examples of all major ecosystem types in national parks and other reserves dates to the early 20th century in North America. The fundamental purpose of these efforts was to have a full array of ecosystem types, in as pristine condition as possible, available for scientific study. The undisputed leader of these early efforts was Victor E. Shelford, the first president of the Ecological Society of America (ESA).

In 1917 Shelford initiated ecosystem conservation research and advocacy within the ESA with the establishment of the Committee on the Preservation of Natural Conditions, which he chaired. As a start, the preservation committee called for "an undisturbed area in every national park and public forest." This goal was quickly expanded into a more visionary resolution to establish "a nature sanctuary with its original wild animals for each biotic formation" across North America, which was accepted by the ESA Governing Board in 1931 (Croker, 1991). That same year a separate but complementary committee devoted to research, the Committee for the Study of Plant and Animal Communities, was formed as an advisory group to the preservation committee. That committee was also chaired by Shelford.

It is important to recognize that Shelford and his colleagues were not interested in merely protecting examples of ecosystem types, as in a stamp collection, but rather were committed to protecting large, intact ecosystems with all native species present, including those that are inconvenient to humans. This requires protection of vast natural and seminatural landscapes. As Shelford noted, "[T]he animals requiring first and most careful consideration are the carnivores, likely to be unpopular with the agricultural (broad sense including game culture) interests" (Shelford, 1933: 244). A later report recognized that "it is in the absence of the large predators that many sanctuaries are not entirely natural and have unbalanced populations of the various species" and that very "large sanctuaries are required to contain the large predators" (Kendeigh et al., 1950–51). Modern proponents of rewilding would do well to pay attention to the intellectual history of ecosystem and carnivore conservation.

Sadly, the committees Shelford founded and led were abolished by the ESA governing board in the late 1940s because of board concerns about advocacy (a no-no for scientists then and, unfortunately, mostly still so today). Undeterred, in 1946 Shelford and colleagues organized an independent group, the Ecologists' Union, to continue the work of the former ESA committees. In September 1950, around the time the Kendeigh et al. (1950–51) report was being completed, the Ecologists' Union was reorganized and changed its name to The Nature Conservancy, which continued the work to protect ecosystems (Croker, 1991). Hence the origin of the coarse filter strategy.

What do I mean by "protection"? This term raises eyebrows these days, especially among people in the social justice community who worry about nature getting more attention than people. Essentially, I mean safeguarding against the destruction, fragmentation, and degradation of habitat, which virtually all conservation biologists recognize as the greatest proximate threat to biodiversity (Noss & Cooperrider, 1994; Wilcove et al., 1998; Haddad et al., 2015). If habitat loss is the greatest direct threat, then habitat protection is the most important strategy for reducing extinction rates and maintaining the healthy ecosystems and "ecosystem services" upon which all species, including humans, depend. However, we cannot neglect the ultimate threats to biodiversity, which are human overpopulation, overconsumption, and anthropocentrism. Fighting these threats is more challenging but no less essential to prevent the loss and degradation of habitat that follows from too many people consuming too much and not caring about their impacts on nonhuman species and ecosystems.

Protected areas of various types have been the cornerstone of conservation for well over a century (Noss et al., 1999; Watson et al., 2014). This emphasis must continue, even as conservation scientists pragmatically embrace other means of conservation, such as "other effective area-based conservation measures" (OECMs), which typically allow a range of land uses that do not seriously impact biodiversity (Convention on Biological Diversity, 2021). The IUCN recognizes six categories of protected areas, ranging from "Strict Nature Reserve and Wilderness Area" (category I) and "National Parks" (category II) to "Protected Area with Sustainable Use of Natural Resources" (category VI). Areas in the latter category generally qualify as OECMs.

How much protection is enough to safeguard Earth's biodiversity? This is a timely question, especially in light of recent proposals to protect at least 30 percent of each nation's land area by the year 2030 (UN Environment Programme, 2020) and more ambitious proposals to protect at least 50 percent of Earth by the year 2050 (Noss et al., 2012; Locke, 2014; Dinerstein et al., 2017). The 50 percent goal was originated by Odum and Odum (1972), the eminent ecologist brothers, who determined through a systems ecology model that at least half of South Florida should remain in natural area to provide what we now call "ecosystem services" to human society. More significantly, they furthermore suggested that "until this kind of systems analysis procedure can be refined and becomes a basis for political action, it would be prudent for planners everywhere to strive to preserve 50 percent of the total environment as natural environment" (Odum & Odum, 1972: 183).

Although the rationale for protecting 50 percent of Earth offered by Odum and Odum was anthropocentric, it was radical for its time. It also has been largely ignored, including by proponents of "Half Earth" (Wilson, 2016). Justifications for protecting half of Earth based on ecocentric values and goals for biodiversity conservation did not emerge until two decades after the Odums' paper. At that time, empirical generalizations and syntheses of systematic conservation plans from many regions led to the suggestion that protection of approximately 25 to 75 percent of an ecoregion (i.e., an average of around 50 percent) is needed to meet well-accepted conservation goals such as representing all ecosystem types, maintaining viable populations of all native species, and sustaining ecological processes and resilience (Noss, 1992; 1996b; Noss et al., 2012; Jung et al., 2021). A review by Pressey et al. (2003) concluded that "recent comprehensive conservation plans have delineated around 50 percent or more of regions for nature conservation."

The range of 25 to 75 percent is broad because ecoregions vary widely in the amount of land needing protection, and capable of being protected in the near term, due to both their inherent qualities and their history of land use (Noss, 1996b). Ecoregions that are physically or climatically heterogeneous, that have large numbers of endemic species, that have spatially expansive disturbance regimes, or that are inhabited by wide-ranging animals with enormous area requirements will require more protected area than ecoregions that are more homogeneous, that have few endemic species, that are characterized by small-scale disturbances, that have lost their wide-ranging animals, or that have had most of their land converted to human land uses. For the latter category of ecoregions, a relatively low level of coverage in protected areas in the short to medium term can be compensated globally by a high level of protection in ecoregions with abundant wild habitat remaining. Canada, for example, has more than 90 percent of its area in natural ecosystems and could easily afford a policy of no net loss of habitat on a national scale (Maron et al., 2020), although it is important to note that some of its more biodiverse southern ecoregions have undergone greater conversion to agricultural and urban land uses.

Protecting an average of 50 percent of each ecoregion on Earth is not as impractical as it might seem. The analysis of terrestrial ecoregions by Dinerstein et al. (2017) found that twelve percent of Earth's 846 terrestrial ecoregions already exceed the qualification of being half protected. Many more ecoregions could achieve 50 percent protection within a few decades with the assistance of habitat restoration. Altogether, more than three-quarters of Earth's ecoregions already have achieved, or could achieve with restoration and rewilding, the status of "half protected." At the same time, quite a few ecoregions have so little natural habitat left that even meeting a 25 percent protection goal is unrealistic within the near future. Some 207 ecoregions globally have had an average of 96 percent of their natural habitat converted to anthropogenic land uses (Dinerstein et al., 2017). Therefore, as a global mission to conserve ecosystems, protection must be complemented by restoration and rewilding.

## Restoration

Representation of ecosystem types is a well-accepted conservation strategy, and most conservation plans pursue this goal through protecting remaining blocks of natural habitat, whether large or small. This approach neglects the historic distribution of ecosystem types (for example, at the time of European settlement) and particularly short-changes those ecosystem types that have lost most of their extent to land conversion. Such endangered ecosystems are of high priority and should be emphasized in conservation plans, with a goal to represent as much as possible of their historic extent—at least half—rather than setting minimalist representation targets based on their current, severely diminished extent.

A review of ecosystem declines in the United States determined that many ecosystem types have suffered extreme losses, some on the order of 95 percent or more (Noss et al., 1995). An interesting finding from this study was that grasslands, savannas, and other open ecosystems have, in general, suffered the greatest losses. Since most of these ecosystems are fire-dependent, fire exclusion is a major cause of their decline. Because grasslands are easier to convert to agriculture than forests, however, agricultural development also played a major role in their loss.

Grasslands and other open ecosystems of the southeastern United States are a case in point. The once extensive grasslands of the region (estimated to have covered more than 100 million acres) have suffered extreme losses, to the point that many otherwise well-educated people do not even know that the region once had extensive open ecosystems (Noss, 2013). Fortunately, recent years have seen a concerted campaign, under the auspices of the Southeastern Grasslands Institute (see https://www.segrasslands.org), to educate the public about the forgotten grasslands of the unglaciated eastern United States, to map the presettlement extent of these grassland types, to identify and protect remnant grasslands, and to restore as much native grassland as possible.

The importance of restoration as part of an overall conservation strategy is well illustrated by southeastern grasslands. A goal of protecting half of each grassland type in the region would accomplish little ecologically if it relied solely on protecting only half of the mostly pitifully small remnants that remain. Protecting at least half of the pre-Euro-American settlement distribution of each type is a more reasonable goal, but it will require a massive investment in grassland restoration. That is an investment worth making, given the extremely high biodiversity value of southeastern grasslands (Noss, 2013). For example, around 85 percent of all plant taxa endemic to the North American Coastal Plain, a global biodiversity hotspot, are associated with fire-maintained pine savannas (a type of grassland, broadly defined) and embedded communities such as small wetlands formed by solution of underlying limestone (Noss et al., 2015).

Although they contain mostly seminatural grasslands, some private ranches in Florida are wild enough to serve as some of the highest-quality remaining habitat for Florida panthers and some other species typically thought of as wilderness associated. However, we cannot rely on the extensive seminatural grasslands of the Southeast to fulfill all important biodiversity conservation objectives. Although many grassland vertebrates do well in these habitats, the richness of native plants is much lower in these grasslands than in high-quality native grasslands. It is imperative that the full spectrum of native grasslands be protected and restored to the point that at least half of their presettlement distributions is represented in protected areas. We must do the same for all other ecosystem types everywhere.

The details of ecological restoration as a component of broad-scale ecosystem conservation are beyond my scope in this chapter. Suffice to say that the level and intensity of restoration needed will vary tremendously among ecosystem types and sites. In some cases, benign neglect will work quite well—just leave the area alone and it will recover. This is especially true for naturally closed-canopy forests, but not for more open ecosystems. Thinning and prescribed burning of historically open-canopy savannas, woodlands, and forests that have been subject to fire exclusion have been demonstrated to restore ecosystem structure and composition, as has letting lightning fires burn, a policy known as "managed wildfire" (Ryan et al., 2013; Noss, 2018; Hessburg et al., 2021). Sometimes, after cutting woody plants that invaded former grasslands, followed by controlled burns, grassland plants that have lain dormant in the seedbank for decades suddenly reappear.

Sadly, many restoration projects are controversial and divide the environmental community. Thinning of small-diameter woody stems and other fuel-reduction techniques in western forests and woodlands that are overly dense due to fire exclusion are opposed by many environmentalists, who naively view logging as necessarily bad. Projects that seek to restore native grasslands in the Southeast by first logging the second-growth hardwoods that invaded after fire exclusion are just as controversial, in some cases sending the local public into an uproar. As for letting lightning fires run wild and reintroducing large carnivores—what I might call the twin pillars of rewilding—here we are likely to encounter even greater public resistance. But other people will be thrilled and energized by such rewilding.

## Rewilding

Rewilding fundamentally means bringing back wildness (Noss, 2020). A more detailed and "unifying" definition and description was offered by Carver and colleagues (2021: 1888):

> Rewilding is the process of rebuilding, following major human disturbance, a natural ecosystem by restoring natural processes and the complete or near complete food web at all trophic levels as a self-sustaining and resilient ecosystem with biota that would have been present had the disturbance not occurred. This will involve a paradigm shift in the relationship between humans and nature. The ultimate goal of rewilding is the restoration of functioning native ecosystems containing the full range of species at all trophic levels while reducing human control and pressures. Rewilded ecosystems should—where possible—be self-sustaining. That is, they require no or minimal management (i.e., *natura naturans* [nature doing what nature does]), and it is recognized that ecosystems are dynamic.

Today there are many interpretations of rewilding, which has produced confusion about its meaning. The first article on rewilding as a conservation strategy was published in *Wild Earth* a quarter of a century ago (Soulé & Noss, 1998). But the idea is actually far older. Victor Shelford, recognizing that many regions of North America no longer contain landscapes sufficiently expansive and wild to represent whole ecosystems, advocated what we now call rewilding in a memo in 1931. Shelford proclaimed, "There needs to be restoration of the primitive as well as protection of the primitive" (quoted in Croker [1991]). This was 67 years before the article by Soulé and Noss scientifically elaborated the rewilding concept. Given Shelford's keen interest in restoring populations of large carnivores, his prescient idea of rewilding aligns closely with the "3 Cs" (cores, corridors, and carnivores) proposed by Soulé and Noss as the fundamental building blocks for rewilding. Shelford and his committees proposed large core areas with surrounding buffer zones to represent ecosystem types across North America, a pretty wild idea. Beginning in the 1940s, Shelford also called for the protection of corridors to link preserves in particular cases (Croker, 1991).

Recent applications of the rewilding concept have varied greatly in ambition and goals, with some interpretations departing significantly from the emphasis on big core areas and large carnivores advocated by Shelford and later by Soulé and Noss (1998). Some European rewilders appear content with livestock and managed pastures as substitutes for native herbivores in natural grasslands (Gillson et al., 2011). Carver and colleagues suggest that "differences in rewilding perspectives lie largely in the extent to which it is seen as achievable and in specific interventions" (Carver et al., 2021: 1890). It is true that reliance on the hypothesis that carnivores are keystone species is a potential weakness of the rewilding paradigm (Noss, 2020). Apex predators do not regulate all food webs. In some ecosystems, control by climate or other physical factors, nutrients, plant diversity, competitors, or fire and other disturbances may be more significant in regulating biodiversity than top-down control by predators (Frederiksen et al., 2006; Scherber et al., 2010).

Nevertheless, because wide-ranging large mammals of all kinds are often umbrella species, whose protection brings along many other species, emphasizing their needs in rewilding projects makes conservation sense. Reintroducing large native mammals is not yet possible in every ecoregion, but this does not mean we abandon goals for rewilding those ecoregions. Just as there is a broad spectrum of wildness, from vacant lots in cities at one end to vast wilderness on the other, there is also a spectrum of rewilding (Noss, 2020; Carver et al., 2021). We should not be such purists that we ignore the biological value of smaller and less pristine areas that serve as critical habitat for wild species in human-dominated landscapes.

Achieving comprehensive representation of ecosystem types in landscapes and ecoregions with higher human population densities and less natural habitat remaining will require far greater investment in restoration and rewilding than in wilder regions. We can still rewild these ecoregions, but for the time being the rewilding will be more modest. In landscapes with a human-dominated matrix, three fundamental actions are critical for rewilding: one, enlargement of patch size by adding area to small reserves and restoring native vegetation; two, restoration of functional connectivity among sites; and three, reintroduction of extirpated species and management (e.g., controlled burning) to simulate natural disturbance regimes. We can rewild at continental scales (Foreman, 2004; Fraser, 2010). It will just take a little time.

## Concluding Remarks

Ecosystem conservation ultimately relies on widespread acceptance of the proposition that ecosystems, as well as species and other levels of biological organization, are good and ought to be preserved. The idea that the land has value for its own sake is not new—it was the fundamental tenet of Aldo Leopold's land ethic (Leopold, 1966). If we see the land as intrinsically valuable and as a community to which we belong, we will accept the ethical obligation to protect, restore, and rewild the land.

Anthropocentric values, appealing to human self-interest, will never be sufficient to inspire bold action to conserve ecosystems (Kopnina et al., 2018). Such values "do not provide the kind of affectively rich and resonant moral languages that are needed to inspire effective political action" (Taylor et al., 2020). Ecocentrism recognizes moral value in ecosystems and all their components and processes. But to work for conservation, ecocentrism must be more than a philosophy—it must be the guiding principle for conservation advocacy. It must direct all our policies and actions. Otherwise, we will protect or restore only what is convenient for us, and that usually means neglecting large carnivores and other creatures that frighten us or cause economic pain, as well as any wild or semiwild areas that have potential for economic development.

Conflicts are bound to occur between the needs of humans and the needs of nonhuman species and the ecosystems they inhabit. There are ways, however, to reduce competition between feeding people and protecting nature, such as by reducing food waste and shifting to largely plant-based diets (Mehrabi et al., 2018). Most important, the human population must be quickly stabilized and then begin declining as soon as possible, while there is still abundant nature left to save. As observed by Crist et al. (2021), "[P]rotecting half the Earth needs to be complemented by downscaling and reforming economic life, humanely and gradually reducing the global population, and changing food production and consumption. By protecting nature generously, and simultaneously contracting and transforming the human enterprise, we can create the conditions for achieving justice and wellbeing for both people and other species." There is no time to waste.

## References

Bland L. M., Nicholson, E., Miller, R.M., et al. (2019). Impacts of the IUCN Red List of Ecosystems on conservation policy and practice. *Conservation Letters*, *12*, e12666. https://doi.org/10.1111/conl.12666

Carver, S., Convery, I., Hawkins, S., et al. (2021). Guiding principles for rewilding. *Conservation Biology*, *35*, 1882–93. https://doi.org/10.1111/cobi.13730

Comer, P. J., Hak, J. C., Josse, C., & Smyth, R. (2020). Long-term loss in extent and current protection of terrestrial ecosystem diversity in the temperate and tropical Americas. *PLoS ONE*, *15*(6), e0234960. https://doi.org/10.1371/journal.pone.0234960

Convention on Biological Diversity (2021). *First draft of the post-2020 global biodiversity framework*. https://www.cbd.int/conferences/post2020

Corlett, R. T. (2016). Plant diversity in a changing world: status, trends, and conservation needs. *Plant Diversity*, *38*, 10–16. https://doi.org/10.1016/j.pld.2016.01.001

Crist, E., Kopnina, H., Cafaro, P., et al. (2021). Protecting half the planet and transforming human systems are complementary goals. *Frontiers in Conservation Science*, *2*. https://doi.org/10.3389/fcosc.2021.761292

Croker, R. A. (1991). *Pioneer Ecologist: The Life and Work of Victor Ernest Shelford, 1877–1968*. Smithsonian Institution Press.

Dinerstein, E., Olson, D., Joshi, A., et al. (2017). An ecoregion-based approach to protecting half the terrestrial realm. *BioScience*, *67*, 534–45. https://doi.org/10.1093/biosci/bix014

Foreman, D. (2004). *Rewilding North America: A Vision for Conservation in the 21st Century*. Island Press.

Fraser, C. (2010). *Rewilding the World: Dispatches from the Conservation Revolution*. Picador.

Frederiksen, M., Edwards, M., Richardson, A. J., et al. (2006). From plankton to top predators: bottom-up control of a marine food web across four trophic levels. *Journal of Animal Ecology*, *75*, 1259–68. https://doi.org/10.1111/j.1365-2656.2006.01148.x

Gillson, L., Laddle, R. J., & Araújo, M. B. (2011). Base-lines, patterns and process. In R. J. Whittaker & R. J. Ladle (Eds.), *Conservation Biogeography* (pp. 31–44). Blackwell. https://doi.org/10.1002/9781444390001.ch3

Haddad, N. M., Brudvig, L. A., Clobert, J., et al. (2015). Habitat fragmentation and its lasting impact on Earth. *Science Advances*, *1*, e1500052. https://doi.org/10.1126/sciadv.1500052

Hessburg, P. F., Prichard, S. J., Hagmann, R. K., et al. (2021). Wildfire and climate change adaptation of western North American forests: a case for intentional management. *Ecological Applications*, *31*(8), e02432. https://doi.org/10.1002/eap.2432

Jenkins, R. E. (1985). Information methods: Why the heritage programs work. *Nature Conservancy News, 35*(6), 21–23.

Jung, M., Arnell, A., de Lamo, X., et al. (2021). Areas of global importance for conserving terrestrial biodiversity, carbon, and water. *Nature Ecology and Evolution, 5,* 1499–509. https://doi.org/10.1038/s41559-021-01528-7

Keith, D. A., Rodriguez, J. P., Rodriguez-Clark, K. M., et al. (2013). Scientific foundations for an IUCN Red List of Ecosystems. *PLoS ONE, 8*(5), e62111. https://doi.org/10.1371/journal.pone.0062111

Kendeigh, S. C., Baldwin, H. I., Cahalane, V. H., et al. (1950–51). Nature sanctuaries in the United States and Canada: A preliminary inventory. *The Living Wilderness, 15*(35), 1–45.

Kopnina, H., Washington, H., Taylor, B., & Piccolo, J. (2018). Anthropocentrism: More than just a misunderstood problem. *Journal of Agricultural and Environmental Ethics, 31,* 109–27. https://doi.org/10.1007/s10806-018-9711-1

Leopold, A. (1966). *A Sand County Almanac, with Other Essays on Conservation from Round River.* Oxford University Press.

Locke, H. (2014). Nature needs half: A necessary and hopeful agenda for protected areas in North America and around the world. *The George Wright Forum, 31,* 359–71.

Maron, M., Simmonds, J. S., Watson, J. E. M., et al. (2020). Global no net loss of natural ecosystems. *Nature Ecology and Evolution, 4,* 46–49. https://doi.org/10.1038/s41559-019-1067-z

Mehrabi, Z., Ellis, E. C., & Ramankutty, N. (2018). The challenge of feeding the world while conserving half the planet. *Nature Sustainability, 1,* 409–12. https://doi.org/10.1038/s41893-018-0119-8

Noss, R. F. (1987). From plant communities to landscapes in conservation inventories: A look at The Nature Conservancy (USA). *Biological Conservation, 41,* 11–37. https://doi.org/10.1016/0006-3207(87)90045-0

Noss, R. F. (1992). The Wildlands Project: Land conservation strategy. *Wild Earth* (Special Issue), 10–25.

Noss, R. F. (1996a). Ecosystems as conservation targets. *Trends in Ecology and Evolution, 11,* 351. https://doi.org/10.1016/0169-5347%2896%2920058-8

Noss, R. F. (1996b). Protected areas: How much is enough? In R. G. Wright (Ed), *National Parks and Protected Areas: Their Role in Environmental Protection* (pp. 91–120). Blackwell.

Noss, R. F. (2013). *Forgotten Grasslands of the South: Natural History and Conservation.* Island Press.

Noss, R. F. (2018). *Fire Ecology of Florida and the Southeastern Coastal Plain.* University Press of Florida.

Noss, R. F. (2020). The spectrum of wildness and rewilding: Justice for all. In H. Kopnina & H. Washington (Eds.), *Conservation: Integrating Social and Ecological Justice* (pp. 167–82). Springer. https://doi.org/10.1007/978-3-030-13905-6_12

Noss, R. F., & Cooperrider, A. (1994). *Saving Nature's Legacy: Protecting and Restoring Biodiversity.* Island Press.

Noss, R. F., Dinerstein, E., Gilbert, B., et al. (1999). Core areas: Where nature reigns. In M. E. Soulé & J. Terborgh (Eds.), *Continental Conservation: Scientific Foundations of Regional Reserve Networks* (pp. 99–128). Island Press.

Noss, R. F., Dobson, A. P., Baldwin, R., et al. (2012). Bolder thinking for conservation. *Conservation Biology, 26,* 1–4. https://doi.org/10.1111/j.1523-1739.2011.01738.x

Noss, R. F., LaRoe, E. T., & Scott, J. M. (1995). *Endangered Ecosystems of the United States: A Preliminary Assessment of Loss and Degradation.* Biological Report 28. USDI National Biological Service.

Noss, R. F., Platt, W. J., Sorrie, B. S., et al. (2015). How global biodiversity hotspots may go unrecognized: Lessons from the North American Coastal Plain. *Diversity and Distributions, 21,* 236–44. https://doi.org/10.1111/ddi.12278

Odum, E. P., & Odum, H. T. (1972). Natural areas as necessary components of man's total environment. *Transactions of the North American Wildlife and Natural Resources Conference, 37,* 178–89.

Pressey, R. L., Cowling, R. M., & Rouget, M. (2003). Formulating conservation targets for biodiversity pattern and process in the Cape Floristic Region, South Africa. *Biological Conservation, 112,* 99–127. https://doi.org/10.1016/S0006-3207(02)00424-X

Ryan, K. C., Knapp, E. E., & Varner, J. M. (2013). Prescribed fire in North American forests and woodlands: History, current practice, and challenges. *Frontiers in Ecology and the Environment, 11,* e15–e24. https://doi.org/10.1890/120329

Scherber, C., Eisenhauer, N., Weisser, W. W., et al. (2010). Bottom-up effects of plant diversity on multitrophic interactions in a biodiversity experiment. *Nature, 468,* 553–56. https://doi.org/10.1038/nature09492

Shelford, V. E. (1933). The preservation of natural biotic communities. *Ecology, 14,* 240–45.

Soulé, M. E., Estes, J. A., Miller, B., & Honnold, D. L. (2005). Strongly interacting species: Conservation policy, management, and ethics. *BioScience, 55,* 168–76. https://doi.org/10.1641/0006-3568(2005)055[0168:SISCPM]2.0.CO;2

Soulé, M., & Noss, R. (1998). Rewilding and biodiversity: Complementary goals for continental conservation. *Wild Earth, 8*(3), 18–28.

Taylor, B., Chapron, G., Kopnina, H., et al. (2020). The need for ecocentrism in biodiversity conservation. *Conservation Biology, 34,* 1089–96. https://doi.org/10.1111/cobi.13541

UN Environment Programme (2020). *Leaders' Pledge for Nature: United to Reverse Biodiversity Loss by 2030 for Sustainable Development.* https://www.leaderspledgefornature.org/

Watson, J. E. M., Dudley, N., Segan, D. B., & Hockings, M. (2014). The performance and potential of protected areas. *Nature, 515,* 67–73. https://doi.org/10.1038/nature13947

Wilcove, D. S., Rothstein, D., Dubow, J., et al. (1998). Quantifying threats to imperiled species in the United States. *BioScience*, *48*, 607–15. https://doi.org/10.2307/1313420

Wilson, E. O. (2016). *Half-Earth: Our Planet's Fight for Life*. Liveright.

# 8

# Coexisting with Africa's Carnivores

TARIK BODASING

Large carnivores are considered as ambassadors for the conservation of biodiversity due to their natural charisma, their role as apex predators, and the place they occupy in the human psyche (Macdonald et al., 2017; Consorte-McCrea et al., 2019). They have a positive influence on biodiversity and human well-being (O'Bryan et al., 2018), as well as on natural processes such as disease control and carbon sequestration (Estes et al., 2011). Yet most of the world's large carnivore species have undergone extreme range contraction due to anthropogenic causes (Wolf & Ripple, 2018). Africa's large carnivore populations are declining rapidly, and several species, including lion, cheetah, and wild dog, are now facing imminent extinction outside of protected areas. Changes in land use from natural habitat to crop agriculture and livestock farming mean that carnivores face fragmented habitats and become easy pickings for poachers and irate farmers (Maxwell et al., 2016; Consorte-McCrea et al., 2019). Addressing the principle causes of the decline—namely, habitat loss and direct persecution—is vital (Maxwell et al., 2016; Galvez et al., 2018). It is here that the importance of protected areas comes to the fore.

## Fences and Defensive Conservation

Law enforcement through fully equipped, highly skilled, and armed rangers is well-established as being essential for effective conservation (Hillborn et al., 2006; Critchlow et al., 2016). Despite backlash from critics of "protectionist conservation," the success of a strong defense model is clear in terms of outcomes for biodiversity conservation. Several African countries have protected and conserved their wildlife through this model for decades (e.g., SANPARKS in South Africa, KWS in Kenya, and DWNP in Botswana). Within the NGO sector, the African Parks Network is currently protecting 17 million hectares of land under conservation and it has succeeded in reintroducing large carnivore species to several former range states, including Rwanda, Malawi, and Zambia (African Parks Network, 2023).

The reason for the success of this approach is that land use outside protected areas is often not compatible with sustained carnivore presence. Intensive agriculture, livestock production, and sport hunting are examples of some activities that are incompatible with the persistence of carnivores in the landscape (Packer et al., 2011; Maxwell et al., 2016). These and other activities have driven a rising carnivore persecution across Africa, with perceived impacts on livelihoods often leading to retaliatory killings of carnivores (Nyhus, 2016).

There is also a considerable body of evidence showing that many large African carnivores reach higher densities and persist longer in fenced protected areas compared with their free-roaming counterparts (Balme et al., 2010; Packer et al., 2013). Fences can ensure a more consistent availability of prey, which results in stable or increasing carnivore populations (Packer et al., 2013). Fences also act as physical barriers, reduce the risk of conflict, and thus help ensure the safety of people and carnivores (Di Minin et al., 2021). Not surprisingly, the operating costs required to achieve conservation objectives differ significantly between fenced and free-roaming populations. The management costs for fenced lion populations to attain high densities average out at an annual budget of US\$500 per $km^2$, while costs for a free-roaming population at half the density amount to US\$2000 per $km^2$ per year (Packer et al., 2013). The latter high costs are largely associated with complex livestock compensation schemes and other actions to mitigate human–carnivore conflict through collaring, tracking, or relocating predators.

These issues have relevance to the sustainability of carnivore conservation in Africa. The vast majority of state conservation departments are grossly underfunded and are forced to operate on severely reduced staff numbers and operational budgets. Securing long-term funding is near impossible in the current donor market, yet this is exactly what is needed to sustain viable numbers of these important species. The successful management of large carnivores thus needs to balance social, financial, and ecological imperatives to develop an integrated and effective approach (Funston et al., 2013).

## Trophy Hunting

The hunting of large carnivores is a global industry and is often cited as a tool for supporting the conservation of these species (Lindsey et al., 2007; Treves, 2009). The premise is that regulated hunting helps increase funding and public support for carnivore conservation (Treves, 2009; Ordiz et al., 2013). Revenue from trophy hunting may act as a source of income to rural communities and provide financial incentives for the preservation of natural carnivore habitat (Lindsey et al., 2012). However, the negative impacts of the trophy hunting industry on carnivore ecology are unquestionable. Lion and leopard populations in Tanzania have declined under hunting pressures, while legalized baited hunting in Zimbabwe has reduced lion numbers and disrupted their social cohesion (Loveridge et al., 2007; Packer et al., 2011).

Additionally, trophy hunting of carnivores often targets the largest or fittest individuals, resulting in the removal of prime animals, and, relatedly, of dominant genetic traits from the population (Ordiz et al., 2013). This may have serious spillover consequences for carnivore population structure and ecosystem integrity. Increased tolerance by landowners around hunting concessions is also disputable given the ongoing persecution of carnivores by livestock farmers under the guise of "problem animal control" (Gusset et al., 2009; Lindsey et al., 2013; Pittman et al., 2016).

The ethical case for an outright ban on trophy hunting is compelling; however, in a world where it continues as a practice (e.g., to secure a piece of land that may otherwise be used for livestock farming), certain measures can be taken to reduce the negative impacts. First, African state conservation authorities need to enforce regulatory mechanisms on the industry to ensure compliance and improve governance of trophy hunting. The setting of quotas needs to be underpinned by scientific rigor and employ a precautionary and adaptive approach (Trouwborst et al., 2020). Frequent audits should be carried out by independent contractors to ensure evidence-based protocols are being applied. At a landscape scale, core areas should be established where hunting is completely excluded (Ordiz et al., 2013), the use of baits discontinued, and well-delineated buffer zones are established around protected areas (Loveridge et al., 2007). At an individual level, the removal of dominant residents and breeding individuals must be banned, as the killing of such animals has disproportionate ecological effects (Balme et al., 2012; Ordiz et al., 2013).

## Carnivores and the Illegal Wildlife Trade

The illegal wildlife trade has grown considerably in Africa, destabilizing rural economies and increasing the risk of zoonotic disease outbreaks (Vandome & Vines, 2018; Di Marco et al., 2020; Cardoso et al., 2021; Tow et al., 2021). It is driven by poverty (the financial incentives to engage in the illegal wildlife trade are high) and is enabled by poor enforcement and weak governance or corruption (Price, 2017). Local trade, however, can be more complex, with traditional belief systems often at the root of the overexploitation of wildlife across the continent.

The trade in bushmeat and animal parts at wet markets, for example, is thought to support approximately 150 million households across rural Africa (Morton et al., 2021). Wet markets are largely unregulated and are hubs for illegal trade in live animals and animal parts (Aguirre et al., 2020). Despite this, many African politicians are unwilling to instigate enforcement actions against the local illegal wildlife trade or its supporters, as it may be perceived as policing of traditional practices (Naude et al., 2020).

African carnivores are extremely vulnerable to domestic and international trade markets, with populations outside protected areas suffering the brunt of the impact. In South Africa, the laundering of bones from poached wild lions into the legal captive lion bone trade with Asian markets remains a serious threat (Williams et al., 2021). The Trade Records Analysis of Flora and Fauna in Commerce (TRAFFIC) found that the poaching of lions to support both domestic and international markets (for teeth, claws, and skin) is rife in Tanzania and Mozambique, with mortality levels in the latter country considered high enough to threaten the species' persistence (Mole & Newton, 2021). Leopards have also suffered from the impacts of the illegal wildlife trade, with large numbers killed for their parts or for derivatives used in traditional practices (Naude et al., 2020). Prior to 2013, more than 800 leopards were killed each year in the southern African region for their skins, which are used as ceremonial garments by members of the Shembe Church and by high-ranking individuals of traditional royal families (see https://panthera/furs-life).

The illegal trade in cheetahs, by comparison, is linked with traditional symbols of status among rich Arab men (Trichorache et al., 2021). A recent article suggests that over a 10-year period (2010–19), more than 4,000 live cheetahs were smuggled out of Africa to several Middle Eastern countries. Trade from Somaliland was especially prevalent and is probably linked to international crime syndicates operating in the eastern Sahel region (Trichorache et al., 2021). This has serious implications for cheetah conservation, given the current estimate of only 7,100 individuals being left in the wild in Africa (Durant et al., 2016).

Such deeply ingrained traditions, as presented above, require novel ideas and outside-the-box thinking to resolve. In a revolutionary piece of work, the nonprofit organization Panthera initiated a demand-reduction program called "Furs for Life," which focused on the creation of *faux* leopard skins to replace the real ones being used in ceremonies. The program found that 95 percent of recipients were satisfied with a faux skin, with demand for an authentic skin decreasing after a three-year period (Naude et al., 2020). This is a remarkable achievement in such a short time frame, and a vital mechanism that can help alleviate the pressure on wild leopard populations.

Such initiatives, however, must be coupled with stronger application of conservation law and policy, and targeted enforcement at multiple scales. There is an urgent need for improved surveillance at land borders, airports, and seaports, as well as for more influential campaigns to promote demand reduction (Trichorache et al., 2021). Social media platforms (e.g., Instagram and Facebook) should be targeted for vastly improved regulation to ensure that posts advertising the purchase of "exotic pet carnivores" are flagged to authorities. Addressing this threat is ultimately about governance and regulation, and the ability of states to enforce conservation laws, with weakly governed states likely to remain the major players in the illicit trafficking of wildlife.

## Livestock Farming and Human–Carnivore Conflict

Community-based conservation through the formation of conservancies has been adopted at national levels in several south and east African countries. The concept is distinctly utilitarian, as communities are granted custodianship rights over natural resources within the designated area (Naidoo et al., 2016). Many conservancies are situated at the edges of large protected areas, with the intention of providing wildlife corridors and land for local communities to practice traditional subsistence farming (Naidoo et al., 2016).

However, despite the initial financial and conservation successes of some conservancies, challenges have emerged that threaten the sustainability of the approach. In my own line of work, it has become obvious that carnivore numbers have dwindled in several Namibian conservancies, to the extent that local populations of lion and wild dog have been all but extirpated in some regions (Lindsey et al., 2013; see also https://lionrangers.org/). Suggestions that traditional livestock grazing is compatible with wildlife conservation appear flawed, for in a world where wild ungulate populations have been severely depleted, carnivores turn to livestock for sustenance (Verschueren et al., 2020). This is being exacerbated by poor land-use planning and minimal benefits for residents, with the result that a number of conservancies make no profit or barely break even (Naidoo et al., 2016). Indeed, certain studies have also indicated that local communities gain little benefit from activities such as trophy hunting (Lindsey et al., 2007; Jorge et al., 2013).

Such acute failures can adversely affect partnerships, cause rifts in the community, and ultimately destabilize the conservancy. Residents may lack the knowledge and skillset to regulate the impact of livestock grazing or trophy hunting, activities that can swiftly threaten carnivore existence (Verschueren et al., 2020). We must also recognize that the nomadic lifestyles of the past may have changed, and many people now want to settle, farm, and engage in commercial trade. This can result in disproportionately large numbers of livestock, and several African states now host over a million cattle, leading to intense rangeland degradation and biodiversity loss (Boronyak et al., 2020; FAO, 2023). Increased rates of conflict with large carnivores become inevitable, leading to retaliatory killings as well as state-sanctioned "problem animal control." Significantly, it has been shown that lion mortalities are highest in countries with the most intensive cattle farming, while cheetah presence is also negatively associated with livestock farming (Packer et al., 2009; Maxwell et al., 2016).

Addressing human–wildlife conflict through integrated approaches is critical. All interventions should incorporate mechanisms for conflict reduction, and directly involve local residents in testing and implementation. Improved livestock husbandry and tracking of carnivore movements, for instance, are both helpful in reducing conflict (Verschueren et al., 2020). Interventions should also include properly aligned land-use plans, provisioning of alternative livelihood opportunities, and educating residents in nonlethal predator deterrence. Ewaso Lions in Kenya have developed a successful model to reduce conflict by engaging members of the community as "Lion Guardians" and providing tangible and sustainable benefits to farmers living alongside large carnivores as an incentive for conserving them (see https://ewasolions.org/).

Compensatory payment schemes or livestock insurance can offer a temporary solution to appease farmers but are ineffective without good governance, accurate verification, and financial sustainability (Wilson-Holt & Steele, 2019). Compensatory mechanisms can also be more likely to succeed in the short-term in sparsely populated landscapes like Namibia. Alternative strategies will probably be required in the more densely populated regions of sub-Saharan Africa. The longevity and integrity of these models will be tested over time, as conflict is dynamic in nature. Risk perception among communities needs to be monitored alongside carnivore ecology in order to stay ahead of the curve should human–wildlife conflict increase at any point.

## Rewilding Carnivores in Africa

The rewilding of native carnivore species to areas of their former range has been part of conservation policy in southern Africa for some time. State conservation agencies in South Africa (e.g., Eastern Cape Parks and Ezemvelo KZN Wildlife) have managed the successful reintroduction of several large carnivore species to both state and private protected areas. At a much larger scale, NGOs such as African Parks have managed the return of lions, cheetahs, and wild dogs to protected areas in Rwanda, Malawi, and parts of Zambia, respectively.

Protected areas offer ideal sites for reintroductions, providing that the main causes of the initial carnivore demise can be controlled and limited. The successful reintroduction of African wild dogs to Gorongosa National Park in Mozambique is a good example of this (Bouley et al., 2021). It was made possible through a combination of effective management and science, strong law enforcement and community engagement, and significant financial support targeting training in essential areas, such as improvement of the criminal justice process for wildlife crime to ensure better rates of conviction (US Agency for International Development, 2019). However, rewilding becomes more complicated outside the protected area network due to certain key criteria required for carnivore persistence. Wolf and Ripple identified the most suitable regions in the world for carnivore rewilding based on the presence of, or proximity to, protected areas, the scale of human impacts, and prey availability (Wolf & Ripple, 2018). They located only two regions in Africa: in the northwest of southern African (Namibia and Angola) and the western Sahel–Sahara belt in northwest Africa (Mauritania, Algeria, and Morocco). These arid landscapes support very low human population densities and contain several large protected areas with healthy populations of wild ungulates. The long-term persistence of large carnivores thus ultimately depends on the availability of large tracts of unsettled and unfarmed land with healthy populations of suitable prey and opportunities for landscape interconnectivity (Wolf & Ripple, 2018).

These results have major implications for large carnivore management across Africa, particularly as no government is willing to address the issue of human population growth and associated impacts. The current mean annual population growth rate across sub-Saharan Africa (2.6 percent) is already more than double the rate of growth in Asia or Latin America, with countries such as Angola, Chad, the Democratic Republic of the Congo, Mali, Niger, Tanzania, and Uganda all increasing at over three percent per annum (World Bank, 2016). Such rapid and sustained population growth (predicted to level off only in 2050), coupled with political instability and extreme poverty, make if very unlikely that there will be many parts of the continent left unsettled or unexploited by people.

## The Path to Coexistence?

While the main drivers for carnivore decline are well understood, the broader mechanisms for change are still not being implemented. At present, few leaders around the world want to address human population growth and economic bloating, as it is complex and controversial. However, a key aspect we can engage in more easily is changing the way we view carnivores and their place in the ecosystem. In this regard, one of the priorities in large carnivore conservation should be to develop strategies to transform and manage people's perceptions of risk (Consorte-McCrea et al., 2019). This has links to the human psyche, and entrenched emotions and beliefs, which are embedded, for example, in human supremacy. Research indicates that a lack of interest in nature is linked to cognitive elements such as fear and misconceptions about wildlife instilled in the formative years (Consorte-McCrea et al., 2017). Zoos and wildlife reserves can make a valuable contribution toward correcting this, by facilitating and promoting opportunities for knowledge transfer and emotional connections between people and carnivores (Kals & Ittner, 2003; Myers, 2007).

The implications of this are important in seeking solutions to address human-carnivore relations now and in the future. Spending time in the presence of large carnivores may foster a closer connection that may alter negative perceptions and ultimately reduce illegal trade and human–carnivore conflict (Nabhan and Trimble, 1994; Consorte-McCrea et al., 2019). Offering communities outside protected areas the opportunity to spend time with carnivores in their natural habitat may be of greater value than tedious questionnaire-based approaches. In the state of Rajasthan in India, for example, local farming communities have lived alongside free-roaming leopards for centuries and hold them in reverence as they believe the big cats are gifts from God (Rahman, 2020). Such examples of successful human–carnivore coexistence are rare, but lessons can be shared and re-created within an African context. Support for the conservation of large carnivores is more likely when people have an emotional connection with them, and providing more opportunities for this may lead to coexistence or at least a greater level of tolerance in the future (Consorte-McCrea et al., 2019).

One of the remaining stumbling blocks is that major international conservation agencies continue to base their arguments and solutions primarily on anthropocentric principles (Taylor et al., 2020). This is highly detrimental to nurturing an appreciation of wildlife, other than in a utilitarian sense. Concepts such as "ecosystem services," "natural capital," and "sustainable trade in endangered species" are all rooted in a utilitarian philosophy, and it is difficult to conceive how continuing to prioritize such strategies will lead to any change in the current trajectories. It is therefore essential that we approach biodiversity conservation from alternative angles that are not dependent solely on human interests or anthropocentric outcomes (Wuerthner et al., 2015; Kopnina et al., 2018). This may foster a better understanding of nature's intrinsic value and would benefit both conservation science and conservation practice (Vucetich et al., 2015).

Linked to the above is an urgent need for a significant shift in the current traditional value systems of several African communities in relation to the way they view and treat wildlife. Among Eastern and Western cultures, there also needs to be a major change in mindset regarding the use of animals or animal parts as status symbols or for medicinal purposes. Many of these traditions and beliefs have no place in the modern world and are driving species extinctions and ecosystem degradation. By removing incentives and transforming traditions that accelerate carnivore declines, and adopting more cooperative actions that value carnivore presence and nurture respect, we may be able to reverse the large-scale extermination of these species outside protected areas.

Ultimately, the measures discussed above are long-term strategies and need to be nested within the broader context for change. They need to be reinforced by direct measures such as law enforcement and robust legal and regulatory frameworks if the demise of large carnivores is to be halted in the short term. The illegal killing of, or trading in, protected species is a crime, and those involved (farmers, hunters, poachers, traders, and state officials among them) should be arrested and prosecuted. Wildlife law enforcement operations are costly and require significant and sustainable financing to run, but they are extremely effective when backed by resources and good governance (Hillborn et al., 2006; Critchlow et al., 2016).

Africa can reimagine itself as well positioned to be a focal point for global biodiversity conservation. Successes here can be adapted and replicated in other regions, and African conservationists, communities, and politicians can inform and influence international conservation policy and practice. The conservation of large carnivores is central to this, given the international interest in the preservation of these charismatic and ecologically vital species. It is now past time for people to recognize a greater value to carnivores, instead of the crude anthropocentric conception of them as resources to be utilized. How we promote that higher value, and how we turn it into positive outcomes for carnivores, will be critical in future biodiversity conservation efforts.

# References

African Parks Network (2023). Our track record. https://africanparks.org/about-us/our-story/our-track-record

Aguirre, A. A., Catherina, R., Frye, H., et al. (2020). Illicit wildlife trade, wet markets and Covid 19: Preventing future pandemics. *World Medical and Health Policy*, *12*(3), 256–65. https://doi.org/10.1002/wmh3.348

Balme, G. A., Slotow, R., & Hunter, L. T. B. (2010). Edge effects and the impact of non-protected areas in carnivore conservation: Leopards in the Phinda-Mkhuze complex, South Africa. *Animal Conservation, 13*, 315–23. https://doi.org/10.1111/j.1469-1795.2009.00342.x

Balme, G. A., Hunter, L., & Braczkowski, A. R. (2012). Applicability of age-based hunting regulations for African leopards. *PLoS ONE, 7*, e35209. https://doi.org/10.1371/journal.pone.0035209

Boronyak, L., Jacobs, B., & Wallach, A. (2020). Transitioning towards human-large carnivore coexistence in extensive grazing systems. *Ambio, 49*(12), 1982–91. https://doi.org/10.1007/s13280-020-01340-w

Bouley, P., Paulo, A., Angela, M., et al. (2021). The successful reintroduction of African wild dogs (*Lycaon pictus*) to Gorongosa National Park, Mozambique. *PLoS ONE, 16*, e0249860. https://doi.org/10.1371/journal.pone.0249860

Cardoso, P., Amponsah-Mensa, K., Barreiros, J. P., et al. (2021). Scientist's warning to humanity on illegal or unsustainable wildlife trade. *Biological Conservation, 263*, e109341. https://doi.org/10.1016/j.biocon.2021.109341

Consorte-McCrea, A., Nigbur, D., & Bath, A. (2017). Implications of teenagers' attitudes toward maned wolf conservation in Brazil. *Canid Biology and Conservation, 20*(5), 16–24.

Consorte-McCrea, A., Fernandez, A., Bainbridge, A., et al. (2019). Large carnivores and zoos as catalysts for engaging the public in the protection of biodiversity. *Nature Conservation, 37*, 133–50. https://doi.org/10.3897/natureconservation.37.39501

Critchlow, R., Plumtree, A. J., Alidria, B., et al. (2016). Improving law enforcement effectiveness and efficiency in Protected Areas using ranger-collected monitoring data. *Conservation Letters, 10*(5), 572–80. https://doi.org/10.1111/conl.12288

Di Marco, M., Baker, M. L., Daszak, P., et al. (2020). Sustainable development must account for pandemic risk. *PNAS, 17*(8), 3888–92. https://doi.org/10.1073/pnas.2001655117

Di Minin, E., Slotow, R., Fink, C., et al. (2021). A pan-African spatial assessment of human conflicts with lions and elephants. *Nature Communications, 12*, 2978. https://doi.org/10.1038/s41467-021-23283-w

Durant, S. M., Mitchell, N., Groom, R., et al. (2016). The global decline of cheetah *Acinonyx jubatus* and what it means for conservation. *PNAS, 114*(3), 528–33. https://doi.org/10.1073/pnas.1611122114

Estes, J. A., Terborgh, J., Brashares, J. S., et al. (2011). Trophic downgrading of planet Earth. *Science, 333*, 301–6. https://doi.org/10.1126/science.1205106

FAO (2023). Africa sustainable livestock 2050. https://www.fao.org/in-action/asl2050/resources/documents/livestock-and-the-environment/en/

Funston, P. J., Groom, R. J., & Lindsey, P. A. (2013). Insights into the management of large carnivores for profitable wildlife-based land uses in African savannas. *PLoS ONE, 8*, e59044. https://doi.org/10.1371/journal.pone.0059044

Galvez, N., Guillera-Arroita, G., St John, F. A. V., et al. (2018). A spatially integrated framework for assessing socioecological drivers of carnivore decline. *Journal of Applied Ecology, 55*, 1393–405. https://doi.org/10.1111/1365-2664.13072

Gusset, M., Swarner, M. J., Mponwane, L., et al. (2009). Human wildlife conflict in northern Botswana: Livestock predation by Endangered African Wild Dog (*Lycaon pictus*) and other carnivores. *Oryx, 43*, 67–72. https://doi.org/10.1017/S0030605308990475

Hillborn, R., Arcese, P., Borner, M., et al. (2006). Effective enforcement in a conservation area. *Science, 314*, 1266. https://doi.org/10.1126/science.1132780

Jorge, A. A., Vanak, A. T., Thaker, M., et al. (2013). Costs and benefits of the presence of leopards to the sport-hunting industry and local communities in Niassa National Reserve, Mozambique. *Conservation Biology 27*(4), 832–43. https://doi.org/10.1111/cobi.12082

Kals, E., & Ittner, H. (2003). Children's environmental identity: Indicators and behaviour impact. In S. Clayton & S. Opotow (Eds.), *Identity and the Natural Environment* (pp. 135–57). MIT Press.

Kopnina, H., Washington, H., Taylor, B., et al. (2018). Anthropocentrism: More than just a misunderstood problem. *Journal of Agricultural and Environmental Ethics, 31*, 109–27. https://doi.org/10.1007/s10806-018-9711-1

Lindsey, P., Roulet, P. A., & Romanach, S. S. (2007). Economic and conservation significance of the trophy hunting industry in sub-Saharan Africa. *Biological Conservation, 134*, 455–69. https://doi.org/10.1016/j.biocon.2006.09.005

Lindsey, P. A., Balme, G. A., Booth, V. R., et al. (2012). The significance of African lions for the financial viability of trophy hunting and the maintenance of wild land. *PLoS ONE, 7*, e29332. https://doi.org/10.1016/j.biocon.2006.09.005

Lindsey, P. A., Havemann, C. P., Lines, R., et al. (2013). Determinants of persistence and tolerance of carnivores on Namibian ranches: Implications for conservation on Southern African private lands. *PLoS ONE, 8*, e52458. https://doi.org/10.1371/journal.pone.0052458

Loveridge, A. J., Searle, A. W., Murindagomo, F., & Macdonald, D. W. (2007). The impact of sport hunting on the population dynamics of an African lion population in a protected area. *Biological Conservation, 134*, 548–58. https://doi.org/10.1016/j.biocon.2006.09.010

Macdonald, E. A., Hinks, A., Weiss, D. J., et al. (2017). Identifying ambassador species for conservation marketing. *Global Ecology and Conservation, 12*, 204–14. https://doi.org/10.1016/j.gecco.2017.11.006

Maxwell, S. L., Fuller, R. A., Brooks, T. M., et al. (2016). Biodiversity: The ravages of guns, nets and bulldozers. *Nature, 536*, 143–45. https://doi.org/10.1038/536143a

Mole, K. H., & Newton, D. (2021). *An Assessment of Trade, Mortalities and Anthropogenic Threats Facing Lions in Tanzania and Mozambique* (TRAFFIC Short Report). https://www.traffic.org/publications/reports/african-lion-trade-an-assessment-of-trade-mortalities-and-anthropogenic-threats-facing-lions-in-tanzania-and-mozambique/

Morton, O., Scheffers, B. R., Haugaasen, T., et al. (2021). Impacts of wildlife trade on terrestrial biodiversity. *Nature Ecology and Evolution*, 5, 540–48. https://doi.org/10.1038/s41559-021-01399-y

Myers, G. (2007). *The Significance of Children and Animals*. Purdue University Press.

Nabhan, G. P., & Trimble, S. (1994). *The Geography of Childhood*. Beacon Press.

Naidoo, R., Weaver, C., & Diggle R. W. (2016). Complementary benefits of tourism and hunting to communal conservancies in Namibia. *Conservation Biology*, 30(3), 628–38. https://doi.org/10.1111/cobi.12643

Naude, V. N., Balme, G. A., Rogan, M. S., et al. (2020). Longitudinal assessment of illegal leopard skin use in ceremonial regalia and acceptance of faux alternatives among followers of the Shembe Church, South Africa. *Conservation Science and Practice*, 2, e289. https://doi.org/10.1111/csp2.289

Nyhus, P. J. (2016). Human wildlife conflict and coexistence. *Annual Review of Environment and Resources*, 41, 143–71. https://doi.org/10.1146/annurev-environ-110615-085634

O'Bryan, C. J., Braczkowski, A. R., Beyer, H. L., et al. (2018). The contribution of predators and scavengers to human wellbeing. *Nature Ecology & Evolution*, 2, 229–36. https://doi.org/10.1038/s41559-017-0421-2

Ordiz, A., Bischof, R., & Swenson, J. E. (2013). Saving large carnivores but losing the apex predator? *Biological Conservation*, 168, 128–33. https://doi.org/10.1016/j.biocon.2013.09.024

Packer, C., Kosmala, M., Cooley, H. S., et al. (2009) Sport hunting, predator control and conservation of large carnivores. *PLoS ONE*, 4, e5941. https://doi.org/10.1371/journal.pone.0005941

Packer, C., Brink, H., Kissui, B., et al. (2011). Effects of trophy hunting on lion and leopard populations in Tanzania. *Conservation Biology*, 25, 142–53. https://doi.org/10.1111/j.1523-1739.2010.01576.x

Packer, C., Loveridge, A., Canney, S., et al. (2013). Conserving large carnivores: Dollars and fence. *Ecology Letters*, 16, 635–41. https://doi.org/10.1111/ele.12091

Pittman, R. T., Fattebert, J., Williams, S. T., et al. (2016). The conservation costs of game ranching. *Conservation Letters*, 10, 403–13. https://doi.org/10.1111/conl.12276

Price, R. A. (2017). *Economic Drivers and Effects of Illegal Wildlife Trade in Sub-Saharan Africa*. Institute of Development Studies.

Rahman, A. P. (2020, September 1). Bera's free-roaming leopards walk on thin ice as tourism grows. *Mongabay*. https://india.mongabay.com/2020/09/beras-free-roaming-leopards-walk-on-thin-ice-as-tourism-grows

Stander, P. (2010). The impact of male-based mortality on the population structure of desert-adapted lions in Namibia. https://lionrangers.org/wp-content/uploads/2020/08/Stander2010Male-basedMortality.pdf

Taylor, B., Chapron, G., Kopnina, H., et al. (2020). The need for ecocentrism in biodiversity conservation. *Conservation Biology, 34*(5), 1089–96. https://doi.org/10.1111/cobi.13541

Tow, J. H., Symes, W. S., & Carrasco, L. R. (2021). Economic value of wildlife trade entering the USA. *PLoS ONE, 16*, e0258523. https://doi.org/10.1371/journal.pone.0258523

Treves, A. (2009). Hunting for large carnivore conservation. *Journal of Applied Ecology, 46*, 1350–56. https://doi.org/10.1111/j.1365-2664.2009.01729.x

Trichorache, P., Yashpe, S., & Marker, L. (2021). Global dataset for seized and non-intercepted illegal cheetah trade (*Acinonyx jubatus*) 2010–2019. *Data in Brief, 35*, 106848. https://doi.org/10.1016/j.dib.2021.106848

Trouwborst, A., Loveridge, A. J., & Macdonald, D. W. (2020). Spotty data: Managing international leopard (*Panthera pardus*) trophy hunting quotas. *Journal of Environmental Law, 32*, 253–78. https://doi.org/10.1093/jel/eqz032

US Agency for International Development (2019). *Conservation and Law Enforcement in Gorongosa and Niassa: A Study of the Criminal Justice Process for Wildlife Crime from Apprehension to Incarceration.* https://pdf.usaid.gov/pdf_docs/PA00TX28.pdf

Vandome, C., & Vines, A. (2018, October 11). *Tackling Illegal Wildlife Trade in Africa: Economic Incentives and Approaches.* Chatham House. https://www.chathamhouse.org/2018/10/tackling-illegal-wildlife-trade-africa-economic-incentives-and-approaches

Verschueren, S., Briers-Louw, W. D., Torres-Uribe, C., et al. (2020). Assessing human conflicts with carnivores in Namibia's eastern communal conservancies. *Human Dimensions of Wildlife*, 452–67. https://doi.org/10.1080/10871209.2020.1758253

Vucetich, J. A., Bruskotter, J. T., & Nelson, M. P. (2015). Evaluating whether nature's intrinsic value is an axiom of or anathema to conservation. *Conservation Biology, 29*(2), 321–32. https://doi.org/10.1111/cobi.12464

Williams, V. L., Coals, P. G., de Bruyn, M., et al. (2021). Monitoring compliance of CITES lion bone exports from South Africa. *PLoS ONE, 16*, e0249306. https://doi.org/10.1371/journal.pone.0249306

Wilson-Holt, O., & Steele, P. (2019). *Human–Wildlife Conflict and Insurance: Can Insurance Reduce the Costs of Living with Wildlife?* International Institute for Environment and Development.

Wolf, C., & Ripple, W. J. (2018). Rewilding the world's large carnivores. *Royal Society Open Science, 5*, 172235. https://doi.org/10.1098/rsos.172235

World Bank (2016). *Analysis of International Funding to Tackle Illegal Wildlife Trade.* https://openknowledge.worldbank.org/entities/publication/2f7ba565-8345-57de-af40-aa723e5c2647

Wuerthner, G., Crist, E., & Butler, T. (Eds.) (2015). *Keeping the Wild: Against the Domestication of Earth.* Island Press.

9

# For the Bounteous Beauty of the Living Seas

EILEEN CRIST

There is no water that is wholly of the Pacific, or wholly of the Atlantic, or of the Indian or the Antarctic. The surf that we find exhilarating at Virginia Beach or at La Jolla today may have lapped at the base of Antarctic icebergs or sparkled in the Mediterranean sun, years ago, before it moved through dark and unseen waterways to the place we find it now. It is by the deep, hidden currents that the oceans are made one.

—Rachel Carson (1951)

The Earth is blue.

—Yuri Gagarin, during his flight into space in 1961

The global ocean is imperiled. What remains of marine life abundance, a fraction of what once was, continues to be afflicted by industrial fishing, human-caused starvations and diseases of nonhumans, warming and acidifying waters from rapid climate change, and pollution from agrochemical runoff, sewage, garbage, and oil spills (Danson, 2011; Crist 2021a). Gigantic amounts of endocrine-disrupting, nonbiodegradable, and toxin-concentrating plastics are killing uncountable animals and fouling the ecosphere's food web (Law & Thompson, 2014; Mooney, 2014; Warner et al., 2020). Persistent organic pollutants have so infiltrated the ocean that the bodies of some marine predators meet the definition of toxic waste (Whitty, 2011). Astounding amounts of fishing gear—including hooks, lines, traps, and nets—are lost in the ocean every year, continuing to kill creatures out of sight and out of mind; the amount of fishing line lost annually is enough to encircle Earth 18 times (Koumoundouros, 2022).

Industrial fishing has devastated the seas through three modes of unrestrained expansion: geographic, bathymetric, and taxonomic (Pauly, 2019). In the wake of serially depleting or extinguishing fish populations, industrial fishing fleets have systematically moved from the Northern to the Southern Hemisphere, and from coastal seas and continental shelves to the high seas (geographic expansion); from relatively shallow seas to ocean depths and seabed (bathymetric expansion); and from depleted species to new ones not previously consumed by people (taxonomic expansion). This assault on marine life has devastated seabed habitats (e.g., oyster beds, reefs, and kelp forests) and massively contracted the populations of marine creatures, both the targeted ones and bystanders such as marine mammals, sea turtles, seabirds, and others labeled bycatch. As a result, "[T]he health of the world's largest ecosystem is at stake" and the end of wild fish is within sight (Pauly, 2019).

Yet ignorance about the ecological history and current state of the ocean is socially pervasive. Unbeknownst to the majority of people, the seas have been divested of their immense populations of fish, invertebrates, marine mammals, sea turtles, and birdlife (Mowat, 1996; Jackson, 2005; Roberts, 2012; Pauly, 2019). It strains the imagination to countenance the destruction of sea creatures that has occurred: to learn from archaeological data, firsthand accounts (such as fishing and whaling logbooks), and historical marine ecology of the erstwhile richness of marine biodiversity even less than one hundred years ago (Schrope, 2006). Marine biologist Callum Roberts writes that "before 20th century industrial fishing took off, European seas seethed with life" (2007: 128). Globally, according to marine researcher Boris Worm, "everywhere you go, in every ocean basin [. . .] hotspots today are only relics of what was once there" (SEAWEB, 2005).

Without confronting this reckless demolition, humanity will remain incapable of aspiring to the return of life-filled seas. Instead, people will settle for an impoverished ocean and the sprawl of industrial aquaculture operations, while seas suffer empty coastlines and estuaries, bulldozed continental shelves and seamounts, offshore and deep-sea mining, massive defaunation and extinctions, jellyfish and algal population explosions, spreading dead zones, and the unthinkable disappearance of coral reefs and coastal ecologies. Humanity may be on the verge of capitulating to the human takeover of the ocean that is leading to its reduction to a "protein" factory, a desalinizing solution for the freshwater crisis, a mineral extraction domain for a "green economy," and a global transit zone for container ships, nuclear-armed submarines, and cables. An exploitable big body of water, in other words. Which is exactly what the ocean is not.

## From Abundance to Destitution

Everything about the ocean—including its delicious scent, which is also disappearing (Upton, 2013)—flows from its polyphony of life. The ocean is a life-creating and life-proliferating crucible, the very place where life itself likely emerged, whose deep past lingers in our intimate fluids of sweat, blood, and tears (Carson, 1951; Helmreich, 2010). Even into the 20th century the seas teemed with life: from the phytoplankton and zooplankton at the bottom of the food web to billions of small prey fish, shellfish, and carnivorous fish to extravagant populations of diverse seabird species to tens of millions of dolphins and whales whose carcasses and poop returned to marine life, including to abyssal critters, food to sustain them (Roberts, 2012).

Abundance nourished and bred abundance, and fish graced with long lives often grew into enormous sizes. In *The Unnatural History of the Seas* (a must-read work about historical marine ecology and the human impact), Roberts reports that sightings of 30-foot great white sharks evoked comparisons to whales, while 20-foot sharks, extremely rare these days, were common when (for example) European colonizers arrived at the islands and shores of the New World (Roberts, 2007). The former numbers and sizes of *all fish* are legendary—not only the cod who fed people for centuries, but also sharks, tuna, marlin, sturgeon, salmon, and swordfish to name a few others. Cod might reach three feet in length, while their astronomical numbers drew analogies to grains of sand. The seafarer who gave Cape Cod its name complained that his boat "was constantly 'pestered' by thick schools of codfish" as he navigated the peninsula (Kurlansky, 2011: 102). The average swordfish today—reflecting the fate of fish in general—is half the size it was 100 years ago (Danson, 2011: 104). Bluefin tuna could reach over four meters in length. Big fish live in the perpetual shadow of being hunted or otherwise killed by human causes. The industrial onslaught on the ocean does not allow fish their natural lifespans—to grow bigger and nurture their milieus with their astounding fecundity.

Indeed, fish size directly correlates with their fertility and regeneration. Many fish are long-lived, and the large female fish are vastly more prolific in the numbers of eggs they produce than the smaller ones (Pauly, 2019). These large females essentially regenerate the populations. The industrial fishing war on marine life has disabled marine biodiversity's inherent capacity to renew its abundances. Extraction by fossil-fuel-powered, government-subsidy-enabled, massive fishing fleets (outfitted with high-tech gear and onboard refrigeration) has not only drained marine life, it has contracted the sizes of fish and thus their fecundity. Climate change is poised to worsen all these effects. Despite frequent and ignorant incriminations of climate change as chief driver of marine life destruction, industrial fishing is far and beyond the major culprit (Pitcher & Cheung, 2013: 510; McCauley et al., 2015; Clover, 2022).

Marine creatures do not get to live as long, eat as heartily, or grow as big as they once did when the seas overflowed with life. In the life-filled ocean, feeding was not a competition nor a struggle with scarcity nor a plastic-ingesting horror show. It was an extravaganza of more-than-plenty to go around. Coastal seas surged with lavish marine populations and wildlife spectacles could be witnessed from the shore (Roberts, 2007; Clover, 2022). Estuaries have been downgraded "from astonishing abundance to abject poverty" (Roberts, 2007: 227). What living vitality there was when the Caribbean, for example, was graced with coral reefs, forested with sea meadows, and dwelled in by innumerable groupers, reef sharks, moray eels, rays, parrotfish, manatees, monk seals, sea turtles, and rainbows of tropical fish. The numbers of the region's sea turtles alone were in the tens of millions; their decimation constitutes "one of the great wildlife exterminations of colonial times" (Roberts, 2007: 62). The Caribbean's goliath groupers, who might reach two meters in length, are today critically endangered. Only 10 percent of the historic Caribbean coral reef habitats remain and their prospects continue to unravel. Indeed, the coastlines and shelves of all continents were once life-constructed and life-dwelling havens; they have been demolished by industrial fishing and especially trawling and dredging, which destroy both the habitats and the living beings who live in them.

The marine environment belied the typical food web pyramid of a profusion of microorganisms at the bottom, followed by abundant plant life and small critters, layered by lesser numbers of midsize predators, and capped by still fewer apex predators. Instead of being triangular, the ocean's food web more resembled a rectangle with abundance at every trophic tier (Jackson, 2005). The plankton and krill; schools of prey fish such as herring, sardines, menhaden, and anchovetas; the larger fish, such as mackerel, cod, haddock, pollock, and sturgeon; the big ones, including sharks, swordfish, sailfish, and tuna; sea turtles and seabirds; marine mammals, such as seals, manatees, dugongs, dolphins, porpoises, and whales; and the habitat-building oysters, mussels, sponges, clams, and corals. These examples are tokens—for how can the multitudes, along with their endemic diversity in different places, be listed? Numbers of species, population masses, astounding sizes, and marine wildlife relations and spectacles were as great as the ocean is wide and deep. This includes the whale nations.

Over the course of centuries, and accelerating from the 18th through the 20th, whales—labeled "fisheries" in the industrial era—were serially decimated population after population, place after place, and species after species. Wherever seafarers found unexploited whale pods, the numbers reported were staggering. The whales often came to see the seafarers, crowding around the vessels. They were killed in response by men trapped and brainwashed by a society of human exceptionalism, men robbed of their earthly birthright for wonder, curiosity, and desire to communicate with nonhumans. At least some of those men suffered trauma from participating in "the stench and brutal reality of the whaling grounds" (Challenger, 2023). Melanie Challenger, who researched firsthand reports of whalers, writes that "what struck me in the diaries of the men who participated in the industry was their regret on killing the animals." We can only imagine how deeply disturbed those whalers must have been to confess such feelings in writing. The coupling of the slaughter and destruction of nonhumans with the debasement and traumatization of humans is a recurring historical and contemporary motif. The key to sanity and reparation is the liberation of all beings, humans included, from the poison of supremacist creeds and the atrocities they drive.

By the end of the 19th century, whaling was global business. Today, even with a moratorium on whaling, 80 percent of the historic biomass of whales (and dolphins) is gone (Walker, 2017). Where once these magical beings sought us, now many humans seek to be near them. We must restore a world in which they thrive again, enriching and cocreating their ecologies. In such a world, humans and whales may meet; in interspecies encounters, all parties are elevated and expand their experience of being alive. Thus, nation-states that continue killing whales must stand down *now* in the wake of the devastation of whales, who are experiencing suffering and dying enough: starvations, ship collisions, entanglements in fishing gear, noise pollution, and intestinal strangulation by plastic and other garbage. In the last decade, whales all around the world are regularly beaching emaciated and with their stomachs full of trash; and what we see is only a tip of the iceberg, since most marine deaths occur out of sight.

Plastic garbage also strangles the digestive tracts of sea turtles, who mistake it for jellyfish. Globally, all species of sea turtles are endangered (Crist, 2019). Uncountable numbers of seabirds, marine mammals, and fish die yearly from eating plastic or getting ensnared in it (Casey, 2010; Warner et al., 2020). The gruesome plastic deaths of whales, sea turtles, fish, seabird chicks, and other beings is a formidable mirror that consumer society should muster the courage to peer into. This is the time to witness, to regret, and to grieve. To make reparations to beings whom we have so reprehensibly wronged. To bring back the bounteous marine life by rewilding the seas through establishing expansive networks of marine protected areas around the globe (Clover, 2022).

To grope in the mind's eye toward the erstwhile life-filled ocean is not some nostalgic pastime. It is about opening toward the essence of earthly life, which is to proliferate abundances and diversities of beings and relationships. It is about nurturing a yearning toward who we humans *need to become* in order to restore marine biodiversity's fullest manifestation and to receive, in turn, the gift of coexisting with that vibrant lifeworld. So much has been lost, yet possibly the greatest harm of all would be for humanity to resign itself to the ocean's (and Earth's) impoverishment and to settle into the debased modalities of unbounded encroachment and willful ignorance.

## Silence = Death

An intimate, rich conversation primordially bonds marine and terrestrial life. Clouds formed over the seas with the help of oceanic microorganisms bring rain to the land, and the rain (with the help of plant roots) loosens nutrients from rocks that flow back to the sea by means of rivers. Abounding nutrients from the seas were once brought inland by abundances of fish, who thus entwined ocean and land ecologies through their epic lifecycles

(Waldman, 2010; Jackson et al., 2011). Such rivers of fish created hybrid ecological zones. For example, they might be pursued inland by predators, such as porpoises swimming up Britain's Thames or bull sharks straying into North America's James River. The salmon, shad, whitefish, sturgeon, eels, and others fed land animals, trees, and soil.

Thus is the natural world knit into patterns of intelligence and reciprocity through life's strivings, sensory pleasures, evolved interfaces, intergenerational reproductions, and mutual feasts. Along with bears, eagles, and trees, Indigenous peoples also feasted after welcoming the fish with ceremony (House, 1999). For millennia the fish returned in numbers that "stretched capacity to believe," appearing to reverse the river's flow, reproducing prodigiously, sustaining the forest ecosystem, and propelling their own destinies (Roberts, 2007: 49; Vickers and McClenachan, 2011).

Stories of fish-filled seas and rivers, of fecund ecotones where ocean and land life mesh, teach us that our ideas about cooperation and mutualism versus competition and struggle for survival—while exhibiting some limited erudition—do not hold a candle to the phenomena of life themselves, which exceed and bewilder our theories. These phenomena are creative and prolific, while also transpiring as relationships between different "species of mind" (Allen & Bekoff, 1999). For millennia, Western civilization kept itself in the dark about the existence, let alone the variety, of nonhuman minds, which represented a cardinal threat to human arrogance. When humans awaken, as is happening in our time, to the diverse forms of awareness on this planet, we surface into awe (Safina, 2015; Simard, 2021). Awe should not be understood as sentimentality or fleeting experience but as a state of grounded being, within which to bring up human children and to anchor human life.

Cultures that live by the credo of humans' distinguished identity do not yet know awe, nor the care and respect it fosters. As Native American writer Jack Forbes explains, supremacists devour the lives of those they consider beneath them, nonhuman or human (Forbes, 2008). The belief in being "superior" or "exceptional" makes it easy to turn others into *just* fish, just trees, just rivers, just meat, or, until not too long ago, just "savages." The fish runs of Europe were wrecked by deforestation, overfishing, dams, and industry as early as the Medieval period, all but silencing one of the planet's rife sea–land conversations (Roberts, 2007).

Europeans then turned to the fish-abounding coasts, and, after emptying them, kept fishing further and deeper afield. Eventually, they came to the New World for its fish—and for its whales, walruses, seals, seabirds, sea turtles, and sea otters. Thus, did "civilized" user behavior toward the natural world continually rehearse itself, except that the destruction of the New World was a palpable bloodbath because of the speed and scale of its unalloyed violence. By the early modern period, voracious markets were devouring the marine (and terrestrial) life of the New World as flesh, eggs, oils, pelts, and feather commodities in an unprecedented performance of Earth desolation (Mowat, 1996).

The repeated response "to local overfishing has been to 'move on' down the food web, toward deeper waters, and to other areas or regions of the world" (Sumaila and Pauly, 2011: 25). This historical pattern *continues*, even as the global fish catch peaked two decades ago (Pauly, 2019). China's industrial fleets have taken the lead, but Russia, South Korea, Spain, Thailand, the United States, and others are rushing to extract the fish of the high seas, of Africa's and Latin America's waters, of seamounts, of any places in the ocean where fish are left (Urbina, 2020). People of developing nations, who often rely on fish from subsistence or artisanal fishing, are deprived of livelihood and nourishment by the industrial-fishing complex (Golden et al., 2016; Pauly, 2019; Clover, 2022). While small-scale and even recreational fishing—especially when powered by fossil fuels—can take considerable toll on local environments, the ecological harm of industrial fishing is incomparable. For example, Chinese distant-water ships can extract as many fish *in one week* as local boats from Senegal or Mexico catch *in a year* (Urbina, 2020).

Along with other marine beings, fish are being exterminated at every tier of the ocean's food web with little ecological accountability through both legal and illegal operations (Vincent and Harris, 2014; Pauly and Zeller, 2016). The majority of fish "stock"—standard jargon that expediently warps the seas into a human food pantry—are so relentlessly exploited that the trend in biomass across species is spiraling downward (Gjerde et al., 2013).

In Roberts's words, "[E]stimates suggest that most of the world's major fishery species have been reduced in numbers by 75 percent to 95 percent or more" (2012: 50). Today, among global "fisheries," 94 percent are either fully exploited or overexploited, while in the Mediterranean 83 percent are overfished (Clover, 2022: xxi, 10). After over a century of industrial fishing, only 10 percent of the historical populations of big fish remain (Myers and Worm, 2005). Coral reef and oyster bed habitats, both huge attractors of marine biodiversity, have suffered tremendous losses. In the past millennium, 90 percent of the world's oyster beds have been destroyed; in the last 150 years, coral cover is gone by half (IPBES, 2019; Clover, 2022: 84). The bludgeoning of the seas' magnificent megafauna has been magnified by the unspeakable cruelty of shark finning operations; almost every shark caught, moreover, has a hook or two lodged in their jaws (Roberts, 2007). The economic and political status quo that is bankrolling and turning a blind eye to these depravities is simply contemptible.

Emptying the seas is depriving marine animals of their nourishment. Vacuuming the herring, menhaden, anchovies, sardines, and other small fish populations is taking its toll on populations of seabirds, sea lions, penguins, dolphins, and whales, among others. Whales are washing up dead of starvation, and on California's coast, sea lions and their pups have experienced famine (Steinmetz, 2014). Florida's manatees have been recently dying in record numbers from starvation (Crist, 2021b). Arctic terns, puffins, albatrosses, and other seabirds are taking nosedives in their numbers; seabird populations have declined by 70 percent since 1970 (van Dooren, 2014). Marine scientists forecast that critters of the deep seabed will face starvation by century's end (Monroe, 2017). With krill branded a "sustainable fishery," humanity is stealing food from whales, seabirds, seals, squid, and others for such consumer niceties as aquaculture feed and health supplements. Since the 1970s, krill populations have declined by 80 percent—illustrating what happens when marine extraction operations are labeled "sustainable" (Taylor, 2018).

From an exuberance of life, the ocean ecosystem has become precarious and unsafe for virtually all its residents, yet governments, the fishing industry, media, and an oblivious consumer public buffer themselves from that knowledge, keeping up the socially fabricated pretensions of fish as "seafood" and of seafood as "health food." The key ingredient of the ocean's depredation is *government subsidies*, which exceed US$30 billion annually to offset the fuel costs that power the fleets; without government handouts, industrial fishing could not be profitable. As scientists Amanda Vincent and Jean Harris state, fisheries' "appalling degradation is powered by widespread government subsidies that make [. . .] abusive practices economically feasible" (2014: 420).

An unsustainable public silence has been kept around the historical and continued demolition of marine life—expedited by toxic-politics-as-usual—spinning new meaning into the outrage of Silence = Death. Fortunately, the silence is increasingly being broken by outspoken marine conservationists and fisheries scientists, as well as by public NGO outreach and documentaries, exposing the desolated state of the seas and the urgent need for action.

## Attend to Reality

The inimitable Dr. Seuss captivates the minds of children with enchanted landscapes and fantastical beings. Yet we inhabit a world that makes Dr. Seuss's creativity a dreamy plagiarism of its creatures, their antics, their peregrinations, their weirdness, and their making of worlds. We inhabit a planet that also enchants children, before they grow into the brainwash that Earth is a human estate composed of "natural resources," which provide "maximum sustainable yields" of (among other things) seafood, which can be eaten by the world's consumers in any amount, at any time, and with smug enthusiasm for its high nutrition value. Yet the days when eating fish was good for human health have receded in the rearview mirror.

Where the continents extend toward ocean depths, they form the once-alive continental shelves. In rampages of demolitions, trawlers have gouged out marine beings and shattered their three-dimensional, life-created habitats. Rolling hills that were once filled with fish, mussels, oysters, crabs, anemones, tubeworms, sponges, and other critters have been smashed and leveled, while underwater glades and forests have turned to muddy flats. "Today," writes Roberts, "there is hardly a scrap of suitable bottom in the world that has not felt the scrape of a trawl." As a result, where there were "rich, complex, and productive habitats," what predominates is "gravel, sand, and mud" (Roberts, 2007: 156). Trawlers should have been decommissioned long ago and recycled into something useful. On the contrary, however, they were pushed by the developed world (and its agencies) onto many developing countries, and their wrecking operations were expanded to greater depths (Pauly, 2019). Trawlers pound and scrape the seabed with grotesque abandon, more than one mile deep. Having leveled and fished out the relatively accessible waters of continental shelves, there are other ocean wonders that trawlers have taken to vandalizing: the mountains of the seas.

Earth's seamounts jut out of ocean depths forming majestic peaks, gorges, and valleys. Life has set up house on them, of course. Deep-sea coral lives there, some hundreds of years old. Slow-growing fish who have evolved extraordinary abilities to withstand extreme conditions of pressure and cold also live there. Transoceanic travelers such as tuna, sharks, and sea turtles make stopovers. Seamounts are places dwelled in by some of Earth's strangest, most long-lived children; they are oases of gorgeous life. We might visualize seamounts as islands submerged underwater (Carson, 1951). And exactly as is the case with islands, much seamount biodiversity is endemic—existing nowhere else. Here come the trawlers with their military high-tech gear, yawning steel mouths, and bellies big enough to park numerous large airplanes, desecrating the seamounts, extracting the fish, and discarding the bycatch. After extinguishing the fish of any one seamount, the same atrocity is repeated on adjacent ones.

Trawling is among the most immoral and destructive assaults on the natural world ever orchestrated. With undiscriminating violence, in a matter of minutes, trawlers level what it took nature hundreds or thousands of years to create. The silt clouds that trawlers stir underwater can be seen on satellite images. Such technologically mediated violence is horror-genre material turned into a reality show in the ongoing staging of human domination over nature. The next chapter of ocean brutality, to be added to industrial fishing, is under preparation by the corporate architects of deep-sea mining and the governments that abet and authorize their ecological crimes. Seamounts, hydrothermal vents, and the deep seabed contain gold, cobalt, nickel, and rare earths among other metals and minerals. Deep-sea mining operations have already begun, and a commercial-scale extraction onslaught is in the works (Niner et al., 2018; Heffernan, 2019).

The consumers who eat the fish are for the most part ignorant about marine biodiversity and the utter madness of its extermination. People know little if anything, for example, about the seamounts' Seuss-like corals, sea fans, and endemic fish who are older than their grandmothers. Most people are unaware of the extraordinary science about those habitats and their endemism or of evolutionary narratives from the big bang to the charm of creatures who make their own light. Fish suddenly appear in the supermarket—the next-in-line species to be consumed to death (taxonomic expansionism). Some of the said species needed new names for better marketing prospects: slime heads were renamed orange roughy and tooth fish rechristened sea bass. Having suffered the fleeting reduction of representing nothing but profit and flesh, with the predictable depletions and collapses that follow, what fragment of real life of our slime head cousins remains and of so many others who have suffered and are suffering the same fate (Dreifus, 2002; Victorero et al., 2018)?

The countercultural bumper sticker "Question Reality" is off the mark. A superior motto would plead "Attend to Reality," which in our world is composed of the ineffable beauty of life. To "Question Social Normalcy," on the other hand, is urgently in order. To question, for example, the mass-extracted shrimp, spooned into one another on mass-produced plastic cocktail trays, with the obligate industrial-vat-made dipping sauce on the side. For every single pound of shrimp caught, ten pounds of sea life are thrown overboard dead and dying. Tens of thousands of sea turtles are killed yearly by shrimp trawlers. Mangroves—whose in-water root systems form enchanting nurseries of marine life—have been massively deforested for shrimp aquaculture operations (Danson, 2011; Keledjian et al., 2014). It is also advisable to question the parade of fish species featured in standardized frozen filets, as well as the factory-farmed, dyed-pink, wild-fish-fed, habitat-polluting, lice-infested, abused (and soon perhaps genetically modified) salmon at the supermarket.

As for those tasty fish on the top of the food-chain, who so efficiently bioaccumulate industrial toxins: "Think about that slab of tuna in the deli case as bushmeat," urges marine biologist Sylvia Earle (2003). Think about that slab of tuna as a crime, marine biologist Jeremy Jackson seconds (2014). Fisheries ecologist Daniel Pauly puts it thus: "Eating a tuna roll at a sushi restaurant should be considered no more environmentally benign than driving a Hummer or harpooning a manatee" (Pauly, 2019). Small fish are being vacuumed out of the Mediterranean to fatten penned tuna before murdering them to make a killing.

Critically important as well is to question fish labels at the restaurant, such as "grouper," which (given what groupers have suffered) are likely *not* a grouper, or, worse, actually are. (Seafood fraud is common [Danson, 2011].) The prestigious swordfish steak: can't we just let the animals be? The tasty scallops? Along with half of the total fish catch, they come from trawling. How about lobsters? For now they are still plentiful, and in some places that is only because their predators have been decimated. Lobsters were once so beneath polite society they were fed to convicts and slaves. But taxonomic expansionism, in the wake of cumulative serial depletions, has bestowed upon lobsters a status upgrade. When lobsters are allowed to live out their natural lifespans, they might grow to be 20 pounds.

Let us broadly question the reduction of sentient beings to flesh (Plumwood, 2013). For example, the octopus on the menu. If you give an octopus in an aquarium a ball, she will bounce it against the glass walls to pass the time. If you pursue an underwater friendship with an octopus teacher, like diver and filmmaker Craig Foster did, she might steal your heart and transform you forever (Foster, 2020). *Who are we alive with, here and now, on this Earth?* Do we actually believe—consciously or not—that consuming Earth as fodder is a worthy destiny for the human?

It is good to question social normalcy on all these registers. It is especially important to question calling sea life "stock" and "marine resources." Marine biodiversity is self-evidently *not* stock. And a resource does not feel or think, nor can it suffer and be brutalized. A resource does not create exquisite worlds nor look you in the eye. It might be "harvested unsustainably" or tagged "bycatch" and thrown overboard like trash. It may be in danger of collapsing. When the threat of depletion or "collapse of the stock" looms, well-meaning calls implore "to harvest it sustainably." The problem with this ostensible corrective to vanishing fish and other marine creatures is that it can never retrieve the primordial condition of *free seas*, of abundant, diverse, creative, ocean-churning life. Many US fisheries, for example, are currently appraised as "sustainable": but the populations they seek to sustain (for the take) are calculated from 1980s baselines when those fish populations were already depleted (Pauly, 2019). Indeed, the goal of "fisheries management," at its best, is to make maximal pilfering perpetual, and not to restore marine life.

From living artwork composed by an unfathomable plenum of creatures and phenomena—with dramatic, life-sustaining reverberations throughout the whole Earth system—the industrial-fishing complex has revamped the ocean into an extraction domain for cheap fish for the global consumer class. About half of the global fish catch today is traded, and consumer markets of developed countries account for two-thirds of the imports of fish and fish products (FAO, 2018; Pauly, 2019). As Pauly explains, "[F]isheries have been warped by the demands of the European Union, the United States, Japan, and China," which all have "devastated local fish populations and insatiable appetites" (Pauly, 2019). The world's consumer class has been draining the living ocean as an all-you-can-eat buffet.

## A Higher Calling Rising

Humanity can make the higher choice of freeing the ocean from industrial encroachment and making reparations to its violated life. To restore marine life bold action is required. Captain Paul Watson, for example, calls for a 50-year moratorium on all commercial fishing "to give the ocean time to repair itself" (Watson, 2018: 152). At the very least, the world must internationally act immediately to end all fishing in the high seas (Mongabay, 2023; Pew, 2023). By prohibiting fishing in the high seas, illegal vessels (which cause even greater harm because their impact is ruthless and unreported) would become readily detectable, making law enforcement feasible.

Beyond full protection of the high seas, we must create an ocean-wide interconnected network of protected areas along coasts, estuaries, islands, and continental shelves, working swiftly to the goal of 30 percent protection (or more) by 2030 (Clover, 2022). Research and experience have repeatedly shown that ecological revival follows in marine protected areas, especially in what are called "no take" or highly protected marine areas, where all fishing and extractive activities are banned (Warne, 2007; Roberts et al., 2017; Clover, 2022). "No take" marine reserves give the best results because a hands-off approach enables all aspects of biodiversity—biomass, diversity, age structure, and reproductive output of fish and other organisms—to recover and the ecological vibrancy of marine areas to return (Roberts et al., 2017; Clover, 2022).

Allowing abundant marine life to return through ambitious protection will revive a world of beauty and preserve a treasure trove of knowledge. The seas will be places we visit but do not remain. With the greatest part of the ocean protected—including high seas, coral reef, mangrove, and sea grass habitats, and networked reserves along coasts, islands, and continental shelves—the ocean can be celebrated as the largest protected area on Earth, where nature is set free into its wild dance.

Humanity must put an immediate end to industrial fishing operations, starting with the abolition of trawling and dredging, longline fishing, gillnets, and purse seine nets, and their indiscriminate massacre of marine creatures (Keledjian et al., 2014). It is time for the industrial war machine to be dismantled, ending the marine habitat destruction, the mass extraction of living beings, the devastation of "bycatch," and the massive pollution and death caused by lost fishing gear.

Regarding the future of fishing, we may welcome the revival of artisanal practices. Artisanal fishers fish by engaging their senses and applying their muscle power. They learn from elders and mentors how to scan the horizons to detect subtle changes in the sea's color and movement that give clues about where the fish might be. They attend to the behavior of seabirds and other living beings for cues. Artisanal fishing gear can be handmade and biodegradable. Moreover, the whole human body is bent upon the art of such fishing—it is not machine mediated. Indeed, artisanal fishers' capacity to take life from the seas is appropriately limited by the amount of bodily energy they can expend. That ability is not determined by fossil-fuel-powered megamachines and behemoth fleets outfitted with onboard storage capacity and high-tech detection devices that no fish and no place can escape. Artisanal fishing is in conversation with the world, not at war with it. It deploys what John Michael Greer calls *ecotechnics*, exhibiting artfulness, cultivated skill, situated knowledge, aesthetic appreciation, and ethical attunement with the nonhuman world (Greer, 2009).

For a life-abundant ocean to return we must also stop polluting it at all sources, and reverse, to the greatest extent possible, the pollution plaguing it. This requires, among other measures, the abolition of plastic production. "What we are witnessing," states scientist Marcus Eriksen, "is a growing threat of toxin-laden microplastics cycling through the entire marine ecosystem" (quoted in Mooney, 2014). Plastic ocean pollution is "a staggering problem" that yields untold numbers of painful deaths, according to a 2020 report from the nongovernmental organization Oceana (Warner et al., 2020). Equally critical for ending ocean pollution is phasing out industrial agriculture and its dead-zone-producing fertilizer and pesticide runoff (Crist, 2021a). Indeed, industrial agriculture is the destructive counterpart of industrial fishing on land. These two modes of mass food production go hand in hand in many ways, most importantly in their refusal to be in reciprocal relationship with the living world, choosing instead appropriation, aggression, violence, and domination (Crist, 2019).

Dietary choice is critical. Choosing not to eat fish and other marine beings at all, or to eat them sparingly, can scale up to make a difference, if ecological citizens promote this course of action courageously instead of shying away from it. The choice of minimal seafood consumption is all but mandatory for global consumers, whose appetite for fish is at the core of the ocean's crisis even though fish is not required for their basic nourishment. In any case, the idea that fish are a "health food" in a polluted world is a sham. The idea that fish do not feel pain, nor suffer, is equally bogus. As Jonathan Safran Foer states, "No fish gets a good death. Not a single one. You never have to wonder if the fish on your plate had to suffer. It did" (Foer, 2009). A dietary shift of saying no to fish consumption, where that is feasible, can play a critical role in ocean restoration in the decades ahead. Beyond this immediate strategy, it is also imperative that we work toward gradually lowering the human population, in order to support both the downscaling of fish consumption and the deindustrialization of all food production into the future (Crist, 2019).

In a world of trading billions, the mass consumption of fish equals the mass extermination of beings and ecologies that humanity may witness and commune with instead of mindlessly eating. "The great majority of sea species are badly depleted," Jackson rues. "But they still exist. If people actually went away, most could recover" (quoted in Weisman, 2007: 266). Humans need not "go away," but we must abolish the fishing military machine and change our view of the planet's largest ecosystem, the ocean. Creating a global culture that passionately protects the ocean and values the arts of underwater photography, snorkeling, scuba diving, and free diving—as much as it ostensibly values the gifts of education and healthcare for all—*that* is a culture worthy of the human spirit. Within this world, we will feast our minds on the pleasures of life's marvels, encountering forms of awareness unlike our own and bathing the fire of our sight in the color and dance of diverse sea animals and plants. A truly *cultivated* global culture is one of ecological and ethical reparation, not only for the sake of the nonhumans whose lives and homes have been vandalized but also for the sake of human well-being and dignity that have been despoiled in tandem.

In lighting up the aspiration to protect the ocean expansively, we have a chance to witness it rewilding itself into its exuberant manifestations of life, second to none in the cosmos. We have a chance to return, ourselves, to the awesome reality we've been graced to belong with. Some may counter that the goal of fully restoring marine biodiversity is a romantic fantasy that has nothing to do with "reality." Far from being a romantic fantasy, allowing sea life to rebound into its inherent glory is a realistic aspiration of the highest order: The order of Earth's life-creating power set free into its self-nature. At the same time, a higher order of human life dawns in the recognition that we are not in the world to eat it, but to witness it, commune with it, and protect its freedom.

## References

Allen, C., & Bekoff, M. (1999). *Species of Mind: The Philosophy and Biology of Cognitive Ethology*. Bradford Books.
Carson, R. (1951). *The Sea around Us*. Oxford University Press.
Casey, S. (2010). Garbage in, garbage out. *Conservation Magazine, 11*(1), 13–19.
Challenger, M. (2023). Unlearning human exceptionalism. Contribution to GTI Forum "Solidarity with Animals," The Great Transition Initiative. https://greattransition.org/gti-forum/solidarity-animals-challenger

Clover, C. (2022). *Rewilding the Sea: How to Save Our Oceans*. Penguin Books.
Crist, E. (2019). *Abundant Earth: Toward an Ecological Civilization*. University of Chicago Press.
Crist, E. (2021a). Got nitrogen? On the links between nitrogen pollution and overpopulation. *The Ecological Citizen, 5*(1), 3–10.
Crist, E. (2021b). WITNESS: Order Sirenia. *The Ecological Citizen, 5*(1), 37–42.
Danson, T. (2011). *Oceana: Our Endangered Ocean and What We Can Do to Save It*. Rodale.
Dreifus, C. (2002, March 5). A conversation with Callum Roberts: A biologist decries the "strip-mining" of the deep sea. *The New York Times*.
Earle, S. (2003). Our oceans, ourselves. Interview of Sylvia Earle. *Wild Earth, 12*(4), 23.
FAO (2018). *The State of World Fisheries and Aquaculture*. https://www.fao.org/documents/card/en/c/I9540EN/
Foer, J. S. (2009). *Eating Animals*. Little, Brown and Company.
Forbes, J. (2008) *Columbus and Other Cannibals*. Seven Stories.
Foster, C. (2020). *My Octopus Teacher* [Documentary]. Craig Foster (Producer).
Gjerde, K., Currie, D., Wowke, K., & Sack, K. (2013). Ocean in peril: Reforming the management of global ocean living resources in areas beyond national jurisdiction. *Marine Pollution Bulletin, 74*(2), 540–51. https://doi.org/10.1016/j.marpolbul.2013.07.037
Greer, J. M. (2009). *The Ecotechnic Future: Envisioning a Post-Peak World*. New Society Publishers.
Golden, C., Allison, E., Cheung, W., et al. (2016). Nutrition: Fall in fish catch threatens human health. *Nature, 534*, 317–20. https://doi.org/10.1038/534317a
Heffernan, O. (2019). Seabed mining is coming—bringing mineral riches and fears of epic extinctions. *Nature, 571*, 465–68. https://doi.org/10.1038/d41586-019-02242-y
Helmreich, S. (2010). Human nature at sea. *Anthropology Now, 2*(3), 49–60.
House, F. (1999). *Totem Salmon: Life Lessons from Another Species*. Beacon Press.
IPBES (2019). *The Global Assessment Report on Biodiversity and Ecosystem Services*. https://ipbes.net/sites/default/files/inline/files/ipbes_global_assessment_report_summary_for_policymakers.pdf
Jackson, J. (2005). When ecological pyramids were upside down. In J. A. Estes (Ed.), *Whales, Whaling, and Ocean Ecosystems* (pp. 27–37). University of California Press.
Jackson, J. (2014). *Healthy Planet Local Heroes Award Gala* [Video]. https://www.youtube.com/watch?v=NyWHSflfiag
Jackson, J., Alexander, K., & Sala, E. (Eds.) (2011). *Shifting Baselines: The Past and Future of Ocean Fisheries*. Island Press.
Keledjian, A., Brogan, G., Lowell, B., et al. (2014). Wasted catch: Unsolved problems in US fisheries. *Oceana Report*. https://oceana.org/reports/wasted-catch-unsolved-problems-us-fisheries

Koumoundouros, T. (2022, October 22). The fishing line lost at sea in a year could wrap around Earth 18 times. *Science Alert*. https://www.sciencealert.com/the-fishing-line-lost-at-sea-in-a-year-could-wrap-around-earth-18-times

Kurlansky, M. (2011). *World without Fish*. Workman Publishing Company.

Law, K. L., & Thompson, R. C. (2014). Microplastics in the seas. *Science, 345*(6193), 144–45. https://doi.org/10.1126/science.1254065

McCauley, D. J., Pinsky, M. L., Palumbi, S. R., et al. (2015). Marine defaunation: Animal loss in the global ocean. *Science, 347*(6219), 1255641-1-1255641-7. https://doi.org/10.1126/science.1255641

Mongabay. (2023, February 2022). Experts pushing for high-seas fishing ban win "Nobel Prize for the environment." https://news.mongabay.com/2023/02/experts-pushing-for-high-seas-fishing-ban-win-nobel-prize-for-environment/

Monroe, R. (2017). Deep oceans face starvation by end of century. Scripps Institute of Oceanography. https://scripps.ucsd.edu/news/deep-oceans-face-starvation-end-century

Mooney, C. (2014, December 10). Good job, humans: The oceans now contain 5 trillion pieces of floating plastic. *The Washington Post*.

Mowat, F. (1996). *Sea of Slaughter*. Mariner Books.

Myers, R., & Worm, B. (2005). Extinction, survival or recovery of large predatory fishes. *Philosophical Transactions of the Royal Society B, 360*, 13–20.

Niner, H., Ardron, J., Escobar, E., et al. (2018). Deep-sea mining with no net loss of biodiversity—an impossible aim. *Frontiers in Marine Science, 5*(53). https://doi.org/10.3389/fmars.2018.00053

Pauly, D. (2019). *Vanishing Fish: Shifting Baselines and the Future of Global Fisheries*. Greystone Books.

Pauly, D., & Zeller, D. (2016). Catch reconstructions reveal that global marine fisheries are higher than reported and declining. *Nature Communications, 7*, 10244. https://www.nature.com/articles/ncomms10244

Pew (2023). Protect high seas. https://www.pewtrusts.org/en/research-and-analysis/data-visualizations/2023/protect-high-seas

Pitcher, T., & Cheung, W. (2013). Fisheries: Hope or despair? *Marine Pollution Bulletin, 74*, 506–16.

Plumwood, V. (2013). Being prey. In L. Gruen, D. Jamieson, & C. Schlottmann (Eds.), *Reflecting on Nature*. Oxford University Press.

Roberts, C. (2007). *The Unnatural History of the Sea*. Island Press.

Roberts, C. (2012). *The Ocean of Life: The Fate of Man and the Sea*. Penguin Press.

Roberts, C., O'Leary, B., McCauley, D., et al. (2017). Marine reserves can mitigate and promote adaptation to climate change. *PNAS, 114*(24), 6167–75. https://doi.org/10.1073/pnas.1701262114

Safina, C. (2015). *Beyond Words: What Animals Think and Feel*. Henry Holt and Company.

SEAWEB. (2005, July 28). Scientists discover pattern of big fish diversity in open oceans. *EurekAlert!* https://www.eurekalert.org/news-releases/780011

Schrope, M. (2006). The real sea change. *Nature, 443,* 622–24. https://doi.org/10.1038/443622a

Simard, S. (2021). Finding the Mother Tree: a conversation with Suzanne Simard [Podcast episode]. *Emergence Magazine.* https://open.spotify.com/episode/6bgBkIgmUZjguk2xFRHkQb

Steinmetz, K. (2014, May 13). Sea lions are starving to death—and we do not know why. *Time,* https://time.com/97041/sea-lions-are-dying/

Sumaila, U. R., & Pauly, D. (2011). The "march of folly" in global fisheries. In J. Jackson, K. Alexander, & E. Sala (Eds.), *Shifting Baselines: The Past and Future of Ocean Fisheries* (pp. 21–32). Island Press.

Taylor, M. (2018, March 13). Krill fishing poses serious threat to Antarctic ecosystem, report warns. *The Guardian.* https://www.theguardian.com/environment/2018/mar/13/krill-fishing-poses-serious-threat-to-antarctic-ecosystem-report-warns

Upton, J. (2013, August 28). Vanishing ocean smell could also mean fewer clouds. *Grist.* https://grist.org/climate-energy/vanishing-ocean-smell-could-also-mean-fewer-clouds/

Urbina, I. (2020, August 17). How China's expanding fishing fleet is depleting the world's oceans. *Yale Environment 360.* https://e360.yale.edu/features/how-chinas-expanding-fishing-fleet-is-depleting-worlds-oceans

van Dooren, T. (2014). *Flight Ways: Life and Loss at the Edge of Extinction.* Columbia University Press.

Vickers, D. (with L. McClenachan) (2011). History and context: Reflections from Newfoundland. In Jackson J., Alexander K., and Sala E. (Eds), *Shifting Baselines: The Past and Future of Ocean Fisheries* (pp. 115–33). Island Press.

Victorero, L. Watling, L., Palomares, M., & Nouvian, C. (2018). Out of sight but within reach: A global history of bottom-trawled deep-sea fisheries from >400m Depth. Frontiers in *Marine Science, 5*(98). https://doi.org/10.3389/fmars.2018.00098

Vincent, A., & Harris, J. (2014). Boundless no more. *Science, 346*(6208), 420–21. https://doi.org/10.1126/science.1255923

Waldman, J. (2010, April 8). The natural world vanishes: How species cease to matter. *Yale Environment 360.* https://e360.yale.edu/features/the_natural_world_vanishes_how_species_cease_to_matter

Walker, M. (2017). Endangered Species Day. Whale and Dolphin Conservation. https://us.whales.org/2017/05/19/endangered-species-day-2017/

Warne, K. (2007). The global fish crisis: Blue haven. *National Geographic,* April: 70–81.

Warner, K., Linske, E., Mustain, P., et al. (2020). Choked, strangled, drowned: The plastics crisis unfolding in our oceans. *Oceana.* https://usa.oceana.org/wp-content/uploads/sites/4/2020/11/25/report_single_pagesdoi_choked_strangled_drowned_final.pdf

Watson, P. (2018). Interview with Paul Watson. *The Ecological Citizen*, 1(2), 152–53.
Weisman, A. (2007). *The World without Us*. St. Martin's Press.
Whitty, J. (2011). *Deep Blue Home: An Intimate Ecology of Our Wild Ocean*. Mariner Books.

10

# The Future of Food Production

Ryan D. Andrews

> The human appetite is the most disruptive force on Earth.
>
> —Chef Bun Lai

> Food is our most intimate and powerful connection to each other, to our cultures, and to the Earth, and to transform our food system is to take one giant step towards healing our bodies, our economy, and our environment.
>
> —HEAL Food Alliance

In many ways the modern food system is incredible, with millions of people along the supply chain growing, raising, processing, packaging, transporting, and stocking foods to ensure that supermarket shelves almost never appear empty. Some countries have a seemingly endless supply of food, calories, and nutrients. But the achievement of this seemingly infinite supply of food has come at a great expense.

The food system is a major driver of climate change, contributing nearly one-third of all greenhouse gas (GHG) emissions, which rivals electricity production. Excessive GHG emissions are leading to changes in ecosystems that limit both the quantity and quality of food that can be grown for future generations (Crippa et al., 2021; FAO et al., 2021; Romanello et al., 2022).

The food system is responsible for some 70 percent of freshwater withdrawals. Many of these withdrawals can be traced back to thirsty crops grown in dry climates along with the inordinate amount of irrigation water used to produce feed crops for confined farm animals.[1] Further, most water pollution is caused by farming, with nearly 80 percent of life-devastating fertilizer pollution coming from agriculture (Poore & Nemecek, 2018).

Of all the food produced globally, about one-third is lost or wasted (Jaglo et al., 2021). This equates to 2,860 large garbage bins of food wasted every second. In the United States specifically, the food that is produced and thrown away yearly draws on agricultural lands equivalent to an area the size of California and New York combined, nearly six trillion gallons of water, 778 million pounds of pesticides, and 14 billion pounds of fertilizer (Jaglo et al., 2021). Not only does this imply we are using a staggering quantity of resources to grow food that is never consumed, but it also hints at a profound societal disconnect from how food is produced.

The food system is built on stolen land and exploited labor. Throughout history, black and brown people have done much of the work on farms, yet people of color barely own two percent of land in the United States (Horst & Marion, 2019). If African American people had been paid US$20 per week for agricultural labor rather than enslaved, they would have nearly US$6.5 trillion in the bank, and this doesn't include reparations for denied credit or property destruction (Penniman, 2018).

Globally, nearly 72 billion "livestock" are slaughtered for food each year (Ritchie et al., 2019). This number is shocking—equating to nine times the global human population. Many of these animals live in crowded, completely unnatural, and unsanitary conditions known as confined animal feeding operations (CAFOs for short), where they are ill-treated as objects of production processes. Confined living conditions make it difficult to keep farm animals healthy without pharmaceutical intervention. In fact, nearly two-thirds of all antibiotics produced globally are given to farm animals. Such inordinate use of antibiotics to keep farm animals alive in unnatural conditions brings humanity closer to the tipping point of widespread antibiotic resistance, a looming public health threat (Tiseo et al., 2020).

The way in which farm animals are raised and the way in which crops are grown for ultraprocessed foods are major drivers of deforestation, wildlands takeover, and freshwater appropriation leading to biodiversity losses and extinctions, both on land and in the marine environment. A thriving biodiversity is essential for ecological integrity and a healthy planet.

Further, when natural habitats are converted to agricultural landscapes, farm animals start to intermingle with wildlife hosts of potential human pathogens, which contributes to the emergence of zoonotic diseases such as H1N1 and bird flu (United Nations Environment Programme and International Livestock Research Institute, 2020).

The modern food system is failing on nearly every possible standard and metric, and the way we produce and consume food is damaging our physiology, our ecology, and our morality. With nearly two billion people not having access to enough nutrient-dense foods and nearly two billion people encouraged to consume too many nutrient-poor foods, altogether what we eat—and don't eat—is the leading cause of death and disability, globally (Swinburn et al., 2019).

The collective well-being of planet Earth and all her residents hinges on how we approach food in the coming decades. There is much that demands to be reimagined and revamped with respect to the status quo. The remainder of this chapter advocates for three keystone ideas for change.

## Idea for Change: Eaters Will Emphasize a Variety of Minimally Processed Plant-Based Foods

> Food is the single strongest lever to optimize human health and environmental sustainability on Earth.
>
> —EAT-Lancet Commission (2019: 5)

In the modern food landscape, there is a preponderance of information about the magical qualities of "superfoods." Many people feel that to attain any kind of positive health outcome, consuming specific foods such as kale, avocadoes, and almonds is essential. Yet, there isn't one superfood that all people around the world need to be eating. In fact, thousands of superfoods exist across this planet. Kale, avocados, and almonds are tasty and nutritious, but they are only three of the 6,000 plants that have been cultivated for food. Currently, just nine plants account for roughly 70 percent of all crop production (sugar cane, maize, rice, wheat, potatoes, soybeans, palm oil, sugar beets, and cassava). This limited variety is compromising both personal and planetary health (FAO, 2019).

Building a dietary pattern around a wide variety of whole (or minimally processed) vegetables, fruits, legumes, grains, nuts, and seeds would help to accomplish three critical outcomes. First, eating a wide variety of real plant foods stacks the odds overwhelmingly in favor of chronic disease prevention (Vadiveloo & Parekh, 2015; Parlasca & Qaim, 2022). This is of paramount importance since chronic diseases are the leading causes of death, disability, and ballooning healthcare costs. Second, growing a wide variety of plant foods encourages better pollinator and soil health (Varah et al., 2020). Third, expanding the variety of crop production can support more flexibility in cultural dietary preferences, will offer freedom to grow crops according to geographic conditions, and will provide more variety for all and options to those with food intolerances.

With whole or minimally processed plant foods providing most nutrients and energy in the future, animal products such as meat, fish, dairy, and eggs can play a less dominant role in human diets. To be sure, it's important to note that there will always be some people who benefit from eating higher quantities of animal products due to particular health conditions, and in some parts of the world there are only limited choices among plant foods. Further, farm animals can be a source of economic stability and food security, and they can be raised in ecological relationship with crops in sustainable systems (more on this later). All that being said, in the developed world in particular, the consumption of animal products must decrease dramatically to achieve a vibrant food future.

Raising enormous populations of farm animals requires enormous amounts of land. Of all the land used for agricultural purposes on the planet, nearly 80 percent is devoted to raising and feeding farm animals. In other words, less than one-quarter of all agricultural land grows crops that directly nourish humans (Poore & Nemecek, 2018). By raising fewer farm animals, far less land will be needed for agriculture, creating exciting opportunities for rewilding and ecological restoration. Raising fewer farm animals will also support the abolition of confinement operations, since intensification will no longer be necessary, and this may enable pastured farms to prosper and animals to be raised in more respectful ways (box 10.1; Van Zanten et al., 2019). Further, where there are fewer farm animals, they can be synergistically integrated with crops: animal waste serves as fertilizer, and the animals can be fed food scraps and other potential sources of wasted food (Van Zanten et al., 2018). Allowing animals to have more space not only respects their innate needs but will also dramatically decrease antibiotic use, which in turn will decrease the likelihood of antibiotic resistance (Van Boeckel et al., 2017).

### Respect for Animals

As long as there are slaughterhouses there will always be battlefields.

– Leo Tolstoy (1885)

Given that nearly 72 billion livestock animals are killed for food each year and many of these animals endure horrific conditions, reflecting on the role of animal products in one's diet is an ethical imperative. For many people choosing a fully plant-based (or vegan) diet supports radiant health along with animal and planetary well-being. But with many people at present uninterested in adopting, or unable to adopt, a vegan diet, the status quo remains strong. Yet this need not be a binary decision. Instead, it is worth exploring the option of responsible animal product consumption.

Responsible animal product consumption is nuanced and varies depending on the person, but it would include foundational factors such as eating less meat and animal products and choosing such products sourced from humane farms. When it comes to showing respect towards fellow beings, the room that humans have for improvement is gigantic. No matter what one thinks about the ethics of eating meat, finding a way to coexist with animals in peaceful and caring ways is an absolute necessity for the soul.

Some people suggest that a solution lies in scaling up plant-based alternatives to meat. While this may be one of many solutions to help ease the suffering of animals, there are environmental and health uncertainties around increasing production of plant-based meats and cell-based meats (Santo et al., 2020; van Vliet et al., 2021), and thus keeping levels of intake similar to that of meat from animals – that is to say as low as possible – may be prudent (Kraak, 2022).

Raising far fewer farm animals and shrinking the land footprint of animal agriculture will lessen the burden on ecosystems and decrease the spread of zoonotic diseases (Springmann et al., 2018; United Nations Environment Programme and International Livestock Research Institute, 2020). While it's difficult to be precise about the ways in which a food system with fewer animal products would influence the welfare of human workers, it can be reasonably assumed that shifting toward an ethical model of treating farm animals will be aligned with providing equitable working conditions for those involved in farming (Parlasca & Qaim, 2022).

## Idea for Change: Farming Will Be Built around Agroecological Systems

The world cannot be fed unless the soil is fed.

—Project Drawdown

Industrialized agriculture is built on an ideology of extracting as much from the soil as possible with the main goals of maximizing calories, yields, and economic gains. In other words, industrialized agricultural is about taking without giving—a relationship of domination. When a relationship is not reciprocal, a state of depletion develops. In the case of agriculture, one kind of depletion is loss of soil health and resilience.

When the same crops are planted year after year across vast landscapes and saturated in chemicals that destroy biological life, dependence on short-term fixes such as synthetic fertilizers becomes entrenched. Further, when soils are tilled to kill "weeds" but then remain barren during the nongrowing season, the organisms in the soil die and there is a significant loss of carbon into the atmosphere (Giller et al., 2021). The current agricultural cycle of planting, chemical saturation, harvesting, and plowing is extractive, unethical, and unsustainable.

An alternative to this kind of system is one that integrates ecology, equity, well-being, and practicality. This kind of approach is generally known as agroecology, but can be thought of more broadly as regenerative farming. Regenerative farming blends time-tested traditional practices with relevant ecologically sound learnings from modern science. It also extends beyond the farm and empowers communities to build a more socially just food system. Regenerative agriculture aims to create reciprocal relations between all living beings. Some examples are presented below. Shifting how food is produced and consumed will require substantial transformations of farming policies in order to support and incentivize regenerative agriculture initiatives.

- *Growing crops appropriate for a given geography:* Just because a crop can be grown in a certain area doesn't mean it should.

Each crop has unique requirements relating to soil type, rainfall, temperature, and various other factors. Selecting the appropriate crop for a given region could not only lead to more nutritious and delicious foods but also help reduce the negative ecological impacts of production.

- *Growing crops that directly benefit soil:* Current practices revolve around which crops are best for farm animal growth, incorporation into processed foods, yields, and profits. With regenerative agriculture, energy and attention will be invested into growing crops (and raising animals) that directly benefit the countless organisms in the soil, thus also supporting carbon storage below ground. In fact, taking full advantage of cover crops could offset eight percent of GHG emissions from agriculture (Poeplau & Don, 2015).

- *Keeping roots in the ground:* Implementing more tree- and perennial-based food production fortifies soil and discourages invasive "weeds" (Jansson et al., 2021; Ickowitz et al., 2022). A corollary to this is minimizing tilling and plowing, which release soil carbon.

- *Minimizing the use of synthetic fertilizers and pesticides:* Instead of relying on chemical inputs, which destroy soil biodiversity, soil can be managed with rest (lying fallow), cover crops, manures (green and animal), food-waste composts, and crop rotation. These regenerative agricultural techniques support and enhance living soils.

For regenerative agriculture to flourish, decentralizing the food system is essential. Practically speaking, this means that food will no longer be produced by a handful of companies. At present, the food system is extremely consolidated, with the number of farms decreasing and the size of each farm increasing. For example, 73 percent of beef processing and 77 percent of beer is controlled by just four companies, while 83 percent of cold cereal is controlled by three companies (Hendrickson et al., 2020).

Instead of such levels of consolidation, foods can be grown and raised in accordance with the local geography, in response to the unique combination of climate, soil, and water availability. These foods would go through only minor processing, such as canning or freezing, and nourish the surrounding community. Producing food in this way allows farmers to explore a wider variety of crops (including cover crops), which will support higher overall levels of biodiversity (Renard & Tilman, 2019).

Decentralization also means greater food system resiliency, since people would no longer rely on a small number of large and remote operations. Decentralization will also be more ecologically viable through small-scale production, crop diversification, and reductions in transportation, packaging (box 10.2), and the demand for cosmetic homogeneity. Improvements in the stability of farmer income also accompany decentralization, as farmers have more power to be price makers instead of price takers. Further, decentralization stimulates the local economy, conviviality, and community; and since the food is spending less time in transit exposed to oxygen, temperature extremes, and ultraviolet light, more of its nutrients are preserved (Farrell et al., 2020). While it might seem difficult to imagine decentralized self-sufficiency in food production, we may keep in mind that at one point after World War II, nearly 40 percent of vegetables consumed in the United States—to give one example—were grown in home and community "victory" gardens (Steinhauer, 2020).

### Single-use Plastic Will Be a Luxury Item

It's difficult to imagine a world where plastic isn't a part of daily life, but as recently as 1950 this was the case. Since then, over eight billion metric tons of plastics have been produced (Geyer et al., 2017), with so much escaping into the environment that plastic pollution has been declared a "planetary crisis" by the United Nations. The top aquatic pollutants are plastic food containers, food utensils, food wrappers, food shopping bags, and beverage bottles and caps (Morales-Caselles et al., 2021).

With the steep ecological cost of production and unreliable recycling options, it's clear that finding food and beverage packaging items that align with a circular model of thinking (ecological design, distribution, and reuse) is imperative. Importantly, alternative packaging materials such as glass and metal can, in theory at least, be reused or recycled indefinitely.

Initiatives that could work toward a dramatic reduction in single-use plastics include deposit schemes to incentivize reuse, effective waste management infrastructure, corporate responsibility schemes, uptake of reusable products (e.g., bamboo utensils and steel water bottles), and bans on certain items.

Unfortunately, many of the people who have deep knowledge and experience regarding regenerative agriculture are people who have been driven off their land. Importantly, then, decentralization is about empowering the rights of communities so that they can shape their own local food systems. This could shift the agricultural work market and allow neighborhoods and local food sheds to take an active role in growing food for their communities. This kind of local land stewardship will be challenging, and decentralization in the food system has some trade-offs, but it will support people to forge new and diverse social networks, spend more time outside, increase their levels of physical activity, and develop a deeper respect for the foods they eat. Collective involvement in growing food as part of daily life will thus contribute to the enrichment of physical, psychological, and community health.

## Idea for Change:
## Food Will Be Valued (and Not Wasted)

> Changing how we eat will not be enough, on its own, to save the planet, but we cannot save the planet without changing how we eat.
>
> —Jonathan Safran Foer (2019)

When profit is prioritized over people and the planet, wasted food is considered part of the "cost of doing business." But with one-third of all food wasted, and nine percent of global GHG emissions related to food losses, food waste constitutes both an ecological and ethical failure of humanity (Jaglo et al., 2021; Crippa et al., 2021).

In the United States alone, if food waste were cut in half this would:

- Free up 75 million acres of agricultural land, an area larger than Arizona, for rewilding and ecological restoration.

- Save 3.2 trillion gallons of irrigation water, equivalent to the annual water use of 29 million American homes.

- Eliminate 640 million pounds of nitrogen fertilizer from being applied, vastly reducing the runoff that leads to large-scale death of aquatic life.

- Prevent 92 million metric tons of carbon dioxide equivalents of GHG from being released, comparable to the annual emissions from 23 coal-fired power plants of average size (Jaglo et al., 2021).

Globally, if wasted food were reduced by 75 percent in the next 30 years it would cut GHG emissions by nearly 100 gigatons of carbon dioxide equivalents (Davis et al., 2022). This would be equivalent to the carbon sequestered by 1.6 trillion tree seedlings growing for 10 years.

Food can be lost or wasted at various points along the entire food supply chain, from field to fork. In developing countries, wasted food is often seen early in the supply chain. It may be left to rot in fields due to labor shortages, pest infestations, or lack of adequate transportation. In developed countries, most food waste happens later in the supply chain, at home and in eatery and retail settings.

Strategies to help solve the problem of wasted food may be focused on individuals or systems, and they include educational campaigns, standardization in expiration date labeling, appropriate portioning of food at restaurants, implementing recess before lunch in schools (students are more likely to rush through eating when lunch is before recess), a redistribution of wasted food from retail establishments (e.g., by nonprofit organizations), and enhanced access to municipal composting. Crucially, reducing the waste of the most resource-intensive foods (e.g., meat, dairy, and eggs) promises the greatest overall societal benefits.

In an ecological future, a closed-loop food system, that is, one that continually sustains itself, will be the norm, with high-quality nourishing food being consumed first by people or being preserved for later use, with leftovers being consumed by animals or composted, and through green and animal manures eventually being incorporated back into soil keeping it healthy.

## Moving Forward

We are all eaters. Providing the food we need to sustain ourselves and flourish is the single most fundamental and important human occupation. How we do it defines our present and determines our future.

—Mark Bittman (2021)

*Itadakimasu* is a phrase from the Japanese vocabulary that is translated as "I humbly receive." It is often said before a meal to express gratitude to anyone and everything that helped to provide the meal. *Itadakimasu* offers a reminder of gratitude to the eater and underscores the main takeaway from this chapter: food deserves our utmost respect and attention. The way in which humans transform and engage with food over the next decade will probably be the single most important collective action we take. Essential steps towards a sustainable food future, as explored in this chapter, will include emphasis on a variety of whole plant foods, the building of farming practices around agroecological systems, and the valuing of food such that it is no longer wasted.

## Note

1. In this chapter, I use "animal" as a shorthand for "nonhuman animal."

## References

Crippa, M., Solazzo, E., Guizzardi, D., et al. (2021). Food systems are responsible for a third of global anthropogenic GHG emissions. *Nature Food*, 2, 198–209. https://doi.org/10.1038/s43016-021-00225-9

Davis, S.M., Hong, A., Mathur, M., et al. (2022). *Reduced food waste*. Project Drawdown. https://drawdown.org/solutions/reduced-food-waste

EAT-Lancet Commission (2019). *Summary Report of the EAT-Lancet Commission*. https://eatforum.org/eat-lancet-commission/eat-lancet-commission-summary-report/

FAO (2019). *The State of the World's Biodiversity for Food and Agriculture*. FAO—Commission on Genetic Resources for Food and Agriculture. https://www.fao.org/state-of-biodiversity-for-food-agriculture/en/

FAO, International Fund for Agricultural Development, UNICEF, et al. (2021). *The State of Food Security and Nutrition in the World 2021*. FAO. https://doi.org/10.4060/cb4474en

Farrell, P., Thow, A. M., Wate, J. T., et al. (2020). COVID-19 and Pacific food system resilience: Opportunities to build a robust response. *Food Security*, 1–9. https://doi.org/10.1007/s12571-020-01087-y

Geyer, R., Jambeck, J. R., & Law, K. L. (2017). Production, use, and fate of all plastics ever made. *Science Advances*, 3(7), e1700782. https://doi.org/10.1126/sciadv.1700782

Giller, K. E., Hijbeek, R., Andersson, J. A., & Sumberg, J. (2021). Regenerative agriculture: An agronomic perspective. *Outlook on Agriculture, 50*(1), 13–25. https://doi.org/10.1177/0030727021998063

Hendrickson, M. K., Howard, P. H., Miller, E. M., & Constance, D. H. (2020). *The Food System: Concentration and Its Impacts*. Family Farm Action Alliance. https://farmaction.us//wp-content/uploads/2020/11/Hendrickson-et-al.-2020.-Concentration-and-Its-Impacts-FINAL.pdf

Horst, M., & Marion, A. (2019). Racial, ethnic and gender inequities in farmland ownership and farming in the US *Agriculture and Human Values, 36*(1), 1–16. https://doi.org/10.1007/s10460-018-9883-3

Ickowitz, A., McMullin, S., Rosenstock, T., et al. (2022). Transforming food systems with trees and forests. *The Lancet Planetary Health, 6*(7), e632–e639. https://doi.org/10.1016/S2542-5196(22)00091-2

Jaglo, K., Kenny, S., & Stephenson, J. (2021). *The Environmental Impacts of U.S. Food Waste*. US Environmental Protection Agency. https://www.epa.gov/land-research/farm-kitchen-environmental-impacts-us-food-waste

Jansson, C., Faiola, C., Wingler, A., et al. (2021). Crops for Carbon Farming. *Frontiers in Plant Science, 12*, 636709. https://doi.org/10.3389/fpls.2021.636709

Kraak, V. I. (2022). Perspective: Unpacking the wicked challenges for alternative proteins in the United States: Can highly processed plant-based and cell-cultured food and beverage products support healthy and sustainable diets and food systems? *Advances in Nutrition, 13*(1), 38–47. https://doi.org/10.1093/advances/nmab113

Morales-Caselles, C., Viejo, J., Martí, E., et al. (2021). An inshore–offshore sorting system revealed from global classification of ocean litter. *Nature Sustainability, 4*(6), 484–93. https://doi.org/10.1038/s41893-021-00720-8

Parlasca, M. C., & Qaim, M. (2022). Meat consumption and sustainability. *Annual Review of Resource Economics, 14*(1), 17–41. https://doi.org/10.1146/annurev-resource-111820-032340

Penniman, L. (2018). *Farming While Black: Soul Fire Farm's Practical Guide to Liberation on the Land*. Chelsea Green Publishing.

Poeplau, C., & Don, A. (2015). Carbon sequestration in agricultural soils via cultivation of cover crops: A meta-analysis. *Agriculture, Ecosystems & Environment, 200*, 33–41. https://doi.org/10.1016/j.agee.2014.10.024

Poore, J., & Nemecek, T. (2018). Reducing food's environmental impacts through producers and consumers. *Science, 360*(6392), 987–92. https://doi.org/10.1126/science.aaq0216

Renard, D., & Tilman, D. (2019). National food production stabilized by crop diversity. *Nature, 571*(7764), 257–60. https://doi.org/10.1038/s41586-019-1316-y

Ritchie, H., Rosado, P., & Roser, M. (2019). Meat and dairy production. *Our World in Data*. https://ourworldindata.org/meat-production

Romanello, M., Di Napoli, C., Drummond, P., et al. (2022). The 2022 report of the Lancet Countdown on health and climate change: health at the mercy of fossil fuels. *The Lancet, 400*(10363), 1619–54. https://doi.org/10.1016/ S0140-6736(22)01540-9

Santo, R. E., Kim, B. F., Goldman, S. E., et al. (2020). Considering plant-based meat substitutes and cell-based meats: A public health and food systems perspective. *Frontiers in Sustainable Food Systems, 4*, 134. https://doi.org/10.3389/fsufs.2020.00134

Springmann, M., Clark, M., Mason-D'Croz, D., et al. (2018). Options for keeping the food system within environmental limits. *Nature, 562*(7728), 519–25. https://doi.org/10.1038/s41586-018-0594-0

Steinhauer, J. (2020, July 15). Victory gardens were more about solidarity than survival. *New York Times Magazine.* https://www.nytimes.com/2020/07/15/magazine/victory-gardens-world-war-II.html

Swinburn, B. A., Kraak, V. I., Allender, S., et al. (2019). The global syndemic of obesity, undernutrition, and climate change: The Lancet Commission report. *The Lancet, 393*(10173), 791–846. https://doi.org/10.1016/S0140-6736(18)32822-8

Tiseo, K., Huber, L., Gilbert, M., et al. (2020). Global trends in antimicrobial use in food animals from 2017 to 2030. *Antibiotics* (Basel, Switzerland), *9*(12), 918. https://doi.org/10.3390/antibiotics9120918

United Nations Environment Programme and International Livestock Research Institute (2020). *Preventing the Next Pandemic: Zoonotic Diseases and How to Break the Chain of Transmission.* United Nations Environment Programme. https://www.unep.org/resources/report/preventing-future-zoonotic-disease-outbreaks-protecting-environment-animals-and

Vadiveloo, M. K., & Parekh, N. (2015). Dietary variety: An overlooked strategy for obesity and chronic disease control. *American Journal of Preventive Medicine, 49*(6), 974–79. https://doi.org/10.1016/j.amepre.2015.06.014

Van Boeckel, T. P., Glennon, E. E., Chen, D., et al. (2017). Reducing antimicrobial use in food animals. *Science, 357*(6358), 1350–52. https://doi.org/10.1126/science.aao1495

van Vliet, S., Bain, J. R., Muehlbauer, M. J., et al. (2021). A metabolomics comparison of plant-based meat and grass-fed meat indicates large nutritional differences despite comparable Nutrition Facts panels. *Scientific Reports, 11*(1), 13828. https://doi.org/10.1038/s41598-021-93100-3

Van Zanten, H. H. E., Herrero, M., Van Hal, O., et al. (2018). Defining a land boundary for sustainable livestock consumption. *Global Change Biology, 24*(9), 4185–94. https://doi.org/10.1111/gcb.14321

Van Zanten, H. H. E., Van Ittersum, M. K., & De Boer, I. J. M. (2019). The role of farm animals in a circular food system. *Global Food Security, 21*, 18–22. https://doi.org/10.1016/j.gfs.2019.06.003

Varah, A., Jones, H., Smith, J., & Potts, S. G. (2020). Temperate agroforestry systems provide greater pollination service than monoculture. *Agriculture, Ecosystems & Environment, 301*, 107031. https://doi.org/10.1016/j.agee.2020.107031

## 11

# Human Identity, Oppression, and the Rigors of Hope

CHELSEA BATAVIA

Driving down Highway 99 south of Sacramento, I squint against the film of dust hovering in the air. After eight days of triple-digit heat, the land has a look of desolation. I'm reminded of Vince Miller's incisive commentary on the recent (and inevitable future) wildfires engulfing the American West, where he suggests change and loss may best be reckoned outside familiar terms and timescales, as beacons to an era of apocalypse (Miller, 2022). "Apocalypse" seems an apt frame to me as I gaze out across parched brown fields; the withering husk of a landscape once alight with life, emptied out and raked over by hot winds blowing low under the relentless sun.

    Confronted with ubiquitous signs of ecological unraveling, many of us are in a fairly constant state of mourning. I think it's generally appropriate to sit with this grief, given the gravity of current circumstances, but I also think hope is essential sustenance for the body, as vital to survival as water or air. So how do we sit with grief and still hold space for hope? Miller writes, "Hope requires open eyes, a hard seeing of the truth of circumstance." I think he means hope is earned. Unless it emerges by seeing (I'd add feeling) difficult realities, hope is hollow delusion. We can make a rightful claim to hope when we've assessed the damage, accepted the odds, understood the diagnoses. Hope is achieved through grief, in spite of the hard truth of circumstance.

"Circumstance" is an interesting word. Its roots trace to the Latin *circum* (around) and *stare* (to stand). Circumstance is not just facts but a situated understanding of those facts and all the surrounding conditions that imbue them with significance. Let's consider a few circumstances, such as buildup of marine plastic pollution in international waters, sea level rise along the coastal United States, or extreme drought and critically overdrafted freshwater supply in California. These circumstances implicate facts, but swirling around the facts are social, moral, and political questions that I distill, at the risk of oversimplification, to a core conundrum: what should we do? Science can't answer questions of this ilk. This sort of question launches us into ethical terrain, and while science critically informs and supports navigations in this space, we can't measure or model our way out. Science is not a surrogate for ethics. Here's a thought experiment: if every human were granted complete, scientifically sound understanding of all the world's workings, would we simultaneously achieve consensus about how to address our most perplexing environmental problems, like climate change or mass extinction? Doubtful. Perfect shared scientific understanding would be convenient, but it wouldn't circumvent the quagmire of values and politics that roils beneath our environmental challenges. To reach a point where hope is warranted through and against current circumstances, we need to see them for all that they are, including their ethical predicaments.

Admittedly, ethics can be hard to see, especially when long-held ethical values and beliefs lie latent as basic assumptions that are sheltered from critical scrutiny. These assumptions get baked into our scientific understandings of the world, which has the circular effect of affirming and confirming those assumptions, and elevating them to the status of fact. In this way, presumed and largely unexamined ethical values and beliefs come to parameterize, seed, and constrain the questions we ask and the solutions we pursue. The example I'll discuss here is the human–nature dualism.

By "dualism" I refer to the idea that there are two types of things in some domain, and every thing in that domain can be classed as one or the other type, but not both. In other words, according to dualistic logic the world can be sorted into binary categories that are mutually exclusive (either/or) and exhaustive (there is nothing else). On a Western dualistic worldview, "nature" and "human" are mutually exclusive categories that, together, account for the totality of the world. Nature categorically excludes humans, and humans are categorically not natural. Dualistic thinking does not admit of ambiguity or nuance. Mind or body, man or woman, reason or emotion: these sorts of dualistic framings foreclose the possibility of crossover or overlap. Dualisms impose stringent and uncompromising boundaries on perceptions, a "black or white" rendering of the world that filters out so many shades of gray and technicolor hues that may otherwise reveal themselves. This ill-conceived metaphysical effort is attended by parallel ethical follies.[1]

The human-nature dualism is encoded with two seemingly contradictory notions of value: (1) humans are the supreme being in a hierarchy of existence, superior to and rightfully dominating over all other forms of life; (2) nature is transcendent, the pure Edenic ideal of pristine wilderness from which humans have fallen. These two fundamental beliefs underpin, respectively, utilitarian resource conservation and preservation movements of the early to mid-20th century (Morales et al., 2022). On the former approach, nature is a repository of resources to be managed efficiently for maximal human benefit and enjoyment. On the latter approach, nature is a haven to be safeguarded by building walls and keeping humans out. Both have yielded devastating outcomes. Per utilitarian resource conservation, the diverse menagerie of life on Earth, in all its splendid complexity, has been reduced to so many goods and services, protected only for and by their commodity value. Per preservation, untold communities have been violently displaced in service of a dualistic "wilderness" ideal that idolizes an unsullied nature free of corrupting "human" influence.

As we have learned more about ecology, evolution, and the myriad ways humans are connected with "nature," dualistic thinking has become increasingly untenable as an intellectual position (Haila, 2000). Still, it is difficult to uproot a mindset that has been entrenched for centuries and woven into the fabric of Western thought. Dualism remains imprinted in proposals such as "nature-based solutions," "natural climate solutions," and "nature needs half." In these cases, "nature" may be invoked merely as shorthand for "nonhuman nature," but even the latter phrase, admirable albeit clunky in its aspiration to integration, remains anchored to a dualistic worldview. "Nonhuman" centers humanness as the norm, grouping everyone and everything else into a coarse negative definition that identifies them only by the commonplace and frankly uninteresting fact that they are not human. Doesn't it seem laughable to speak of "fairy shrimp" and "non–fairy shrimp nature"? No less absurd than "human" and "nonhuman nature," I'd argue, yet the latter terminology is well established. I use it myself.[2] We're accustomed to thinking there is something categorically different about humans and, in spite of so many scientific and intellectual advances indicating otherwise, I think many of us are still conditioned to think of humans as somehow outside of nature.

As evidence I would point to environmental interventions that purport to protect "nature" by removing "human" or "anthropogenic" influence. Consider, for example, programs to control or eradicate species labeled "nonnative" or "invasive." Ostensibly these species are managed based on adverse impacts to ecosystem functions or processes (e.g., Dick et al., 2017), but it is because of their association with humans (based, e.g., on abundance or current distributions) that these species' impacts are interrogated in the first place. Suspected as carriers of anthropogenic influence, "invasive alien" species are found guilty while "natives" are presumed innocent; or, rather, "natives" are spared any such judgmental scientific scrutiny because they, and their place in the ecosystem, are simply accepted as a "natural" (Wallach et al., 2020).[3] Similarly, restoration sites and protected areas are designed to create or retain "natural" or "ecological" conditions (Batavia & Nelson, 2016a), based on reference systems that predated a (frequently unstated) Eurocentric notion of "human" interference that ignores the long history of human habitation and stewardship in those ecosystems (Fletcher et al., 2021).

I find something perverse and frankly sad in this general approach to environmental protection. We're effectively trying to erase ourselves. This can be interpreted as an act of attrition—attempts to reverse the outcomes of a heady modern history of unrestrained expansion. But I also think it bespeaks a fundamental sense of estrangement from the world around us, and a deep-seated sociopsychological pain that, filtered through our dualistic mindset, we struggle to understand and so cannot relieve. Instead we act out, channeling our pain into aggression against humans who are perceived as too natural (e.g., Indigenous peoples) and more-than-human beings considered too human (e.g., "invasive alien species"). These subversives who straddle our clean categories shirk the dualism that structures our basic sense of reality and moral order in the world, so we attempt to destroy them. Fiercely we guard a dualistically defined human identity, even if it displaces us from our larger community of life, because we don't know who or what we are without it. Perhaps it is precisely because of deep existential insecurity that we insist on asserting the superiority of our species. We lash out to quell the sting of failing to feel at home in a world that we believe rightfully belongs to us.

But I've been sloppy and nondescript talking about "us."

By "us" I mean those (like myself) who have come up in a Western dualistic culture. "We" certainly do not speak for the entire human species (or "we" shouldn't). Yet if "our" dualistic worldview is not universal or inherent, it is extremely influential. From its stronghold as bedrock of the Western intellectual tradition, the human–nature dualism permeated the institutions and norms of modern globalized society courtesy of the European colonial enterprise. And this leads to my next point about dualisms: they are rarely innocent. Dualisms serve agendas.

Dualism is a basic mechanism of what Val Plumwood calls the "logic of oppression" (Plumwood, 1993). Plumwood argues that all modes of oppression are rooted in a common, hierarchical, and dualistic way of thinking, or "logic." Stated simply, in all the ways the world is bifurcated into two different types of things (a dualistic metaphysic), one of those things is better than the other (a moral hierarchy). It is on this reasoning that, per the human–nature dualism, "humans" reign supreme at the top of a pyramid of moral worth. Conversely, entities who are construed as "natural" (based on biology, physical form, perceived emotional or cognitive capacities, etc.) are inferior. It is with minimal or no scruple that such "subhuman" beings are rightfully manipulated, exploited, repressed, destroyed . . . in a word, oppressed.

With so much at stake in humanness, it behooves us to ask: on the logic of oppression, what exactly is a "human"?

The "human" of the human–nature dualism possesses certain, perhaps predictable traits. He is White and of European descent. He was assigned the biological sex of "male" at birth and he identifies as a man. He is upper class (ideally landholding). He is heterosexual, able-bodied, and neurotypical. He is Christian. This is the reference "human" of the human–nature dualism. Let's call him *Homo dualismus*. *Homo dualismus* is the paragon of Mankind: at once ideal and norm, he is the antithesis of nature and the human against whom the personhood of all others is measured. "Others" may fall into any or all of multiple categories that are socially constructed and socially depreciated in contrast to the categories that define *Homo dualismus*, such as "Black," "woman," "queer," and/or "disabled." And of course, "others" include more-than-human beings, who are categorically excluded from the social and moral status of "humans."

The logic of oppression creates a conceptual order within which *Homo dualismus* make sense. It also undergirds what I will call "projects of oppression." If the logic of oppression constructs the power of *Homo dualismus* in the abstract, projects of oppression engineer, incubate, and ignite his power materially in the world. Generally, projects of oppression involve the appropriation of physical, sociopolitical, and/or discursive space to expand the privilege, material wealth, and social status of *Homo dualismus*. Examples include the colonial imposition of racialized femininities to create and enforce the moral and political superiority of White masculinity (Lugones, 2007); the colonial dispossession, genocide, and erasure of Native American Indigenous peoples (Quijano, 2000); the historic and ongoing state-sanctioned enslavement, commodification, and violation of Black bodies to advance capitalist-colonial interests (Iheme, 2022); and the symbolic and material transmutation of more-than-human relations into lifeless and inert resources to be cultivated and disposed in service of patriarchal ego and colonial empire (Batavia et al., 2019). While different projects yield unique forms and experiences of oppression, they are rooted in a common logic and serve a common agenda, so they are all intertwined and mutually reinforcing. Veiled by narratives of ingenuity and progress, these projects are normalized as "the way things are" or, worse, "the way things ought to be."

I believe there has been a sustained equivocation on the concept "human" in environmental thought and practice. When scientists point to "anthropogenic" impacts as harbingers of environmental doom, the underlying reference is to an apolitical concept of "human" that is seemingly just descriptive of a species. "Human" is used as a synonym for *Homo sapiens*. "Humans" in this apolitical, descriptive-species sense are not the root cause of environmental crisis, but dualistic logic embeds oppression at the core of human identity, and herein lies the equivocation. When we say "humans are responsible," we seemingly implicate *Homo sapiens* when we should implicate *Homo dualismus*. And to clarify, when I say *Homo dualismus* I'm not referring to any specific humans who instantiate the qualities that imbue *Homo dualismus* with power.[4] In implicating *Homo dualismus*, I refer to the social reality of *Homo dualismus*; the underlying, hierarchical logic that confers and consolidates power in the concept of *Homo dualismus* as the normative being, and the projects that actualize his power through the suppression and violation of human and more-than-human beings who are "othered." My argument, in short, is that the core problem is not humans. The core problem is oppression.

With a refined understanding of the problem comes a shift in the imagining of solutions. We should push back against environmental interventions (or noninterventions) presupposing that protecting the environment requires reversal or elimination of "human" influence, per se. These entrenched, pseudoscientific approaches only reinforce the logic that actualizes and animates *Homo dualismus*. Instead, environmental efforts should seek to scale back human influence only (but entirely) insofar as it is underwritten by the logic of oppression. In other words, environmental energies should be directed toward identifying and interrupting projects of oppression, in all their permutations; and at the same time, cultivating conditions that advance multispecies, cross-societal flourishing. Others have highlighted intersections of multispecies and ecological justice with social and environmental justice (e.g., Washington et al., 2018; Treves et al., 2019; McGregor et al., 2020). Building on these arguments, I propose what I think of as a program of "revisionist environmentalism." By "revisionist," I refer to a re-visioning of environmentalist goals and values, moving away from oppressive efforts that presuppose and perpetuate a dualistic worldview, and toward holistic efforts that identify and address interlinked projects of oppression. I will briefly outline how this might look for four mainstream approaches.

*Conservation:* Many mainstream conservation approaches function as instruments of oppression. I refer not only to the obvious suspects, like sustained-use and wildlife management, but also nonutilitarian interventions like protected areas and biodiversity conservation. These and other conservation approaches embed principles, practices, and underlying philosophies that presume and reinforce power structures that emerged through the European colonial-capitalist enterprise. Today, conservation largely remains embedded within a racialized, utilitarian-anthropocentric hierarchy of power (Batavia et al., 2019; Wallach et al., 2020; Kashwan et al., 2021; Morales et al., 2022). On a personal level, this is hard for me to acknowledge. Years ago I wrote, "Conservationists should be heroes" (Batavia & Nelson, 2016b). Though I stand by these words, I've also come to realize that heroism is not tenable within current conservation paradigms. A revisionist concept of conservation—one that could proudly call itself a positive force for a holistic vision of justice—would advance broader agendas of *decolonization*. On this account, "conservation" would seek to dismantle colonial systems and practices that repress the potential of Earth's biological and cultural diversity for transformative becoming and belonging (Massarella et al., 2022). Decolonizing conservation would mean discontinuing practices that exemplify a mindset of entitlement and conquest, and replacing them with practices that reclaim and honor the rights of all beings to exist with integrity and authenticity. In North America, for example, promoting Indigenous-led conservation and returning land to support Native American stewardship of multispecies, kincentric communities is a good start (Salmón, 2000; Artelle et al., 2021).

*Wilderness preservation:* Wilderness has been debated ad nauseum (Nelson & Callicott, 2008). I won't weigh in here, except to argue that we should reject any wilderness ideal defined by an absence of humans. It's insulting and inaccurate. In lieu of preserving wilderness in some narratively fabricated, static or semistatic "prehuman" state, I propose a revisionist account of wilderness that inspires exploration and exercise of *agency* in multispecies spaces. By agency, I don't necessarily refer to intentional or deliberative action. I mean agency more broadly, as a process by which an entity may "intervene in the world's becoming" (Barad, 2003: 827). Agency may take different forms for different beings, whether a stream, an insect, or a vascular plant, each according to their capacities and gifts. For humans, agency is inseparable from ethics. I see wilderness as a context in which human beings build and exercise moral agency by exploring their responsibilities for presence and absence, and action and inaction, within a nonhierarchical community of life.

*Restoration:* As practiced, restoration often aims to "restore" desired features or functions of an ecosystem (e.g., ecosystem services, multibenefits, or beneficial uses). These objectives are predicated on anthropocentric resource-utilitarian logic, focused on what (certain) human beneficiaries need, want, and get from an ecosystem (e.g., Martin & Lyons, 2018). In a revisionist framing, I propose that restoration should seek to repair bonds and renew relationships that have been severed by projects of oppression (Kimmerer, 2011). To center relationships, I propose that restoration should be approached through the lens of *reparation*.[5] Reparation is an other-oriented framing in which restoration presents as an apology, in efforts to heal both the specific and systemic wounds of oppression. This is achieved largely by repairing mutualistic relationships predicated on love and respect. Repairing relationships requires efforts to understand and fulfill the diverse needs of all humans and our more-than-human fellows—needs, like safety or space, that have so long been denied and overridden. It also requires us to collectively move through traumas wrought by resource-extractive processes that physically scarred Earth and violated her living communities, while enacting racial and class-based processes of social exploitation and marginalization (e.g., Claire & Surprise, 2021). Restoration should at heart mend ruptured relationships, which requires that these interlinking layers of harm be acknowledged and materially redressed.

*Sustainability:* "Sustainability" begs questions. Sustain what, in what state? And to what ends and for whom? From my observations, sustainability baselines are generally calibrated to the norms and values of current society. In case I've been too subtle, I'll be blunt now: I don't think the dominant norms and values of society should be sustained. Sustainability is a false promise unless the conditions sustained are sustainable for all. There is no sustainability when the powerful elite seize and maintain their privilege by standing on the necks and tails of others. A revisionist imagining of sustainability should be nested within an overall agenda of *liberation*. Perhaps one day we'll achieve a state of authentic freedom in which no one's flourishing is predicated on exploitation. Liberation means that all beings have the latitude to exist in their individual and collective power, and none feel entitled or compelled to expand their power by encroaching upon others. I would argue that this state—nothing short of it—is what we should strive to sustain. Until we arrive there together, we should set our eyes on moral progress and growth, rather than bolstering oppressive and corrupt mechanisms of the status quo.

My brief vignettes are intended to provoke reflection and discussion, recognizing that each requires far more analysis than I can provide here. Like the problems they purport to address, these revisionist agendas are interconnected, and none of them are intended to be zero-sum departures from current practice. If there are elements of conservation, wilderness, restoration, and sustainability that are nonoppressive, by all means let's carry them forward. But we must be exacting in excavating these fields to root out oppression in all its guises. At this juncture, nothing less than transformative change is required.

Still, if conceptually we can (and should) differentiate the influence of oppression from the influence of humans, in practice they often overlap. This is simply because so many dominant modes of human behavior are intricately habituated to oppressive systems. As such, I expect many efforts undertaken under the aegis of revisionist environmentalism would, for a long while, look much like withdrawal, that is to say a scaling back of "human" influence. But we mustn't forget that withdrawal is meant to be antioppressive, not antihuman. Though it may be a fine distinction at times, I think it will play out in important ways into the future. *Homo dualismus* has extended across all corners of Earth—indeed, the colonizing impulse to extend and expand is core to the logic of oppression. Retreat may be essential at this stage, but going forward we must also work to carve out a positive identity for human beings, one that is independent of and antithetical to oppression.

☙

Sometimes I walk with my mother. Though we share space, we move through different worlds. I tend to be enmeshed in my inner emotional landscape, the surrounding landscape mere backdrop for rumination. Not so for my mom; on her walks, she observes the subtle harmonies of river flow and the quick, colorful flits of songbirds. I believe her interface with the world is more sensory than mine, which is largely introspective and affective. Now I sit here writing on my computer at the kitchen table and pause for a moment to peer down at my dog. He blinks up at me, politely inquisitive. I can only wonder about his inner world, and how it is reflecting the outer world back to him.

These anecdotes are partially tangents—a glimpse into the musings of my inner world. But they are also leading to a larger point, which is that something sort of marvelous happens when you realize your view of the world is filtered. It's decentering and humbling, but also empowering and revelatory of new realms of possibility. I used to be deeply rankled to think that there is no "God's-eye view" or, in secular terms, what Hannah Arendt (1998) calls the Archimedean point from which absolute and universal reality is defined. Intellectually I don't think it's tenable to maintain the existence of any such point (Haraway, 1988), but for many years I craved that solid touchstone. I suppose part of me still does. But as I grow older, I also find comfort contributing to the communal project of arranging our kaleidoscopic world in all the ways it can be known. Perhaps there is similar freedom and empowerment to be found in decentering at the species level.

I'd like to return to my earlier claim that humans are not The Problem. I think articulating this in itself has a palliative effect. Humanness is not a blight upon Earth or a cancer to be cut out. *It is okay to be a human.* Really, being human isn't such a big deal. We're animals; etymologically, Earthlings. Readers versed in scholarly debates around the Western human–nature dualism may feel I have at best remixed familiar arguments or, at worst, simply restated the dull truism that "humans are part of nature." I know the ground I've covered here is well-trodden, but respectfully, I think many of us still need to internalize the truism. It's time to stop apologizing for what we are, and instead set to work holding ourselves accountable for our actions, motivations, and characters. Once humanness is no longer viewed as either the crowning achievement of evolution or a pernicious genus of planetary rot, human action and moral responsibility can also be recast. There is space for our species, as there is for all species. I believe we can develop the generosity, humility, and wisdom needed to navigate a complex topography of coexistence within a multispecies landscape. However, discerning the contours of this space will require a radically inclusive effort at a global scale, and an acuity of perception that will emerge only if we recover and fully engage our ethical instincts as moral animals. The question of where we belong is inseparable from the question of how we ought to abide in the world. I see this as our crucible, and the great work of our era: learning to inhabit Earth in ways that reflect embodied and ecologically situated understandings of human identity and moral agency.[6]

The paths we follow to create or reclaim a human sensibility as one species embedded in larger Earth ecologies are bound to be winding and contested. Our morally defunct systems are also structurally sound, and dismantling them will incur damage. I'll admit I'm apprehensive, considering that things I personally value would likely change, diminish, and perhaps vanish in any broadscale redistribution of power. This is all abstracted, but I'd like to think that, faced with the choice, I would bear my losses gracefully and with a sense of purpose.

Some years back I discovered the term "moral residue" (Batavia et al., 2020), which points to a discrepancy between morally upright action (what one ought to do and ideally would do in a perfect world) and morally defensible action (reflecting the best decision possible under the circumstances). When the two don't match, the best possible decision still has some element of moral wrongdoing. That element of wrong is a moral residue. According to philosophers, we know residue as an emotional response, such as regret or remorse. This is the insight I find especially resonant. I want to act in alignment with my values—values such as compassion, benevolence, and justice—but I consistently fall short. Even basic choices (e.g., about food, housing, energy, or travel) seem unavoidably injurious to someone, whether directly or indirectly. I am riddled with guilt all the time, and finding the language for "moral residue" crystallized the meaning of this feeling. It's a chronic sense of moral failure. There are various philosophical explanations for residue, but particularly compelling to me is Tessman's (2010) argument that humans exercise moral agency within a web of moral binds, the byproduct of a society constructed by so many projects of oppression. The system is built to maintain privilege of a few at the expense of many. Structurally, it discourages morally upright action.

I see moral residue accruing like a thick film on the collective conscience of society. The quality of our moral atmosphere is compromised, fittingly analogous to the physical air quality dangers we increasingly confront with extreme wildfires in the western United States. If I may be permitted a final digression, I'll recollect some memories from the 2020 wildfires in Oregon. The golds and coppers of late summer were tarnished to a bilious orange haze. There was so much ash. At first it dropped—picture an incineration of angels' wings, soft as snowfall only sadder. But then it stayed suspended in the atmosphere for weeks, the air stagnating and acrid. It felt like a glimpse of apocalypse, right down to a smell I liken to the reek of time in its slow decay to eternity. I remember gulping water, desperate to dissolve the wad of tar congealing in my throat, to no avail. Breath was toxic. I think we are similarly suffused in a thick smog of moral contamination created by the cumulative residue of our combined decisions. Imagine being released from the binds of structural oppression, to a world where we could breathe the crisp, clean air of moral integrity. To me, that vision is worth the fallout.

The work ahead is disruptive and unflinchingly self-reflective, and we cannot fall back on familiar dualisms for reprieve. The time for simple seeing has passed. The defiant necessity of impossible transformation stands before us—plain to see, formidable to face. Face it we must, and face it we should, with open eyes; and then, hope.

## Notes

1. Technically a dualism articulates a metaphysical belief about the fundamental structure of reality. However, metaphysics and ethics tend to correspond. Beliefs about fundamental reality inform notions of value and associated moral beliefs about how we ought to act (Batavia & Nelson, 2016a).

2. I personally prefer the equally awkward "more-than-human," which at least points to a positive characterization but is still subject to the same critique as "nonhuman."

3. See also, e.g., Ecological Society of America (2023; click "What is invasion ecology?") and Smithsonian Tropical Research Institute (2023).

4. Through words and deeds any of us may (and many of us do) contribute to environmental destruction, but there is nothing innately problematic about being a human of any type.

5. I use this word generally to highlight processes of repair. "Reparations" has a specific meaning in the context of US slavery, and I seek neither to override nor to appropriate this specific meaning.

6. My views are conditioned by my upbringing, lifestyle, and privilege. Intellectually I reject the human-nature dualism, but socially and psychologically it remains central, even instinctual, to how I navigate the world. This is not so for many people whose cultural worldviews don't presuppose a moral and metaphysical cleft between humans and everything (everyone) else. To these readers: I hope you still found something entertaining in my 5,000 words.

## References

Arendt, H. (1998). *The Human Condition* (2nd edition). University of Chicago Press.

Artelle, K. A., Adams, M. S., Bryan, H. M., et al. (2021). Decolonial model of environmental management and conservation: Insights from Indigenous-led grizzly bear stewardship in the Great Bear Rainforest. *Ethics, Policy, & Environment, 24*(3), 283–323. https://doi.org/10.1080/21550085.2021.2002624

Barad, K. (2003). Posthumanist performativity: Toward an understanding of how matter comes to matter. *Signs, 28*(3), 801–31. https://doi.org/10.1086/345321

Batavia, C., & Nelson, M. P. (2016a). Conceptual ambiguities and practical challenges of ecological forestry: A critical review. *Journal of Forestry, 114*(5), 572–81. https://doi.org/10.5849/jof.15-103

Batavia, C., & Nelson, M. P. (2016b). Heroes or thieves? The ethical grounds for lingering concerns about new conservation. *Journal of Environmental Studies and Sciences, 7*, 394–402. https://doi.org/10.1007/s13412-016-0399-0

Batavia, C., Nelson, M. P., Darimont, C. T., et al. (2019). The elephant (head) in the room: A critical look at trophy hunting. *Conservation Letters, 12*(1), e12565. https://doi.org/10.1111/conl.12565

Batavia, C., Wallach, A. D., & Nelson, M. P. (2020). The moral residue of conservation. *Conservation Biology, 34*(5), 1114–21. https://doi.org/10.1111/cobi.13463

Claire, T., & Surprise, T. (2021). Moving the rain: Settler colonialism, the capitalist state, and the hydrologic rift in California's Central Valley. *Antipode, 45*(1), 153–73. https://doi.org/10.1111/anti.12777

Dick, J. T. A., Laverty, C., Lennon, J. J., et al. (2017). Invader Relative Impact Potential: A new metric to understand and predict the ecological impacts of existing, emerging and future invasive alien species. *Journal of Applied Ecology, 54*(4), 1259–67. https://doi.org/10.1111/1365-2664.12849

Ecological Society of America (2023, January 4). *Invasion Ecology Section of the Ecological Society of America.* https://www.esa.org/invasion/

Fletcher, M. S., Hamilton, R., Dressler, W., & Palmer, L. (2021). Indigenous knowledge and the shackles of wilderness. *PNAS, 118*(40), e2022218118. https://doi.org/10.1073/pnas.2022218118

Haila, Y. (2000). Beyond the nature-culture dualism. *Biology and Philosophy, 15,* 155–75. https://doi.org/10.1023/A:1006625830102

Haraway, D. (1988). Situated knowledges: The science question in feminism and the privilege of partial perspective. *Feminist Studies, 14*(3), 575–99.

Iheme, W. (2022). Black bodies in America as the metaphors for oppression, poverty, violence, and hate; Searching for sustainable solutions beyond the Black-letter law. *Journal of Black Studies, 53*(3), 290–319. https://doi.org/10.1177/00219347221074060

Kashwan, P., Duffy, R. V., Massé, F., et al. (2021). From racialized neocolonial global conservation to an inclusive and regenerative conservation. *Environment: Science and Policy for Sustainable Development, 63*(4), 4–19. https://doi.org/10.1080/00139157.2021.1924574

Kimmerer, R. (2011). Restoration and reciprocity: The contributions of Traditional Ecological Knowledge. In D. Egan, E. E. Hjerpe, & J. Abrams (Eds.), *Human Dimensions of Ecological Restoration: Integrating Science, Nature, and Culture* (pp. 257–77). Ecological Society of America. https://doi.org/10.5822/978-1-61091-039-2_18

Lugones, M. (2007). Heterosexualism and the colonial/modern gender system. *Hypatia, 22*(1), 186–219. https://doi.org/10.1111/j.1527-2001.2007.tb01156.x

Martin, D. M., & Lyons, J. E. (2018). Monitoring the social benefits of ecological restoration. *Restoration Ecology, 26*(6), 1045–50. https://doi.org/10.1111/rec.12888

Massarella, K., Krauss, J. E., Kiwango, W., & Fletcher, R. (2022). Exploring convivial conservation in theory and practice: Possibilities and challenges for a transformative approach to biodiversity conservation. *Conservation and Society, 20*(2), 59–68.

McGregor, D., Whitaker, S., & Sritharan, M. (2020). Indigenous environmental justice and sustainability. *Sustainability, 43,* 35–40. https://doi.org/10.1016/j.cosust.2020.01.007

Miller, V. (2022, March 2). Tears and ashes. *Commonweal Magazine, 149*(3). https://www.commonwealmagazine.org/tears-ashes

Morales, N., Lee, J., Newberry, M., & Bailey, K. (2022). Redefining American conservation for equitable and inclusive social-ecological management. *Ecological Applications, 33*(1), e2749. https://doi.org/10.1002/eap.2749

Nelson, M. P., & Callicott, J. B. (Eds.) (2008). *The Wilderness Debate Rages On.* University of Georgia Press.

Plumwood, V. (1993). *Feminism and the Mastery of Nature.* Routledge.

Quijano, A. (2000). Coloniality of power and Eurocentrism in Latin America. *International Sociology, 15*(2), 215–32. https://doi.org/10.1177/0268580900015002005

Salmón, E. (2000). Kincentric ecology: Indigenous perceptions of the human-nature relationship. *Ecological Applications, 10,* 1327–32.

Smithsonian Tropical Research Institute (2023, January 4). *Invasion biology.* https://stri.si.edu/discipline/invasion-biology

Tessman, L. (2010). Idealizing morality. *Hypatia, 25*(4), 797–824. https://doi.org/10.1111/j.1527-2001.2010.01125.x

Treves, A., Santiago-Ávila, F. J., & Lynn, W. S. (2019). Just preservation. *Biological Conservation, 229,* 134–41. https://doi.org/10.1016/j.biocon.2018.11.018

Wallach, A. D., Batavia, C., Bekoff, M., et al. (2020). Recognizing animal personhood in compassionate conservation. *Conservation Biology, 34*(5), 1097–1106. https://doi.org/10.1111/cobi.13494

Washington, H., Chapron, G., Kopnina, H., et al. (2018). Foregrounding ecojustice in conservation. *Biological Conservation, 228,* 367–74. https://doi.org/10.1016/j.biocon.2018.09.011s

12

# Respecting Nonhuman Life
## The Guide for a Better Pathway in Outdoor Recreation

### Joe Gray and Ian Whyte

Before I learned to respect rattlesnakes I killed two, the first on the San Joaquin plain. [. . .] I felt degraded by the killing business [. . .] and I made up my mind to try to be at least as fair and charitable as the snakes themselves, and to kill no more save in self-defense. [. . .] Since then I have seen perhaps a hundred or more in these mountains, but I have never intentionally disturbed them, nor have they disturbed me to any great extent, even by accident, though in danger of being stepped on.

—John Muir (1898: 629–30), in an account of animal life in Yosemite Valley

A quarter of a century ago, when I made this journey, Grand Canyon was largely untraveled below its Rims. So I did certain things that at the time seemed legitimate. I lit occasional campfires, for example. I had three supply drops parachuted from lowflying aircraft. I killed a rattlesnake. [. . .] I hope you will understand that because of today's heavy travel in the Canyon by backpackers and river-runners such acts would now be neither legitimate nor legal.

—Colin Fletcher in an introductory note to the 1989 edition of his account of a 1963 hike through the Grand Canyon (first published in 1968)

Times are changing for all the major facets of modern human life. This includes the focal topic of this chapter, outdoor recreation, which can be defined as the breadth of activities that people choose to undertake in nature-rich settings for reasons not directly related to subsistence or financial gain. As we will explore, the ways in which we go about these activities has a major impact on well-being and flourishing in the more-than-human world. Any vision for an ecological civilization must surely, then, call for recreational pursuits to be undertaken with a vigorous respect for nonhumans and their needs as living beings. Before elaborating upon this idea, we will begin with a contemporary portrait of outdoor recreation.

Recent developments in the area can be distilled into three interconnected trends. The first is the growing awareness that contact with wider nature is not only a cornerstone of human well-being (Bratman et al., 2019) but also a catalyst for conservation support and other proenvironmental behaviors (Miller, 2005; Mackay & Schmitt, 2019; Whyte & Gray, 2020; Miller et al., 2022). The second trend relates to the emerging body of evidence from a research field known as recreation ecology, which describes the complex negative impacts that outdoor pursuits can have on wild places and wild beings (box 12.1; Marion et al., 2016). Such impacts have been identified, to one degree or another, for a range of activities extending well beyond those that are starkly problematic—such as trophy hunting and high-decibel motorized recreation (Wuerthner, 2007; Dellinger, 2019)—to include pursuits as seemingly benign as birdwatching (Jones & Nealson, 2005). Considered at large, recreational activity has been described as being equivalent to reducing habitat area and as contributing to behavior-driven habitat fragmentation (Hambler & Canney, 2013; Hennings, 2021). For more sensitive species, such as the Eurasian lynx, evidence points to human disturbance as being the key limiting factor in their distribution (Ripari et al., 2022).

In light of the growing awareness of both the importance of time in nature and the negative impacts of recreation, we would very much like to be able to defend a stance here that calls for increased access to wild nature *and* a reduction in the harm to nonhuman life associated with outdoor pursuits, but to do so would ignore the fact that the former would inevitably undermine the latter. Instead, in accepting the validity of both truths, we will need to advocate a position that lies somewhere between the extremes of encouraging everyone to roam everywhere and closing modern civilization off in habitable bubbles. In line with the thrust of this book, the position will be ecocentrically oriented, meaning that

> **Some Examples of the Negative Impacts of Recreational Activities on Wild Beings and Wild Places**
>
> - Compaction or erosion of soil and prevention of plant regeneration from trampling.
> - Introduction and spread of nonnative species (e.g., from seeds in boot treads or from the movement of recreational boats between waterbodies).
> - Degradation of water quality through chemical contamination, nutrient influxes, and the stirring of sediment (e.g., during wild swimming or motor-boating).
> - Killing of wildlife (e.g., from vehicle collisions).
> - Disturbance of wild animals, leading to their excess energy usage and temporal or spatial displacement from more favorable to less favorable habitat.
> - Altering of the feeding strategies of wildlife, through learned food-attraction behaviors associated with human presence.

the well-being and freedom of nonhuman life are considered important in their own right, rather than being significant—solely or principally—in terms of their contribution to human well-being.

The tension that exists between the desire for better access to experiences in nature and the imperative to reduce the harm that we cause nonhuman life, during these times of anthropogenic mass extinction, is demonstrated in the third of the aforementioned interconnected trends. This is the increasing number of visitors—and the resulting escalation of pressure placed on wild nature—in already-popular places, such as national parks, which are among the most important corners of the planet for safeguarding biodiversity. Trend lines on graphs that describe the popularity of recreational pursuits in nature-rich places during the past 100 years do not tell of a steady year-on-year growth, as there have been periods of stasis and even decline, but a comparison between now and a century ago reveals a huge upsurge (Pergams & Zaradic, 2008; Simmonds et al., 2018). The numerous drivers of this upsurge include, among others, road construction, increased ownership of cars, an ever-growing human population, a rising global middle class, and the facilitation by social media of a "snap-and-share" culture.

During this period of growth for outdoor recreation, we have begun to rediscover in our modern lives that recurring motif of indigenous wisdom: an intimate respect for the more-than-human world. This personal philosophy is one that developed for John Muir back in the 19th century, as evidenced in the first of the introductory quotations. While we are not suggesting that Muir's attitudes are generalizable (yet) across humanity—to do so would be like offering the peak of Kilimanjaro as being representative of land in East Africa—we believe that modern civilization is making headway toward the metaphorical summits that he encouraged us to scale. At the same time, the escalating pressure on wild places and beings has necessitated changes in societal norms and laws, as noted by Colin Fletcher in the second rattlesnake-themed quotation.

In the next section, we consider some of the guidance that has emerged to encourage responsible behavior in the outdoors, including through the codification of respect for nonhuman life. Before moving on, though, we must note that there is an obvious complementary means of relieving, if not resolving, the tension between a desire for better access to experiences in nature and the imperative to reduce the harm that we cause nonhuman life. As Gray and Noss have commented, "In order to facilitate human interactions with nature without overwhelming the wild, it is necessary for land conservation programmes to be greatly expanded. This ranges from protection of undeveloped areas within city limits, outward to the wildest remaining landscapes" (Gray and Noss, 2021: 56).

## Codes for Recreational Pursuits

In introducing some established codes for recreational pursuits, we should stress that they are not exclusively focused on reducing harm to nonhuman life. Rather, their remit extends to also cover individual- and humanity-centered concerns—including outdoor safety, impacts on the experiences of other humans, and broader sustainability issues. As is exemplified by some of the other discussions in this book, however, human well-being is intimately tied to the thriving of nonhuman life; thus we will not attempt to disentangle ecocentric and anthropocentric motivators for regulating outdoor activities.

What is arguably the best-known guidance for recreational pursuits comes from the seven principles of Leave No Trace (box 12.2a; see https://lnt.org/why/7-principles/). In this code, only the last of the seven principles is focused solely on human interests. Each of the first five covers both human and nonhuman interests to varying degrees, and the sixth strongly foregrounds the latter (box 12.2b; see https://lnt.org/why/7-principles/respect-wildlife/). While having its roots in the United States, the Leave No Trace movement now has an uptake that extends far beyond the boundaries of that country. For instance, researchers in Taiwan—where hiking has become a "highly popular outdoor recreational activity"—found that knowledge of the seven principles of Leave No Trace among visitors to Shoushan National Nature Park increased after the introduction of an educational program (Wu et al., 2021: 2). Other codes that exist are less broadly applicable, having been developed for particular groups or shaped by the political landscape. Tread Lightly!, for example, is an organization in the United States that provides guidance targeted for users of motorized vehicles (see https://treadlightly.org/). In Scotland, to provide a different example, most land and freshwater is open for public access but privately owned, and the national outdoor access code has a notable focus on landholder interests, such as in the stated responsibility to "help land managers and others to work safely and effectively" (see https://www.outdooraccess-scotland.scot/).

Leave No Trace is not without its critics. One major theme to emerge in the literature is that the implication of its very name—that recreational pursuits can be undertaken without impact—is either disingenuous or blinkered from reality. Moskowitz and Ottey (2006: 16), for instance, have commented, "[T]he notion that it is possible to live in the natural world without leaving a trace [. . .] conflicts with fundamental principles of ecology [and] encourages wilderness visitors to view the natural world as an environment in which humans do not belong, disconnecting them from the landscape."

These authors add that the principles "do not address larger environmental issues and day-to-day patterns of behavior" (Moskowitz and Ottey, 2006: 16). Reinforcing this point, Alagona and Simon have observed that Leave No Trace "disguises the larger social and environmental consequences of outdoor recreation in countries with consumer-oriented economies" (Alagona and Simon, 2012: 122). The code, they go on to argue, "could not exist in its current form without a plethora of consumer products," and this "does not erase environmental impacts [but] only displaces them from the sites of consumption to sites of production, distribution, and

> **The Seven Principles of Leave No Trace**
>
> 1 Plan ahead and prepare
> 2 Travel and camp on durable surfaces
> 3 Dispose of waste properly
> 4 Leave what you find
> 5 Minimize campfire impacts
> 6 Respect wildlife
> 7 Be considerate of other visitors
>
> **Extracts from the explanatory text for the "Respect wildlife" Leave No Trace principle**
>
> - "Do not disturb wildlife or plants just for a 'better look.'"
>
> - "Observe wildlife from a distance so they are not scared or forced to flee."
>
> - "Travel quietly and do not pursue, feed or force animals to flee."[†]
>
> - "In hot or cold weather, disturbance can affect an animal's ability to withstand the rigorous environment."
>
> - "Allow animals free access to water sources by giving them the buffer space they need to feel secure."
>
> - "Washing and human waste disposal must be done carefully" so that "animals and aquatic life are not injured."
>
> [†]Here, the explanatory text notes: "One exception is in bear country where it is good to make a little noise so as not to startle the bears." This mirrors the approach that John Muir developed, back in the 19th century, subsequent to his first encounter with a bear in the High Sierra: "Thenceforth I always tried to give bears respectful notice of my approach and they usually kept well out of my way" (Muir, 1898: 619).

disposal" (Alagona and Simon, 2012: 122). By way of a remedy, Alagona and Simon (2012) suggest that an eighth principle be added to the code: Leave No Trace starts at home. In contrast, Moskowitz and Ottey (2006), whose criticisms are broader, have proposed a more holistic set of seven principles, which they call Conscious Impact Living (box 12.3). In an expansion of Leave No Trace's "Respect wildlife" principle, this alternative

## The Seven Principles of Conscious Impact Living

1. Live simply
2. Think globally and plan ahead
3. Follow the precautionary principle
4. Reduce, reuse, recycle, relearn
5. Follow nature's lead and blend into one's surroundings
6. Use appropriate technology and use technology appropriately
7. Show respect and compassion for all forms of life

code concludes, "Show respect and compassion for all forms of life." Also worth noting is their inclusion of the precautionary principle. In their words, "if the consequences of an action are unknown, but hold the potential for grave or irreversible damage, then it is better to act as if the risks will come to pass" (Moskowitz and Ottey, 2006: 18). More recently, with the growth of social media, a further suggested addition to the Leave No Trace principles is one that cautions against geotagging (sharing location details with photos and videos), which can lead to high visitor levels in once-quiet locations (discussed in Usher [2021]).

## Practicing Respect for Nonhuman Life

As is described in the previous section, respect for nonhuman life in outdoor recreation features prominently in the well-established Leave No Trace code and also in the more holistic Conscious Impact Living principles. Such respect, at the level of the individual, draws on both a willingness to honor nonhuman interests and a cognizance of how these interests can be affected by human activity (on this latter point, we cannot assume, for instance, that everyone subscribes to the *Journal of Outdoor Recreation and Tourism*). Let us consider, as an example, a person who is walking a dog in the spring or summer in a place with ground-nesting birds. Practicing respect for these birds involves not just a desire to avoid or reduce negative impacts on them from the activity but also a knowledge that they are present, that the parents may be flushed from their nests by a free-roaming dog, and that this can lead to a failure of eggs to hatch, the death of chicks from a lack of warmth or food, and an increased vulnerability of nests to predators. Writing more generally about awareness of the adverse impacts of recreation, the conservationist Roy Dennis (1999: 30) observed, "I must place on record my worry about the increasing penetration of wild places crucial to sensitive wildlife by large numbers of people. [. . .] These people often criticise others in the countryside who damage or destroy wildlife through their [land use] activities, without recognising that their leisure activities may also [be] causing change and damage." Simon Leadbeater, one of the other authors in this volume, has elsewhere described the negative impacts of recreation as something that "all of us see but tend not to notice" (Leadbeater, 2019). Contributing to limited awareness is a phenomenon recently discussed in an online presentation by researcher Lori Hennings. On the one hand, she noted, people think, "I saw wildlife, so I must not be disturbing them." And on the other, "I didn't see any wildlife, so I must not be disturbing them" (Hennings, 2021). Also exacerbating the issue is the tendency of many humans to judge themselves by more lenient standards than they apply to others.

To help remedy this situation, we feel that there is an obligation not just on participants in recreation to learn about the potential consequences for the nonhuman world of their actions but also on landholders and land managers to assist with this through the provision of information on signs, in leaflets, and with other media. This education will encompass place-specific nuances, such as the needs of the locally present species who are more sensitive to human disturbance, as well as more broadly applicable learnings. Much good work is already being done by landholders and land managers in this area, but its importance demands that we emphasize the case for it. Enhancing our understanding of the impacts we have on the wider world in such ways is a crucial facet of lifelong ecological learning and the practice of respect for more-than-human life. Through personal development, we can cultivate ecologically kinder habits in the great outdoors. And here, we believe, there is a special onus on the nature lovers of today to lead the way in making better choices.

For recreation at any given location, these choices might include *restricting ourselves spatially*, by keeping to well-used paths and waterways, in order to help minimize human disturbance in quieter areas. The choices might also include *restricting ourselves temporally*, by refraining from visits during certain periods of the day or particular parts of the year, in order to honor sensitive lifecycle activities of nonhumans. For instance, during times of the year when there are dawn gatherings of birds at lekking sites (patches of ground used for communal display), recreationists can consider avoiding visits in the early part of the day. Similarly, in places that are hot and arid, where wildlife might be more active at night, one could choose to stay clear of drinking sites once darkness approaches. And in places where winter days are short and cold, consideration can be given to staying away so as to avoid exacerbating the daily struggle of sensitive animal species to achieve a sufficient calorie intake for survival. Or, as the kindest decision of all, one might choose to avoid a place altogether, if, say, human disturbance is particularly detrimental there.

To promote spatial and temporal avoidances, landholders and land managers might go beyond the provision of information by introducing physical barriers to access, either permanently or at particular times of the year. One example of the introduction of year-round barriers is in the Abernethy National Nature Reserve, in the Scottish Highlands. Here, a large surviving fragment of Caledonian pine forest provides crucial habitat for the capercaillie—a grouse species of serious conservation concern with a marked intolerance of human presence. In order to inhibit recreational access to core areas for this species, the Royal Society for the Protection of Birds, which owns and manages the land, has allowed a thick cover of vegetation to return to some of the tracks that were previously used for forestry operations, thus significantly decreasing the possibility of recreational activities in certain parts of the nature reserve (Summers, 2018).

Here, support could be lent to such strategies of access restriction through higher-level legal measures, at least until such a time as our culture as a whole has grown sufficient respect for wild nature that the measures become redundant. To expand on the example of dog walking introduced above, and using Great Britain for illustration, signs to encourage the keeping of dogs under close control are common in nature reserves in this country, but they are often ignored. This has led the conservationist Chris Packham, in his *People's Manifesto for Wildlife*, to call for a ban on the walking of dogs in any area designated as a nature reserve (Packham et al., 2018). Nevertheless, it is worth observing that regulations—even strictly enforced ones—can only go so far in promoting ecologically respectful behavior

Following the recommendations of Moskowitz and Ottey (2006), as well as Alagona and Simon (2012), to think more holistically about the impacts of recreational activities, we also want to note that practicing respect for nonhuman life plays out more broadly in our choices as consumers (in regard to clothing and equipment, for instance), in any implicit support we lend to ecologically harmful infrastructure (such as that associated with downhill snow sports), and in the overall footprint of our travel. Regarding travel, specifically, a strong case can be made for individuals seeking a large proportion of their recreational experiences in the vicinity of their home. People who live in inner-city locations may need to travel further, of course, but the principle holds as a general one. The literature on recreation that has emerged during the COVID-19 pandemic includes a call by Houge Mackenzie and Goodnow for a renewed focus on microadventures "in nearby nature that are low-carbon and human-scaled" (Houge Mackenzie and Goodnow, 2021: 62). In addition to reducing the footprint of activities, local recreation—in our increasingly urban civilization—will, more often than not, mean recreation in anthropogenically shaped places, where the wild beings are likely to be more tolerant of human presence. Indeed, urban parks that are pleasant and well frequented have a significant role to play in reducing the stress that recreation can place on wilder places.

A further angle to consider here, for any chosen place for recreation, is the extent to which we can reduce the net negative impact of our presence on nonhuman life by undertaking positive actions. In some cases, just being present in a place can have a beneficial impact on some species. For example, it is known that common aspen struggles to regenerate in parts of the Scottish Highlands where the now-extirpated gray wolf once reduced levels of browsing by deer. By discouraging browsing, the presence of walkers and cyclists can help aspen gain a foothold in a zone adjacent to moorland tracks (Summers, 2018). In general, though, positive impacts will require deliberate actions such as picking up litter, participating in conservation-focused citizen science projects, reporting problems to landowners and land managers, and encouraging other recreationists to behave in ways that minimize the negative impacts (Gray, 2022). Relatedly, Miller and her colleagues have proposed a model for understanding interactions between recreational activities and nonhuman life envisioned in four quadrants: positive impacts of nonhuman life on recreation; positive impacts of recreation on nonhuman life; negative impacts of recreation on nonhuman life; and negative impacts of nonhuman life on recreation (Miller et al., 2022).

It is clear from the discussion above that there are many angles to consider in striving to be more respectful of nonhuman life in the ways that we go about recreation. A further illumination of this—in the form of questions that we might ask ourselves, before or during recreational activities, from the perspective of a deep respect for nonhuman nature—is presented in box 12.4. These questions are not intended to be exhaustive, as they do not cover, for instance, the choices we make relating to

## Questions That We Might Ask Ourselves, from an Ecocentric Perspective, before or during Recreational Activities

Example questions to consider before recreational activities:

- Could I undertake recreation closer to home or in a place where wildlife is less sensitive to disturbance by humans?
- Can I walk my dog in a place where their presence is going to be less detrimental to wildlife?
- Is there a better time of the year for my visit, in terms of minimizing the negative impact on wildlife?
- Can I choose a more ecologically sound means of travel to the place of recreation?
- Am I supporting ecologically harmful infrastructure by choosing a certain type of recreation?
- Is riding a mountain bike compatible with the thriving of nature in the area I intend to visit?
- Is there a risk that I will be introducing nonnative species into the area that I am visiting?
- If I am taking medication and am going to need to urinate, can I avoid the negative impact on wildlife of chemical pollution?
- Do I need to take something with me to help in the ecologically sound disposal of excrement?
- Do I need to learn more about the nuances of the local wildlife before I visit a place?
- What routes can I follow to minimize the negative impacts associated with my presence?
- If water is likely to be scarce for all life in the place I am visiting, am I going to be entering with sufficient liquid for myself?
- Is there some equipment I can take to help me do something positive (e.g., a litter-grabber)?

*continued on next page*

> Example questions to consider during recreational activities:
> - Am I minimizing harm to nonhuman life in my behavior as a hiker?
> - Should I avoid certain parts of the lake while canoeing?
> - Might approaching wildlife to take photographs cause them distress?
> - Is there a nonhuman being who might need a forageable good more than I do?
> - Can I be doing something positive for wildlife (e.g., picking up litter)?
> - What can I do to help other visitors develop a love of nature?
> - Am I taking full advantage of the opportunity to be attentive to the nonhuman world?

clothing and equipment, but they can serve as a prompt. Where answers are unknown, the precautionary principle is a useful guide.

## Concluding Thoughts

Recreation ecology is praiseworthy for shining a light on the negative impacts for nonhuman life that arise across the gamut of outdoor activities. If a civilization is to emerge in which humans truly live in harmony with wider nature, a crucial aspect of our lives will be undertaking recreational activities in ways that deeply respect nonhuman lives, both in places of recreation and more broadly. In other words, we must learn to connect with wild nature without undermining its flourishing. We can do this through experiencing nonhuman beings and their homes as inherently meaningful and worthy of our deep affection. Indeed, time spent immersed in wild nature is invaluable in our growth as ecological citizens, through the opportunities that it presents for studying, respecting, and nurturing a love of our fellow Earth inhabitants, while simultaneously cultivating our physical and spiritual self-care. In the words of Moskowitz and Ottey (2006: 19), "Approach all living things with respect, compassion, gratitude, and awareness that each plays a part within the whole. By recognizing that humans are only one small part of the world, dependent on the myriad natural systems and life forms of the planet, we can act in large and small ways with gratitude and concern, remaining humble and aware of our place in the world."

## References

Alagona, P., & Simon, G. (2012). Leave No Trace starts at home: A response to critics and vision for the future. *Ethics, Policy and Environment, 15*(1), 119–24. https://doi.org/10.1080/21550085.2012.672695

Bratman, G. N., Anderson, C. B., Berman, M. G., et al. (2019). Nature and mental health: An ecosystem service perspective. *Science Advances, 5*(7), aax0903. https://doi.org/10.1126/sciadv.aax0903

Dellinger, M. F. (2019). Trophy hunting—a relic of the past. *Journal of Environmental Law and Litigation, 34*, 25–60. https://doi.org/10.2139/ssrn.3137742

Dennis, R. (1999). The birds and mammals of Rothiemurchus. In T. C. Smout & R. A. Lambert (Eds.), *Rothiemurchus: Nature and people on a highland estate, 1500–2000* (pp. 22–31). Scottish Cultural Press.

Fletcher, C. (1989). *The Man Who Walked through Time*. Vintage Books.

Gray, J. (2022, February 14–16). *Treading Lightly and Giving Back to Nature: The Need for a New Culture in Recreational Activities* [Online presentation]. ILAS-HUFS HK+ 2nd International Conference. https://deepgreen.earth/pdfs/treading-lightly-and-giving-back-to-nature.pdf

Gray, J., & Noss, R. (2021). Fostering a love of the living world—or, the need for a grand revival of natural history. In J. Gray (Ed.), *Visions for a Post-Covid World: Defining a Radically New Normal* (pp. 45–59). Dixi Books. https://deepgreen.earth/publications/fostering-a-love-of-the-living-world.pdf

Hambler, C., & Canney S. M. (2013). *Conservation* (2nd edition). Cambridge University Press. https://doi.org/10.1017/CBO9780511792472

Hennings, L. (2021, July 1). *Using Wildlife Fright Distances to Inform Trail Planning* [Online presentation]. Advancing Trails Webinar. https://www.americantrails.org/training/using-wildlife-fright-distances-to-inform-trail-planning

Houge Mackenzie, S., & Goodnow, J. (2021). Adventure in the age of COVID-19: Embracing microadventures and locavism in a post-pandemic world. *Leisure Sciences, 43*(1–2), 62–69.

Jones, D., & and Nealson, T. (2005). *Impacts of Bird Watching on Communities and Species: Long-term and Short-term Responses in Rainforest and Eucalypt Habitats* (Technical Report). CRC Sustainable Tourism. https://hdl.handle.net/10072/8438

Leadbeater, S. (2019, September 14). The sixth driver of the Sixth Extinction. *Nearby Wild*. https://nearbywild.org.uk/sixth-driver-of-sixth-extinction/

Mackay, C. M. L., & Schmitt, M. T. (2019). Do people who feel connected to nature do more to protect it? A meta-analysis. *Journal of Environmental Psychology, 65*, 101323. https://doi.org/10.1016/j.jenvp.2019.101323

Marion, J. L., Leung, Y. F., Eagleston, H., & Burroughs, K. (2016). A review and synthesis of recreation ecology research findings on visitor impacts to wilderness and protected natural areas. *Journal of Forestry, 114*(3), 352–62. https://doi.org/10.5849/jof.15-498

Miller, J. R. (2005). Biodiversity conservation and the extinction of experience. *Trends in Ecology & Evolution*, *20*(8), 430–34. https://doi.org/10.1016/j.tree.2005.05.013

Miller, A. B., Blahna, D. J., Morse, W. C., et al. (2022). From recreation ecology to a recreation ecosystem: A framework accounting for social-ecological systems. *Journal of Outdoor Recreation and Tourism*, *38*, 100455.

Moskowitz, D., & Ottey, D. (2006). Leaving Leave No Trace behind: Towards a holistic land use ethic. *Green Teacher*, *Spring*, 16–19.

Muir, J. (1898). Among the animals of the Yosemite. *The Atlantic Monthly*, *82*(493), 617–31. https://scholarlycommons.pacific.edu/jmb/248/

Packham, C., Barkham, P., & MacFarlane, R. (Eds.) (2018). *A People's Manifesto for Wildlife* (draft one). http://www.chrispackham.co.uk/wp-content/uploads/Peoples-Manifesto-Download.pdf

Pergams, O. R. W., & Zaradic, P. A. (2008.) Evidence for a fundamental and pervasive shift away from nature-based recreation. *Proceedings of the National Academy of Sciences of the United States of America*, *105*(7), 2295–300. https://doi.org/10.1073/pnas.0709893105

Ripari, L., Premier, J., Belotti, E., et al. (2022) Human disturbance is the most limiting factor driving habitat selection of a large carnivore throughout Continental Europe. *Biological Conservation*, *266*, 109446. https://doi.org/10.1016/j.biocon.2021.109446

Simmonds, C., McGivney, A., Reilly, P., et al. (2018, November 20). Crisis in our national parks: How tourists are loving nature to death. *The Guardian*. https://www.theguardian.com/environment/2018/nov/20/national-parks-america-overcrowding-crisis-tourism-visitation-solutions

Summers, R. W. (2018). *Abernethy Forest: The History and Ecology of an Old Scottish Pinewood*. Royal Society for the Protection of Birds.

Usher, P. (2021, December 6). Leaving "no trace" at beauty spots should include a ban on social media. *inews*. https://inews.co.uk/inews-lifestyle/travel/leave-no-trace-responsible-travel-wilderness-countryside-beauty-spots-social-media-1334092

Whyte, I., & Gray, J. (2020). Field guides as a gateway to appreciating more-than-human concerns. *The Ecological Citizen*, *3*(2), 119.

Wuerthner, G. (Ed.) (2007). *Thrillcraft: The Environmental Consequences of Motorized Recreation*. Chelsea Green.

Wu C. C., Li, C. W., Wang, W. C., et al. (2021). Low-impact hiking in natural areas: A study of nature park hikers' negative impacts and on-site leave-no-trace educational program in Taiwan. *Environmental Impact Assessment Review*, *87*, 106544. https://doi.org/10.1016/j.eiar.2020.106544

Section Three

# Reverence

## 13

# Enchantment, Modernity, and Reverence for Nature

PATRICK CURRY

In this chapter, I shall sketch a philosophical genealogy of ecocidal "Western" modernity, now global, taking it as read that scientifically uncontroversial indicators confirm the dire and worsening effects on Earth and its creatures of anthropogenic climate chaos, including global warming; biodiversity loss, including mass extinctions; and industrial agriculture and husbandry.

Without underestimating the importance of politics, economics, society, or culture, I concentrate on the metaphysical dimension of this phenomenon. I don't view it as the primary cause of where we now are but as at least an integral part of the mixture, and I have no doubt that it plays a role in enabling ecocide.

I shall then describe the most basic characteristics and dynamics of enchantment as the experience of wonder, culminating in reverence, especially its rootedness in the more-than-human natural world.[1] (This term, from Abram [1997], refers to the world of nature that includes but vastly exceeds human beings.) I go on to suggest that there is an elective or inner affinity between enchantment and nature, sharing as they do the quality of wildness, which I contrast with the quality of the fundamental project of modernity: will-driven mastery. I conclude by inferring that the former has the potential to counter the latter, provided one doesn't fall into the trap of regarding wonder as a useful resource.

With such a large subject it is possible, within the limited space available, only to present the main concerns and developments, often leaving others—even when they are almost as important, and certainly of interest—to be noted in passing. But I do not think this is a good reason not to discuss the topic at all.

❧

In tracing the course of contemporary ecocide, I believe the single most concentratedly toxic sentiment at work was succinctly expressed by the god Silenus, as quoted by Aristotle, via Plutarch. A fragment of Aristotle which Plutarch quotes asserts, "That not to be born is the best of all, and that to be dead is better than to live." And Silenus avers that "the best thing for all men and women is not to be born; however, the next best thing to this, and the first of those to which man can attain, but nevertheless only the second best, is, after being born, to die as quickly as possible" (Plutarch, 1928).[2]

Notice what this worldview entails, not strictly logically but in practice and no less influentially for that: since both men and women are born of women, women are associated with—and in another very short step, blamed for—the misfortune of being alive. By the same token, birth is blamed for death, with the descent of the soul into the body at birth seen as a fall.[3] Furthermore, given the ancient and widespread association by men of women with Earth, thanks to the latter's purported emotionality and therefore greater degree of animality, plus the fact that Earth is the home of life, the final link in the pathological concatenation is that Earth itself, the very source and sustainer of life, comes to be feared and hated. This attitude is further encouraged by Heaven supposedly being up above and Hell down below—where Earth is.

This worldview, for want of a better word, is an amalgam of feeling or emotion plus conceptualization or theory. It readily lent itself to further development in both Gnosticism and Platonism. In both, the material and sensuous world of changing so-called appearances—in a word, nature—was condemned as inferior, untrue, and, in the most extreme case, by Parmenides, nonexistent. According to the Gnostics, this world was the flawed creation of a malevolent demiurge (god), and therefore itself evil. Parmenides sacrificed life, the realm of endless becoming, which includes both birth and death, for a statically perfect, unchanging, and eternal Being.

Plato softened Parmenides's conclusion to the extent of positioning the natural world as merely a flawed and inferior copy of the real (and therefore true) world of eternal and bodiless spiritual Ideas or Forms, rather than nonexistent. But in the *Phaedo* (82d) and the *Gorgias* (493a) he described the body as a prison for the soul; in the *Cratylus* (400) as a tomb and again a prison, being a place of punishment; and, famously, in the *Republic* (7, 514a–515), he compared earthly life to living in a cave deprived of light and truth. But whether from tomb, prison cell, or cave, one's duty is to escape, by dying; that is the definitive return to a heavenly home. Practicing philosophy is merely a rehearsal and preparation for the real thing.[4]

Although the philosophy of death did not originate with Plato, he gave it enormously influential expression. Through Saint Paul, it passed directly into Christianity. Almost repeating Socrates welcoming death in the *Phaedo*, Paul said he "wanted to be loosened asunder"—"he" being entirely identified with his disembodied soul—in order "to be with Christ" (Philippians 1:23), and he bemoaned "[t]his body of death" and "these bonds" (Romans 7:24). Equally influentially, this theology of Thanatos was taken up by Saint Augustine. The result was a Platonizing Christianity, in the Western church especially, marked by an enduring ascetic hatred and fear of the body, sex, and women.

It hasn't had it all its own way, being at odds with the humbling of God incarnating as a limited and vulnerable human being, the complicating interrelationality of the Trinity, and the stress laid on the resurrection of the body, implying its integrality to the person. The resulting tension within Christianity is effectively unresolvable. Meanwhile, the Christian Platonic philosophy of death passed into Islam, but tracing its influence there is beyond my scope here.

The next phase of the philosophy of death, alongside its continuing career in theistic religion, was its secularization in the course of the early modern Scientific Revolution, especially the philosophy of Descartes—the implausibilities and logical failures of that proved, once again, no barrier to widespread influence—supported by Bacon's human imperialism and misogyny. Cartesianism carried forward the Platonic split between spirit and matter but arguably radicalized it by denying any subjectivity or agency whatsoever to matter—that is, nature—equating the latter with pure mechanism and reserving the former for the human mind alone, increasingly a placeholder for spirit.

Subsequent formal philosophy changed nothing of importance about this arrangement. Kant's transcendental idealism valorized human reason even while limiting it, arguing that the external world was unavoidably structured by the categories of human cognition and was therefore ultimately a world of mere appearances, rather than "things in themselves." Hegel's all-determining World Spirit was just that—spiritual—even though it manifests through and as the world, while Schopenhauer's misanthropy and misogyny returned to the values of the original root-philosophy.

Essential to the mode of the philosophy of death is a series of hierarchical and value-laden essences: spirit versus matter, mind versus body, man versus woman, culture versus nature, subject versus object, and so on. They are linked because the first and usually more valued terms of each binary are elided into one, as are those of the second set of terms.[5] Sometimes the valuing was reversed, as with Marx's materialist inversion of Hegel's spiritualism. Such reversal is widespread, but the schizoid mode remains. Against the long-standing dominance of theistic metaphysics, in particular, it was integral to the scientific naturalism that developed in the 19th century and that continues, putting the physical and matter (now most commonly as neurophysiology) in the place of honor. But the choice of materialism is, of course, just as metaphysical as that of supernaturalism.

It is probable that Alfred North Whitehead's organicist and nondual "process philosophy" could be enlisted as an ally here. (It is not possible to enlist his student David Ray Griffin's *Enchantment without Supernaturalism*, despite its promising title, since it seems to vaunt theism *and* scientific naturalism, both of which I am rejecting here for all the reasons given.)

What doesn't change in that choice is the phenomenon of "two competing monisms" (Jonas 1982: 16), as each school tries to reduce and absorb the opposite term while tacitly accepting a radical difference, a split (more than a mere distinction, which is perfectly defensible) between the two.[6] Why does this matter to us here? Because in the words of Ludwig Wittgenstein (1979: 77e), "Physiological life is of course not 'life.' And neither is psychological life. Life is the world." And both "life" and "nature" can be understood as cognate with nature, as the more-than-human natural world that includes all nonhuman as well as human life.

For this reason Gregory Bateson (1987: 59) called supernaturalism and mechanism "two species of superstition," which he similarly accused of tacitly colluding in obscuring while supporting the assumed split they share.[7] And that split itself falsely legitimates an anthropocentric ascendancy, whether materialist or spiritualist, which treats nature—including human nature—as something to be dominated, used, and ultimately transcended.

That indeed is how Val Plumwood (1993) described the defining project of modernity, whether in one mode or the other: *the rational mastery of nature*, including human nature, by certain humans, paradigmatically male. (A few women adopting the same mode doesn't alter its dominant gender dynamics.) This androcentrism, combined with hatred and fear of the female and Earth, resulted in them becoming inextricably entangled such that any attempt to resist and retrieve one will sooner or later meet the other. (Hence Plumwood's self-designation as an ecofeminist.) But this point too takes us beyond what can be traced here.

The outcome that we must face is that the philosophy of death condemns the natural world to servitude—that is, "ecosystem services" and "natural capital"—when not outright slavery, as with industrial agriculture, meat and fisheries, and extermination, as the statistics concerning the plummeting numbers of wild animals confirm. Indeed, Isaac Bashevis Singer's description of our collective treatment of animals—that we are, for them, "an eternal Treblinka"—seems entirely justified.[8] Key to this process is the spell summed up in the word "resources." It magically converts living nature, with its own nonhuman subjectivities and agency that are therefore appropriate "others" for relationships and ethics, into a uniform set of lifeless objects, supposedly dead, inert, and quantitative rather than qualities, which are therefore morally inconsiderable and can be commodified, exploited, and extinguished without qualms.[9]

I think the current apotheosis of this program is transhumanism, that twisted neo-Gnostic hybrid of spiritual transcendence and magical thinking (promising personal immortality, no less) plus technoscientific materialism (AI, robotics, and binary code algorithms). It would be a *reductio ad absurdum* of modernity if it wasn't taken frighteningly seriously, especially by those with very big budgets. But it's not their success I fear; it's the damage resulting from their attempt.

As the accounts above by some anti-Platonic philosophers imply, there is and has been some resistance by an honorable counterhegemonic tradition. One important member is Friedrich Nietzsche (1989: 17), whose courage in calling out the metaphysical Emperor's lack of clothes can be applauded without buying into his entire philosophy. "The 'apparent' world," he proclaimed, "is the only one: the 'true' one is merely added by a lie." (Note that Nietzsche's point applies whether the putatively true world is "spiritual" or "material.") Others not so far mentioned include William James, with his emphasis on protean experience as primary, and the agonistic value-pluralism of Isaiah Berlin. Personally, I take heart from the long strange journey of Michel de Montaigne, from uncritical adherence to the Platonic practice of philosophy as merely an ascetic preparation for death to a robust and profoundly sane appreciation of life as a gift and of life's gifts, from food and sex to friendship.[10]

Make no mistake, however: these have been voices in the wilderness, proponents of a distinctly minority view. That is why in 1919, Max Weber (1991: 155) could describe "[t]he fate of our times" as "characterized by rationalization and intellectualization and, above all, by the 'disenchantment of the world.'"

But what of reverence? Weber (1991: 282) described the splitting we have been considering as the fundamental act of disenchantment, the paradigmatic way the world, including humans, become disenchanted. By implication, the world is *not* already, necessarily, or fundamentally disenchanted. The declaration that it is (notoriously by Descartes, after Plato) is again nothing other than the dark magic of modernist epistemology, which typically disguises as a disinterested description of the world what is actually an intervention intended to bring it about. In this case, enchantment is actually more-than-human nature's natural condition, and reverence, when and where possible, is the appropriate response. (Am I guilty of *tu quoque* here, or double standards? No, because my description doesn't pretend to an impossible objectivity but admits its own involvement in part-describing, part-creating its subject-object.)

Weber continues that in the historical process of the disenchantment of nature, "[t]he unity of the primitive image of the world, in which everything was concrete magic, has split into rational cognition and mastery of nature, on the one hand, and into 'mystic' experiences, on the other." And as Weber (1991: 282) added, "The inexpressible contents of such experiences remain the only possible 'beyond,'" when they can no longer be found in the sensuously perceptible world. They are therefore ecologically irrelevant at best.

So the reverence that I am going to advocate is not in any degree mystical or supernatural (literally, above nature), and its transcendence is immanent in and as the more-than-human natural world. But that is no undue restriction, because to borrow an aperçu by G. K. Chesterton (not coincidentally an acute critic of modernity), "in everything that matters, the inside is much larger than the outside" (quoted in Leys [2013: 104]).

This is where enchantment comes in. I have already mentioned some important aspects of it, but let me briefly review more of its characteristics and dynamics in terms of what Wittgenstein (2001: 27e–28e) termed its family resemblances. The experience at the heart of enchantment is sheer existential wonder, and it comes, as William James (1897: 154) noticed, "as a gift or not at all." There is no place for willing, making, or consciously doing here, so enchantment and activities like these are immiscible, like oil and water, even when they are circumstantially entangled. The appropriate attitude to it was therefore nicely summed up by Freya Stark (2013: 107) as "fearless receptivity."

This fundamental aspect of enchantment is particularly to the point because it is the precise contrary of the will to power, power-knowledge, program, and system that characterize the project of modernity, from its Platonic and earlier antecedents to its present technoscientific incarnation.

The wildness and unbiddability of enchantment are also clear in the fact that it is relational: wonder *at*, enchantment *by*. In any relationship properly so-called, no one is in charge; it is recursive, each party affecting and being affected by the other. To the extent that one party alone consistently dominates, controls, or manages the other, the result lacks wildness, which discourages this quality essential to both true relationship and the special kind thereof called enchantment.

Borrowing from Weber, and with Wittgenstein's warning against one-sided "explanations" also in mind, I have described it as concrete magic, both subjective *and* objective, material *and* spiritual or ideational, natural *and* cultural, particular *and* universal, and therefore neither solely one or the other. It is, in Henri Bortoft's excellent metaphor, "upstream" of all those separations upon which the modernist project depends (Bortoft, 2012: 103). Enchantment always takes place in a precise set of circumstances, an amalgam of concrete place (not space) and moment (not time) that are nonetheless deeply, indeed inexhaustibly mysterious or "magic." Differences and distinctions remain—they do not disappear into a mystic void—but they are crossed, connected, and transcended in the moment of relational encounter.

Enchantment therefore resists being carved up by modernist conventions according to which it must be either psychological (a state of mind) or physical, often neurophysiological (a condition of the world)—not to mention whether it is real, which they confuse with objective, or subjective, which they confuse with unreal. This is just the kind of questioning, and self-questioning, condemned by D. W. Winnicott (2005) for its destructive and specifically disenchanting effects—a point whose relevance extends well beyond psychoanalysis.

In this respect, enchantment is an ontological metonym, an intensification, an exemplar, and a lineament of life, the world, and nature itself. In other words, wonder is how we experience life when we are truest to it, which is something that happens most often in moments of enchantment. As I've said, these moments, short but deep,[11] are always relational, and what the experience reveals is the intrinsic value of the enchanting other, free from all market, utilitarian, or instrumentalist calculations—again, the very currencies of modernity. In this important respect, then, enchantment doesn't involve casting a spell or being under a spell. On the contrary, it is an awakening to reality in which a *truth* is revealed, which breaks the deadly spell of modernist banality or despair.

Now, despite their variety, humans are a particular kind of animal with many shared characteristics (and limitations). So it is not surprising that they tend to find some others particularly enchanting. Among the most frequent, or at least frequently attested, are natural beings: creatures, plants, perhaps especially trees, free-flowing water, and places; and when this happens, it is their intrinsic value to which enchantment will have opened our eyes, most likely strengthening our resistance to their appropriation or extermination. Not without reason did Tolkien (2005: 101) define enchantment as "love: that is, a love and respect for all things, 'animate' and 'inanimate,' an unpossessive love of them as 'other.'"

But enchantment is natural in another way, too. It is the kind of experience that only an embodied, embedded natural being such as ourselves can have. So in that important sense, all experiences of enchantment, even the most rarified—art, music, ideas, and so on—are fully natural. Enchantment is our birthright, so to speak, and in all its incalculable, unusable, ineffable, awkward inconvenience it is finally ineliminable for humans (and, I have no doubt, for other species as well).

As such, it is a sign of the limits of modernism and its programmatic disenchantment. In fact, natural enchantment is inherently subversive of that project, with its belief that one can (in Weber's [1991: 139] words) "master all things by calculation"—of which binary-based algorithms are of course the apotheosis—and its hubristic anthropocentric and androcentric will-driven ambition for power over nature. It is an infuriating impediment to the latter, reminding modernists that their projects cannot finally be completely realized. (Hence the hatred, fear, and mockery to which modernists subject enchantment: "superstitious," "immature," "unrealistic," mere "projection," and all the rest of the hypercritical armory.) But to ecocentrics it is a blessed affirmation of life as the ultimate value, to which no figure can be attached, and which is not for sale!

It follows that the only way the modernist project could succeed would be by replacing human beings not with an "advanced" version but with something else altogether, and not with a "managed" Earth but, again, somewhere else. And that is indeed what transhumanism ultimately envisions. The murderous seduction of a revolutionary Year Zero beckons yet again. So collective suicide and ecocide proceed together in a danse macabre.

But despite this inherent limitation, short of a fatally Pyrrhic victory over nature, the philosophy of death remains integral to the project of modernity, and the ecocidal damage it has done, still is doing, and will continue to do (unless stopped) is also incalculable. So does enchantment hold out any hope in this regard? I believe so, and we will come to that in a moment. But first I would ask you to notice a trap awaiting the unwary, no matter how idealistic and progressive. To put it bluntly, enchantment, and the reverence for nature's intrinsic value that it partly reveals and partly creates, can help only if it is not *used* to do so. For as soon as wonder is treated as a resource—part of a program, say, to "re-enchant" nature or the world—then even with the best of intentions, it has been sacrificed to the will to power and subsumed in the mind- and value-set that is a key part of the problem. From there it is a very short step to targets, outcomes, managers, corporate sponsors, Disneyworlds, and all the rest of the modern bureaucratic, calculative, and instrumentalist apparatus.

In short, we must learn to love nature *for its own sake*.

Does this consign us to passivity or quietism? Not at all. We cannot create or order wild enchantment at will, but there are things we can, indeed must, do. One is to create the conditions it favors, which encourages it to happen. Those conditions include, in this case, the opportunity to experience relatively wild nature on its own terms, including encounters with nonhuman natural others as open-ended relationships between equals, accompanied by a tacit awareness that all that lives ultimately deserves not only to be respected and protected but revered. (This of course is an ideal the realization of which will not always be possible. I am talking about the difference resulting from an ecocentric horizon, so to speak, rather than a human-centered one.)

In this context, any micromanagement and hypercontrol of such encounters, say, strongly discourages wonder. Nor will it survive unscathed from being restricted to the mediation of TV, film, and video; no matter how artfully orchestrated, there must be the opportunity for some relatively direct and therefore unmediated experience.

By the same token, we can resolve to work *with* enchantment, as between cooperating equals—to learn *from* it—and to make that a matter of principled openness. Note that in all these instances, there is something positive for the will to do; indeed, what I am advocating, whatever its field—education, art, public policy, and so on—requires a great deal of both will and skill. And notice too how it is attended throughout by humility, in significant contrast to the arrogance of the modernist project. *Will* here is, as it should be, in service of the other, not itself a bloated object of worship. (Not for nothing is the poison of Ayn Rand a staple in Silicon Valley.)

I would add that those taking the lead in helping open people's eyes to the wonder of nature—and, incidentally, the nature of wonder—must themselves love the natural world for its own sake, rather than merely being engaged in doing what they are told and ticking the box. Sometimes we are less easily fooled than we think.

The basic point is this: all the vital dimensions of enchantment—wonder, wildness, relationality, and concrete magic—are ones it shares with living more-than-human nature, and they are equally essential to both. In other words, their core qualities are held in common.[12] We could equally say that the moment and place of wild wonder takes in the "magic" ("inside") of its "concreteness" ("outside").

Thus even if it's only a glimpse, needing a much fuller exposition to become a view, I hope to have shown that enchantment exists in deep sympathy and resonance with the more-than-human natural world, including human beings, and in deep antipathy and repugnance with ecocidal modernity and its instruments.

By implication, the enchantment of and by nature, which culminates in reverence, offers a hopeful basis to resist the anthropocentric appropriation of the wild natural world, its exploitation and finally elimination—maybe to begin to roll it back—and even to help rewild it. To create, in this way, a successful countercultural movement in the direction of sanity will need a lot more than reverence alone, including scientific knowledge, public policy, political activism, and more. But I dare say that without wonder to give us the heart and courage to act, with hope or without it, then whatever else we do will fall short.

## Notes

1. For more on this subject, see Curry (2019; 2021a; 2021b) and Washington (2018).
2. Cf. Sophocles, *Antigone*, 466.
3. For an indispensable guide to this process, see Cavarero (1985).
4. For Plato's foundational antiecocentrism, see Plumwood (1997).
5. Another indispensable guide in this territory, along with Cavarero, is Plumwood (1993).
6. On this doomed but destructive struggle, see Viveiros de Castro (2004).
7. Cf. the lucid formulation of this point in Abram (1997: 67).
8. See Patterson (2002), and cf. Coetzee (1999).
9. See Curry (2019: chapters 9 and 10).
10. See Screech (2000).
11. A phrase by Etel Adnan, seen in an exhibition of her art.
12. For the next step, positing an identity between the two, see Curry (2019: 25–6), drawing on Bateson, himself drawing on Charles Saunder Peirce's "abduction."

## References

Abram, D. (1997). *The Spell of the Sensuous: Perception and Language in a More-Than-Human World*. Vintage Books.
Bateson, G. (1987). *Angels Fear: Investigation into the Nature and Meaning of the Sacred*. Rider Books.
Bortoft, H. (2012). *Taking Appearance Seriously: The Dynamic Way of Seeing in Goethe and European Thought*. Floris Books.
Cavarero, A. (1995). *In Spite of Plato: A Feminist Rewriting of Philosophy* (transl. S. Anderlini-D'Onofrio & A. O'Healy). Routledge.
Coetzee, J.M. et al. (1999). *The Lives of Animals* (ed. Amy Gutman). Princeton University Press.
Curry, P. (2019). *Enchantment: Wonder in Modern Life*. Floris Books.
Curry, P. (2021a). The experience of enchantment and the sense of wonder. *Green Letters*, 25(2), 115–29. http://www.patrickcurry.co.uk/papers/The%20Experience%20of%20Enchantment%20and%20the%20Sense%20of%20Wonder.pdf
Curry, P. (2021b). The enchantment of nature and the nature of enchantment. In L. McLoughlin (Ed.), *Honoring Nature* (pp. 142–47). Human Error Publishing. http://www.patrickcurry.co.uk/papers/The%20Enchantment%20of%20Nature%20and%20the%20Nature%20of%20Enchantment%20-%20final%20draft.pdf
James, W. (1897). *The Will to Believe and Other Essays in Popular Philosophy*. Longman.

Jonas, H. (1982). *The Phenomenon of Life.* University of Chicago Press.
Leys, S. (2013). *The Hall of Uselessness: Collected Essays.* Black Inc.
Nietzsche, F. (1989). *Twilight of the Idols* (transl. D. Large). Oxford University Press. [The author has very slightly modified the translation here.]
Patterson, C. (2002). *Eternal Treblinka: Our Treatment of Animals and the Holocaust.* Lantern Books.
Plumwood, V. (1993). *Feminism and the Mastery of Nature.* Routledge.
Plumwood, V. (1997). Prospecting for ecological gold among the Platonic forms: A response to Timothy Mahoney. *Ethics and the Environment, 2*(2), 149–68. https://www.jstor.org/stable/40338938
Plutarch (1928). *Consolatio ad Apollonium* (vol. 2 of the Loeb Classical Library edition; transl. F. C. Babbitt). Harvard University Press. https://penelope.uchicago.edu/Thayer/E/Roman/Texts/Plutarch/Moralia/Consolatio_ad_Apollonium*.html
Screech, M. A. (2000). *Montaigne and Melancholy: The Wisdom of the Essays* (2nd edition). Rowman and Littlefield.
Stark, F. (2013). *Perseus in the Wind.* I. B. Tauris.
Tolkien, J. R. R. (2005). *Smith of Wootton Major* (extended edition). V. Flieger (Ed.). HarperCollins,
Viveiros de Castro, E. (2004). Exchanging perspectives: The transformation of objects into subjects in Amerindian cosmologies. *Common Knowledge, 10*(3), 463–84.
Washington, H. (2018). *A Sense of Wonder towards Nature.* Routledge.
Weber, M. (1991). *Essays From Max Weber in Sociology.* H. H. Gerth & C. W. Mills (Eds.). Routledge.
Winnicott, D. W. (2005). *Playing and Reality.* Routledge.
Wittgenstein, L. (1979). *Notebooks, 1914–1916* (revised edition; transl. G. E. M. Anscombe). G. H. von Wright and G. E. M. Anscombe (Eds.). Basil Blackwell.
Wittgenstein, L. (2001). *Philosophical Investigations* (transl. G. E. M. Anscombe). Blackwell.

14

# There Are Gods Here Too

## For an Inhumanist Animal Aesthetics

Matthew Calarco

The ecological catastrophes that mark our age bear disproportionately adverse effects for many animals. Climate change has drastically affected the range and food supplies of many animal populations (Foden et al., 2019); wildlife suffers from astonishing levels of defaunation (Dirzo et al., 2014), and some 50 percent of animal species face possible extinction within the next 50 years (Román-Palacios & Wiens, 2020); modern transportation systems have radically fragmented animal habitats, and automobile use is responsible for the deaths of millions of animals daily (Schilthuizen, 2022); the hundreds of millions of tons of plastics that end up in landfills and oceans each year threaten countless animals with entanglement and death from ingestion (Sigler, 2014). These ongoing catastrophes are situated amid the long-standing problems that animal activists have sought tirelessly for many decades to curb: the slaughter of animals for food (which takes the lives of tens of billions of animals globally per annum); scientific and medical experiments on animals (which are responsible for the sacrifice of hundreds of millions of lives each year); and the litany of negative welfare and environmental consequences of factory farms and animal agriculture.

The established order consistently downplays and even disavows the severity of these crises and injustices. Yet, there are a growing number of people who have begun to recognize the need to address the issues at hand and to establish better and more respectful ways of living in common with our animal kin. The aim of this chapter is to explore what I take to be an essential component in this task of reconstituting human–animal relations; in particular, I aim to examine the *aesthetic* dimension that lies at the heart of an affirmative response to the crises of our age. Aesthetics is a theme that is almost wholly neglected, however, in the field of animal philosophy (the field in which I primarily work).[1] At first glance, the neglect of aesthetics in this context is understandable. In the face of the sorts of crises just mentioned, aesthetics—with its traditional focus on beauty, art, and related matters—would seem to be rather beside the point, a toothless instrument in the fight against the anthropocentric and capitalist forces that are presently obliterating animal life and ravaging the planet as a whole. The problems involving animals appear to be clearly economic, political, ethical, and legal in nature and seem to require solutions that operate at that level. If philosophy has any role to play here, surely, one might assume, it would be the more "normative" aspects of the discipline that would be most relevant and effective.

As someone who has spent much of his adult life engaged in various struggles on behalf of animals, I can readily appreciate why animal philosophers and activists gravitate toward a more explicitly normative approach. Indeed, part of what drew me to philosophy as a young person was that many contemporary philosophers took animal issues seriously and thought that philosophy had important things to offer for challenging status quo attitudes about animals. The philosophers I studied during my formative years made a strong case that the cause of the mistreatment of animals was, at bottom, ethical and that the solution to this problem lay in ethical reform. The essential thesis of this approach, articulated by such formidable philosophers as Peter Singer (2001) and Tom Regan (1983), is that nonhuman animals are, for all ethical intents and purposes, so similar to human beings that they should receive the same basic ethical consideration. To fail to extend such consideration to animals, these philosophers argue, is a form of "speciesism"—an unethical prejudice based on the dogmatic belief that the human species bears higher value than all other animal species.

Starting from these very simple premises, Singer and Regan draw truly revolutionary conclusions. Singer argues, for example, that many of our standard practices concerning animals, including consuming and experimenting on them, must be fundamentally changed; there is, he maintains, no persuasive reason for subjecting animals to painful lives on factory farms or to invasive experiments that yield only trivial results. Regan goes even further than Singer, arguing that all animals who display strong forms of subjectivity should be seen as individuals with full moral rights that protect them from unnecessary violence; as such, Regan believes we should not just reform animal-abusing institutions and practices but abolish them altogether. These ethical approaches have served as the founding principles and ideals of several national and international proanimal organizations and have inspired many theorists and activists over the past several decades.

Although I was and remain generally sympathetic to the ideals and stakes of this sort of ethical approach to animal issues, it was clear to me early on that it suffers from certain critical limitations. On the one hand, the ethical vision that motivates this work is too narrow. In taking standard notions of human ethical worth as their starting point and then enlarging those notions to include animals, this approach risks restricting the scope of ethics only to animals who are sufficiently "like us." In other words, on this approach, if a given animal or animal species does not demonstrate sufficiently robust levels of sentience or subjectivity, then they are in danger of being denied moral consideration; furthermore, this approach explicitly leaves the entire nonanimal world (plants, water, ecosystems, and so on) completely outside the scope of direct consideration and potentially reduces that world to the status of mere "resources" for human and animal use. On this issue, I was and remain on the side of environmentalists who argue that ethical concern does not stop at the border of the combined set of human beings and animals who are sufficiently "like us" but extends well beyond this limit.

Another problem with standard approaches to animal ethics is that they are largely prohibitive in nature and lack a genuinely affirmative component. If, for instance, we were to follow the logic of animal liberation (Singer) or animal rights (Regan), it is clear that we would have to restrict or eliminate the use of certain foods and medicines, and modify or abolish certain institutions. Such prohibitions and restrictions are all well and good—and, given the widespread violence directed at animals, entirely necessary. It would be better both for us and for animals to reduce and even eliminate a whole swath of common human–animal interactions. But curbing violent and unjust practices is one thing; learning to establish healthier and more loving relationships with animals is another. What is more, in a crowded world like our own, where many of our day-to-day decisions and actions have profound effects on animal life, and where animals are ubiquitous even in many spaces dominated by human beings, we have no choice but to think more carefully about establishing alternative kinds of human–animal relations.

At the same time that I was grappling with the promises and limitations of standard approaches to animal ethics, I was also learning about how theorists such as Carol Adams (2015) and Josephine Donovan (1990) bring feminist theory and politics into fuller dialogue with animal and environmental issues. By contrast with the mainstream philosophical frameworks just mentioned, these feminist approaches to animals and environmental issues place an emphasis on developing loving and caring relationships with the more-than-human world. Although justice and rights are certainly a concern in this context, such political matters are understood to be grounded in and to emerge from ethical relationships of caring for others and as a way of institutionalizing and politicizing such care as fully as possible. Here, then, I found an approach that recognized the need not just for stopping or restricting certain behaviors but also for forming new and better sorts of relationships with the wide variety of animals that inhabit the planet.

In recent years, this trend of seeking to build and institutionalize more affirmative relations with animals has led to a "political" turn in the field, headed in large part by the philosophers Sue Donaldson and Will Kymlicka (2011). In their influential work, *Zoopolis*, Donaldson and Kymlicka make a persuasive case that proanimal discourse and activism must move beyond a focus on negative rights (the sorts of restrictions and prohibitions mentioned above) and pivot toward a positive consideration of how to reconfigure human–animal relations at various levels. The chief advance in Donaldson and Kymlicka's work is their attempt to make room in political discourse for a variety of human–animal relations and responsibilities. Although their framework is not meant to be exhaustive of all such relationships, they suggest that we can begin to make better sense of our obligations if we understand our interactions as occurring with three distinct sets or kinds of animals: domesticated animals who lives with and among us; wild animals who live largely outside human communities; and liminal animals who live among us but not within human homes or institutions. And since we interact with these various kinds of animals in differing ways, they argue we need a correspondingly variable and flexible set of political categories. Employing key concepts from the framework of citizenship theory, Donaldson and Kymlicka argue that domesticated animals should be seen as full *citizens* of human communities; that wild animals should be treated as independent, *sovereign communities*; and that liminal animals should be understood as *denizens* with the rights corresponding to that class.

As admirable as this approach is (and I emphasize that I am not at all dismissive of its animating sentiments and aims), there are serious problems with its implementation. Perhaps its chief limitation is that it presupposes and ultimately reinforces the ongoing legitimacy of settler nation-states (in this instance, as arbiters of political rights for animals) in the face of long-standing challenges by Indigenous peoples who seek to maintain alternative practices of sovereignty and relations with animals, land, and other kin outside the purview of state apparatuses (Belcourt, 2014). But even in view of this limitation, it is clear from the generally positive reception by theorists and activists of Donaldson and Kymlicka's work that the proanimal movement has reached a point where serious consideration of how to reconstitute human–animal relations in a more affirmative direction is squarely on the table. The time is past in which questions concerning animals could be reduced to prohibitions and to consumer preferences in the marketplace. The political turn, along with other developments in feminist, decolonial, and critical race theoretical approaches to animal issues, have made it abundantly clear that we need fundamental structural change in order to move in the direction of more just relations with the animal world.

## For an Aesthetic Turn

What is largely missing from the field at present, though, is a fuller consideration of what it is that grounds and sustains such radical changes. I think the feminist proanimal thinkers have seen more clearly than others that a primarily theoretical and logical commitment to ethical, legal, and political rights will not suffice for the task at hand. In order to bring about the sorts of changes it will take to address the planetary-scale crises we face at present, it will be necessary to become the kinds of individuals and collectives who aim for more than just respecting animals and the more-than-human world; we must, frankly, come to care passionately for them and love them. I understand that many pragmatists in the proanimal and environmental movements think that this is asking too much of us, that we would be better off building a movement based on egocentric and anthropocentric premises and seeking out win–win strategies and policies that will simultaneously benefit both human beings and animals. It would be naive, of course, to deny that some version of this pragmatic approach to politics is necessary at present; but it would be equally naive to trust that we can work our way through the problems at hand without a genuine transformation of who we are and what we love and value most.

But how to become these sorts of impassioned people, both as individuals and as collectives? As the title of my chapter suggests, I think an "aesthetic turn" is needed in proanimal discourse and activism, a turn that takes a fundamentally "inhumanist" orientation. Although the term *inhumanist* carries several senses, I use it here to refer in a strong and direct way to the nonhuman (or what is sometimes called the "other-than-human" or "more-than-human") world. The most proximate source for this sense of the term *inhumanism* derives from the poetry of Robinson Jeffers, who uses it to name the underlying philosophical vision animating his work. Jeffers's mature poetry is aimed throughout at encouraging readers to "turn outward" toward inhuman realities and to move beyond the human narcissism characteristic of so much of contemporary culture (Jeffers 1988–2001, 2: 418). For Jeffers, our anthropocentric myopia regarding the sources of meaning and value constitutes the chief source of our contemporary psychological, social, and ecological ills.

In line with Jeffers's philosophical and poetic vision, the inhumanist approach I am sketching out here takes as its aim a fundamental conversion in our individual and collective dispositions and aesthetic sensibilities. By *aesthetic*, I have in mind the common use of the term as denoting the domains of beauty and the arts but also the etymological sense of *aisthēsis* as naming the general capacity for perception and discernment concerning matters of ultimate importance. In this sense, an inhumanist aesthetics aims at shifting our perception and attention—and, ultimately, our loyalties, loves, and entire way of life—to the beauties and majesties of more-than-human registers of existence. It is by way of the repeated practice of inhumanist modes of seeing and living that we can begin to appreciate the more-than-human world as a realm that precedes and exceeds the orbit of the human subject and its concerns. From an inhumanist perspective, the human no longer serves as the measure of things; instead, the more-than-human world itself stands as the ultimate measure and source of meaning and as the matrix in and through which human existence emerges. Inhumanist ways of seeing and living reveal that human beings and their practices are but a partial and contingent mapping of an incredibly small slice of social, planetary, and cosmic existence.

In a related vein, the environmental philosopher Brian Henning (2009) offers what he calls a *kalocentric*, or beauty-centered, orientation for thinking about our normative interactions with animals and the more-than-human world. For Henning, an aesthetic approach to social and ecological problems is grounded in a fundamentally different disposition and perspective than those on offer in either the dominant culture or in standard forms of ethical discourse. The guiding intuition behind his *kalocentric* approach (which shares much in common with Jeffers's inhumanism) is that human beings are part of a rich, beautiful whole; concomitantly, ethics can be understood as the task of trying to make any given situation, as well as things as a whole, more beautiful. On Henning's account, then, ethics is not simply a matter of my extending rights to others based on some ethically relevant similarity but rather of asking whether our actions add to or detract from "the achievement of the most beautiful whole possible in each particular situation" (Henning, 2009: 118). It is precisely this disposition and end that are at stake in adopting an aesthetic turn in animal theory and activism.

## Beyond Animal Subjectivity

So, how might an inhumanist aesthetics and disposition help reframe and reinvigorate contemporary proanimal theory and activism? I would suggest that an aesthetic turn is crucial here, first and foremost, for effecting a shift away from an almost exclusive focus in contemporary proanimal theory and activism on the subjectivity of individual animals. Whether in its traditional ethical, feminist, or political form, proanimal discourse is nearly always centered on the singularity and subjectivity of individual animals. The logic at work here is that, since the bulk of dominant normative practices and institutions are grounded in respect for individual human subjects, if it can be shown that animals are also individual subjects, this will provide a persuasive reason for extending those practices and institutions to individual animals.

Despite the undeniable effectiveness of this strategy, such a limited focus on individual animals poses serious problems. First—and I say this as someone who maintains an extremely generous opinion of the cognitive capacities and sophistication of animal life and animal cultures—it must be acknowledged that the bulk of animals on the planet fall well short of meeting the criterion for subject-standing in the ethical and legal senses commonly invoked by theorists and activists. Sentience, being a subject-of-a-life, intentionality, and self-consciousness (which are the standard sorts of criteria invoked) are certainly manifest among certain animals, but to greatly varying degrees; and the presence of such characteristics tends to shade off among many animal species to the point of being functionally nonexistent—at least from the point of view of a human observer. But we ought not conclude, as these frameworks subtly encourage us to do, that the animals who seemingly fail to exhibit a robust form of subjectivity or sense of individuality are any less remarkable or less significant. Animals can provoke wonder and be cherished in manifold ways that have nothing to do with the presence or nonpresence of subjectivity. But if we aim our gaze at them solely in view of finding fellow subjects who are "like us" in relevant ways, we will tend to miss the wild, strange, rich, and remarkable aspects of the animal world that exist beyond the bounds of subjective life.

One of the central inspirations for an inhumanist aesthetic approach to animal life of this sort is Aristotle, from whom I have borrowed the title of this chapter. Aristotle employs the phrase "there are gods here too" (Aristotle 1987: 645a) in describing a famous scene involving Heraclitus, the renowned ancient Greek philosopher. As the story goes, some admirers of Heraclitus ventured to visit him, but when they arrived at his abode, they found him simply standing there and warming himself by the fireplace. The visitors were disappointed by this initial encounter, perhaps expecting a sage like Heraclitus to be engaged in loftier, more theoretical pursuits. Sensing their disappointment, Heraclitus beckons the visitors to enter anyway, assuring them that "there are gods here too," even here in this humble room, standing here in front of this small fire, in the simple act of warming oneself.

Philosophers are fond of recounting this anecdote, as it nicely captures the ways in which philosophy seeks to return us to the myriad wonders that pervade even our mundane lives. But what is often overlooked about this passage is that it stands at the beginning of a lengthy treatise on animal life. What is it doing there? Aristotle feels the need to recall this anecdote at the outset of his discourse on animals because he wants to assure his readers that studying animals in fine-grained detail—which is what Aristotle does in the bulk of his animal philosophy—is worth their time. Aristotle is keenly aware that his readers will expect him, like the visitors expect Heraclitus, to be focused on seemingly loftier matters—affairs that are at least human in orientation, if not divine. His readers will certainly not expect him to descend into the messy realities of animal existence: the very parts of animal bodies, ordinary animal behaviors, the varied ways in which they reproduce, and so on. But this is precisely what Aristotle plans to do, he tells his readers, and he beckons them to join him regardless—for there are gods here too.

Scholars note that Aristotle's biological writings constitute some 25 percent of his existing corpus. These writings are clear testimony to his fascination with animals and to his belief that earthly, embodied existence, if studied with sufficient care, will illuminate matters essential to the philosophical life.[2] Ancient philosophy scholar Pierre Hadot (1995) suggests, and I think correctly, that Aristotle initiates a revolution in aesthetics in these writings, endeavoring to convert our attention and understanding of wonder and beauty from an exclusive focus on the eternal-heavenly ideals of order and symmetry to the messy and dynamic realities of earthly existence. To be sure, Aristotle himself is certain that a deeper order underlies the messiness of animal and earthly existence, and that persistent study of animals will eventually reveal this order. But those of us who have followed in his wake have learned that animal and earthly life, while certainly not devoid of certain kinds of order and patterns, do not always reduce to persistent structures. Animal life is irreducibly dis-organized at certain levels, filled with surprising novelty, variation, and unpredictable behaviors and relations. Developing a taste for and an appreciation of this messier side of animal life is one of the key features in learning to cherish animal life today. For when we turn, genuinely turn, our attention to the animal world, it is this strangely beautiful, unpredictable, exuberant—in a word, inhuman—world we encounter. This is a world that will never disappoint us, as long as we learn to see (with and beyond Aristotle) the remarkable beauty of its order and disorder, its organization and disorganization, its tenacity and vulnerability.

This sort of aesthetic approach to animal life is equally crucial in an era in which many animal species and much of the more-than-human world as a whole are subject to forces of degradation and are clearly in a period of decline. The problems noted at the outset of this chapter indicate that animal life and embodied existence are fragile, and that the species, behaviors, and regularities we take to be persistent structures inherent to life are anything but invariant. To the contrary, the remarkable creatures with whom we share the planet are all-too-vulnerable and all-too-exposed to the pressures of population, competition for water and food, the fragmentation of habitats, and the general loss of biodiversity. To turn our attention to animals, today, is thus to open ourselves to the fragility of exposed beings who find themselves pushed beyond their standard living range, struggling to find reliable sources of water and food, and dealing with overwhelming amounts of pollution and waste. And when we fight alongside and on behalf of our animal kin, we are not fighting simply for the integrity of individual animal subjects but for the ongoing existence of the rich, complex, and creative play of the inhuman world in all of its subjective and nonsubjective forms.

## An Aesthetics of Existence

> For what we love, we grow to it, we share its nature.
>
> —Robinson Jeffers (1988–2001)

To accomplish such a shift in perception and attention, in our ultimate loyalties and loves, it is clear that we must become something fundamentally different from who we are at present, something different from our familiar, all-too-human selves. We must, in other words, re-shape and re-form ourselves into something and someone other-than-human. Most of us have been formed since birth by the dominant culture to pursue the ideals, commodities, and routine behaviors central to a hyperconsumerist lifestyle—and it is alongside those "treasures" that our dominant sense of who we are and our "hearts lie also." While increasing numbers of people are coming to recognize the meaninglessness and unsustainability of such ideals and the emptiness and restlessness that accompanies their pursuit, such intellectual recognition often fails to bring about the sort of transformation necessary to change our lives in a fundamental way. Thus, even though we know in an abstract, intellectual sense that the ways we move, eat, clothe, shelter, heal, and entertain ourselves often have profoundly violent and deadly consequences for ourselves, other animals, and the planet as a whole, it can be hard to break the grip of these deep-seated behaviors and institute genuine alternatives.

Philosophers have, for the most part, tended to believe that rigorous arguments and critical thinking are sufficient tools for helping to wake us up to the problems in our lives and to effect the necessary changes.

The problem with this intellectualist approach, though, is that we did not arrive at our current form of life primarily through reasons or careful argumentation. It was something we picked up through repeated practice as we became acculturated to the social and economic patterns of the established order; and the habitual behaviors that we learned in this context have hardened over time into relatively stable and hard-to-unravel dispositions. We will not break these patterns of behavior solely through clear-sighted recognition of the problems at hand, critical thinking skills, and better arguments (although such things can certainly play a role in that process). Rather, we need to undertake what Michel Foucault (1985) referred to as an *aesthetics of existence*—an intentional effort to practice the art of living well, an art that involves adopting deliberate changes in our daily routines and habits—in order to become different selves with different affective and attentive orientations.

An aesthetics of existence of this sort is premised on the idea that we change our selves not primarily by changing our minds but by repeatedly *practicing* different modes of living and being attentive. And this is why a different *aisthēsis*, a different way of seeing and attending, is crucial for us today—especially if we hope to change our relations with our animal kin. In repeatedly practicing the sort of aesthetic sensibility described in the previous section, we gradually develop new ways of attending to and relating with the world and with animal life. Bit by bit, new channels of affect are opened, new passionate attachments are formed, new tastes and inclinations are established, new habits are ingrained, and new dispositions begin to emerge. Enacting such practices in a habitual manner is very different from merely recognizing at an intellectual level that some of the animals who populate the world are subjects like us and are thus deserving of equal consideration. Intellectual awareness of the latter sort is not enough to sustain a conversion in our sense of self or in our way of life toward better human–animal relations. What *does* have the potential to capture and redirect our hearts, to transform our sense of self and institute new relations, is an altogether different "treasure" from those on offer in the dominant culture: the treasure of living alongside and attending to the unbridled and inexhaustible beauty of animal existence.

In redirecting our focus beyond animals who are "like us" to the unpredictable, strange, and boundless beauty of animal existence, an inhumanist aesthetics encourages us to see the more-than-human world as opening up myriad and unanticipated possibilities for living differently and living well. Animals display enormous creativity and potentiality. They play in varied and delightful ways. They show us how to live earnestly and simply. They teach us important things about living and dying well. They expose us to surprising forms of bonding and love. They challenge us to understand friendship in new and deeper ways. They manifest remarkable strength and ethically potent forms of fragility and vulnerability. In all these ways and many others, they expand our sense of what is possible and of the forms a true and beautiful life might take. These inhuman, more-than-human realities, if we give ourselves to them as fully and persistently as possible, can impassion and enable us to become something other than who we are. The more we love our animal kin, and the more we attend to and engage with their inhuman potentials, the more *we* become *like them*.

## Notes

1. For important exceptions to this general neglect of animal aesthetics, see Brady (2014), Henning (2009), Hettinger (2010), Parsons (2007), and Rolston (1987).

2. I should note that I do not mean to imply that Aristotle's approach to animals ultimately leads him to adopt an antispeciesist or antianthropocentric attitude toward the more-than-human world. To the contrary, Aristotle's ethical and political writings consistently aim to place animals and the rest of the more-than-human world within a teleological schema that justifies their instrumental use by human beings (or, rather, by privileged classes of human beings). I discuss this other side of Aristotle's work at more length in Calarco (2015).

## References

Adams, C. J. (2015). *The Sexual Politics of Meat: A Feminist-Vegetarian Critical Theory*. Bloomsbury.

Aristotle (1987). Parts of animals. In J. L. Ackrill (Ed.), *A New Aristotle Reader*. Princeton University Press.

Belcourt, B. R. (2014). Animal bodies, colonial subjects: (Re)locating animality in decolonial thought. *Societies*, 5(1), 1–11. https://doi.org/10.3390/soc5010001

Brady, E. (2014). Aesthetic value and wild animals. In M. Drenthen & J. Keulartz (Eds.), *Environmental Aesthetics* (pp. 188–200). Fordham University Press. https://doi.org/10.1515/9780823254521-014

Calarco, M. (2015). *Thinking through Animals: Identity, Difference, Indistinction*. Stanford University Press.

Dirzo, R., Young, H. S., Galetti, M., et al. (2014). Defaunation in the Anthropocene. *Science, 345*(6195), 401–46. https://doi.org/10.1126/science.1251817

Donaldson, S., & Kymlicka, W. (2011). *Zoopolis: A Political Theory of Animal Rights*. Oxford University Press.

Donovan, J. (1990). Animal rights and feminist theory. *Signs, 15*(2), 350–75.

Foden, W. B., Young, B. E., Akçakaya, H. R., et al. (2019). Climate change vulnerability assessment of species. *WIREs Climate Change, 10*(1), e551. https://doi.org/10.1002/wcc.551

Foucault, M. (1985). *History of Sexuality, Volume 2: The Use of Pleasure*. Random House.

Hadot, P. (1995). *Philosophy as a Way of Life: Spiritual Exercises from Socrates to Foucault*. Blackwell.

Henning, B. (2009). Trusting in the "efficacy of beauty": A kalocentric approach to moral philosophy. *Ethics and the Environment, 14*(1), 101–28. https://doi.org/10.2979/ete.2009.14.1.101

Hettinger, N. (2010). Animal beauty, ethics, and environmental preservation. *Environmental Ethics, 32*(2), 115–34. https://doi.org/10.5840/enviroethics201032215

Jeffers, R. (1988–2001). *The Collected Poetry of Robinson Jeffers* (vols. 1–5). Stanford University Press.

Parsons, G. (2007). The aesthetic value of animals. *Environmental Ethics, 29*(2), 151–69. https://doi.org/10.5840/enviroethics200729218

Regan, T. (1983). *The Case for Animal Rights*. University of California Press.

Rolston III, H. (1987). Beauty and the beast: Aesthetic experience of wildlife. In D. Decker & G. Goff (Eds.), *Valuing Wildlife: Economic and Social Perspectives* (pp. 187–196). Westview Press.

Román-Palacios, C., & Wiens, J. J. (2020). Recent responses to climate change reveal the drivers of species extinction and survival. *PNAS, 117*(8), 4211–17. https://doi.org/10.1073/pnas.191300711

Schilthuizen, M. (2022, April 12). Roadkill literally "drives" some species to extinction. *Scientific American*. https://www.scientificamerican.com/article/roadkill-literally-drives-some-species-to-extinction.

Sigler, M. (2014). The effects of plastic pollution on aquatic wildlife: Current situations and future solutions. *Water, Air, & Soil Pollution, 225*, 2184. https://doi.org/10.1007/s11270-014-2184-6

Singer, P. (2001). *Animal Liberation* (3rd edition). Ecco/HarperCollins.

15

# Rediscovering Tree Sentience and Our Reverence for Life

SIMON LEADBEATER AND HELEN KOPNINA

"Nowadays" is a civilization in which the prime emblems of poetry are dishonoured. In which serpent, lion and eagle belong to the circus-tent; ox, salmon and boar to the cannery; racehorse and greyhound to the betting ring; and the sacred grove to the saw-mill.

—Robert Graves (1952: 14)

Long ago King Erysichthon decided to cut down the tallest oak in a grove sacred to the goddess of the harvest, Demeter, to use in the construction of his palace's new banqueting hall. Upon entering the grove his servants refused to fell the oak, knowing that around his base dryads—nymphs whose lives were bound to the fate of their trees—danced. Angered, the king seized an axe and struck the oak, whose pain Demeter felt. She arrived immediately to admonish the king, at first as Nicippe, priestess of the grove. Only when the king threatened her too did Demeter assume her true form and condemn him to everlasting hunger. The king's appetite became insatiable; he ate himself out of house and home, and finally consumed himself.

The story concerning the sacrilegious conduct of this mythological ruler is well-known. The significance of the oak and of the dryads—the two being indivisible, as both were understood to be sentient, possessing "the capacity to feel," is largely ignored (Harnad, 2019). Yet recognizing plant sentience can rekindle the reverence once widely felt for trees, by undoing their transformation into "senseless, bio-mechanical matter" back to the sacred beings with whom we can once more have meaningful relationships (Haberman, 2013; Abbott, 2021: 1060).

This chapter links the plight of the world's forests today to the development of Western thought. We forge what to many may seem unlikely answers, but in reality, we argue, are the only solutions, in terms of encouraging human behavioral change in response to the increasing evidence for animal—and more recently plant—sentience, and particularly that of trees. In so doing we take readers on a journey "back to the future," and along the way we relearn ancient and indigenous epistemologies within which lie true hope for renewing our reverence for nature.

## Scoping the Scale of Loss

Human activities have reduced the world's forests by one-third (Welch, 2022: 50). Ten thousand years ago forests cloaked 57 percent of Earth's habitable land—some six billion hectares. This was reduced to 38 percent—4 billion hectares—by 2018, and a full half of this reduction has occurred since 1900 (World Economic Forum, 2022). Vertiginous losses continue unabated, with one estimate suggesting that 17,500 hectares of wilderness were lost per day between 1990 and 2017, comprising mostly mangroves and tropical and subtropical forests (Carver, 2022; Carver, 2023: 93). It can hardly be a surprise to learn that almost 17,000 of the world's 58,000 known tree species are threatened with extinction (Fauna & Flora International, 2022: 34).

Remaining woodland is largely of recent origin, with (excluding Russia) only two percent of Europe's old-growth forests remaining, or, in British Columbia, three percent, and this continues to be logged (Simard, 2022; Brindley, 2022). Felling remains the main threat. For example, in the Amazon, between August 2020 and 2021, 1.3 million hectares were lost, an increase of 22 percent on the previous year (Welch, 2022). We may now, however, be approaching the point when changes in the climate become the primary peril (Welch, 2022). Wildfires in some parts of the world form a natural component of a forest's ecosystem. But fires are becoming bigger, hotter, and more frequent. Jessica Richter and colleagues have traced their development over 20 years, culminating with

2021's apocalyptic vista of forests aflame across swathes of Russia, North America, and southern Australia (Richter et al., 2022; Welch, 2022). When forests burn or old-growth stands are felled, it is not merely the loss of an assemblage of trees to mourn. All manner of life dies when trees are killed, including the one billion animals who perished in Australia's wildfires of 2019–20 (Welch, 2022). Extremely concerning are the signs that forests are beginning to lose their capacity to heal; regeneration, after what were normal cycles of fire and repair in Yellowstone, for instance, appears to have been disrupted (Welch, 2022).

The scale and range of threats stemming from two related causes—deforestation and climate change—are overwhelming, with *defaunation* an equally pressing and cognate concern. The most urgent requirements, as summed up by Jane Goodall, are "to prevent clear-cutting," to "protect our remaining old growth forests," and to deal with "these terrible fires" (Goodall, 2022). Forests across the world account for 90 percent of global terrestrial carbon storage, and felling ancient forests releases up to 65 percent of carbon also contained in the soil (Vestin et al., 2020; Simard, 2022).

## The *Intractable Quandary*

In contemporary Western thinking, discussions surrounding sentience began with a concern for animals. When extended to plants, we are invited to consider, from both a historical and a cross-cultural perspective, how trees, in particular, are viewed to have a capacity to feel. In this chapter we raise the following questions: What are the implications of recognizing plants as sentient, as recent studies urge, and what importance will this new understanding have in terms of ameliorating the exigencies highlighted above? If tree sentience is embraced, as has been remarked by Peter Wohlleben, a forester and author of the best-selling *Hidden Life of Trees*, "we would have to radically change the way we interact with them, because we'd find ourselves facing the same kinds of issues that we face with factory farming" (Wohlleben, 2021). Unlike in the case of animal products, however, there is what we term the *intractable quandary*, namely, that "we cannot survive without consuming plants" (Harnad, 2019). Yet, as Paco Calvo in *Planta Sapiens* opines, the "inconvenience and apparent 'absurdity'" of challenging this reality "is not a valid argument against" doing so (Calvo 2022: 218).

For two cardinal reasons the fate of forests, surprising as it may seem, is thoroughly entwined with our treatment of animals and understanding of sentience. First, deforestation is in large part driven by animal agriculture; since 1960, 65 percent of forests and other wild habitats have been lost to both graze and feed farm animals (Harwatt & Hayek, 2019). A global transition to a mostly plant-based diet would take us halfway to limiting climate warming to 2°C, by supporting the reforestation of areas lost to agriculture. Almost half of the UK's land, for example, is dedicated to animal agriculture, and a Harvard case study demonstrated that this could all be reforested while at the same time improving human food security (Harwatt & Hayek, 2019). Second, animal rights activists compellingly argue that we should transition away from animal-based diets because animals are sentient. According to Marc Bekoff, for instance, "[I]t's not enough to say that animals think and feel. This knowledge should affect our actions," catalyzing a "paradigm shift, one that values compassion above all" (Bekoff, 2014: 2–4). Analogously, recognizing tree sentience would not just be an intellectual leap but should catapult behavioral transformation. There may be a third additional connection associated with our concern for animals, having recognized their sentience, but we will come to that presently.

## Sacred Forest Protections in Antiquity to the Present Day

Secular attempts to protect life, while essential, are proving insufficient. If people regard wooded landscapes as sacred or spiritual, they are more likely to be protected. We revere what we hold sacred. One reason for couching natural phenomena in sacred terms, therefore, is their religious associations. Colin Tudge in *The Secret Life of Trees* suggests that the architecture of redwood and beech groves inevitably evokes comparisons with great cathedrals: "[T]he silence; the green, filtered, numinous light." Tudge goes on to state that cathedral and mosque designs emulate "innately holy" trees (Tudge, 2005). Perhaps it was David Chidester who provided the definitive religious essence of what it is to be sacred, namely, that which possesses ultimate meaning and transcendent power (Chidester, 1987). Patrick Curry, however, has stated that "there is a religious version of the sacred, but it is not the only one," offering a broader definition, as "that which is beyond human control, intrinsically valuable, wondrous and . . . not for sale" (Curry, 2011: 139).

Within this interpretive framework, we recognize sacredness in sentient personhood. Inanimate objects, unless infused with cultural significance, are not generally valued in sacred terms. But if a living being, such as a tree, can *feel*, this quality transforms a "what" into a "who," and a "who" is a person (see Haberman [2013: 155–59]). Persons are always intrinsically valuable, and selling them unthinkable.

Historically, and to this day, some trees have been and are venerated as individuals (Haberman, 2013). There was once a "ubiquity of sacred forests, trees and groves throughout the world" (Greenberg, 2015: 380). Sir James Frazer referred to the longevity of sacred groves throughout antiquity, as people vigilantly preserved particular groups of trees because they viewed them as imbued with divine significance (Frazer, 1926). Joy Greenberg, Carol Cusack, and Matthew Hall have all explored how woodland groves came to be considered sacred. Greenberg described how Artemis, daughter of Zeus and Leto, dwelt in sacred groves where wild animals enjoyed sanctuary, and that her very name may derive from the Greek for "sacred enclosure" (Greenberg, 2015). To the Celts of mainland Europe, some groves were also holy places. Cusack cited Tacitus, born around 56 CE, who observed that "reverence is paid to the grove," where Druids performed ceremonies on behalf of the community (Cusack, 1998: 253–4).

## All That Is Holy Is Profaned

We should be careful to avoid overstating the degree to which the veneration of trees preserved forests. Keith Kirby has pointed out that in Britain the Celts cleared forests as much as later invaders did, and suggests that "there is no hard evidence" for large-scale tree worship in Britain (Kirby, 2021). Across the world, however, there are illustrations of tree felling being constrained for cultural or religious reasons, and deforestation being advanced when alien cultures were imposed on indigenous peoples. Artemis's presence inhibited the "human invasion" of sacred forests, and for centuries her worship is credited with saving significant portions of the Greek landscape from deforestation (Greenberg, 2013, 2015). Helen Kopnina, referring to Frazer's *The Golden Bough*, has discussed rituals associated with the violation of tree taboos in Germany, in which, for example, "the culprit's navel was to be cut out and nailed to the part of the tree" they had accosted (Kopnina, 2016; Frazer, 1926: 9). Conversely, there is the story from northern India of Amrita Devi and her daughters, who were the first of 359 people to die while hugging trees that the local Maharaja wanted to use to burn lime for the construction of his new palace (Haberman, 2013). When the Maharaja learned of his men's actions, which had been ordered by one of his ministers, the trees were saved, and the inspiration behind the Chipko movement was born.

While evidence of tree veneration protecting forests is perhaps incomplete, the reverse impact caused by dismantling the cultural mores that revered nature has been at least partially documented. By the fourth century BCE, Plato was complaining about deforestation around Athens, but, in fact, it was his *intellectual* deracination of the sacred groves dedicated to Artemis—rendering the myths surrounding her meaningless—that desacralized them and fueled widespread tree felling (Greenberg 2013). For another example, during the time of the British Raj, trees became commercially exploited for new railway lines and shipbuilding, and these new forest policies "caused radical changes for certain segments of Indian society in their relationships with forests and trees," resulting in even more widespread deforestation (Haberman, 2013: 42). Perhaps strongest of all were the early American colonizers' antinature cultural values, iconically expressed by Puritan minister Cotton Mather in his description of the vast New England forests as being the "Devil's Land" and in need of subjugation (Haberman, 2013).

There are numerous examples evidencing that an alien, colonizing culture can instigate deforestation that otherwise, at that point in time, may not have occurred. Such historical events represent profound schisms in our relationship with nature. David Haberman insightfully illustrated how our conceptions of trees are framed by either a dualistic or monist cultural background, drawing on the work of Lynn White, Jr., and others. By *dualistic*, we mean (borrowing words from Thomas Berry) the presumption of "a radical discontinuity between the human and other modes of being," the latter "having reality and value only through their use by the human" (Berry, 1999: 4). Monism, in contrast, entails "reverence for all that exists in nature" and for "all that is alive, from plants to human species, belong[ing] to the same family" (Haberman, 2013: 43). We can trace the shift from monism to dualism as far back as Plato and Aristotle—with the invention of an anthropocentric worldview based on the great chain of being (*scala naturae*).

It was Sir Edward Tylor, in *Primitive Culture* (1871), who coined the term *animism* to revive the most ancient religious beliefs, which were generally polytheistic and recognized spirit (sentience and personality) in nonhuman lifeforms (Haberman, 2013). Tylor, in Haberman's reading of him, explicitly viewed religious beliefs in terms of historical progression, advocating a more rational, scientific basis of understanding the world. The progressive mind steadily "shifts divinity away from the natural world to ever more transcendent realms," as advanced, for example, by 19th century Christian missionaries operating in India (Haberman, 2013: 18). Lynn White's famous 1967 essay claimed that Christianity, by overthrowing paganism, made it possible to exploit nature because it instilled in people no regard for the feelings of natural objects: "The whole concept of a sacred grove is alien to Christianity," he wrote. "For nearly two millennia Christian missionaries have been chopping down sacred groves [. . .] because they assume spirit in nature" (White, 1967: 1206). A famous vignette concerning felling sacred trees is that of Boniface in eighth-century Germany, who used timber from the Geismar oak dedicated to Thor to build his church. Ultimately, trees lost much of their religious significance in Europe, with rare exceptions such as the Glastonbury Thorn—the original one having been cut down during the English Civil War of 1642–51 (Cusack, 1998).

After White's work, Haberman turns to Berry, who claimed that the "deep aversion to the natural world" began with the Great Plague of 1347–49, suggesting that, previously, the medieval period adopted a more empathetic approach to knowing nature wherein the human and natural worlds were "fundamentally akin" (Berry, 1999: 77). By the end of the 17th century, however, the Renaissance zeitgeist cast humans as the measure of all things, and a pivotal figure of this cultural arena, René Descartes, "desouled the Earth," declaring nature as inanimate and devoid of subjectivity (Berry, 1999: 78). And thus monism's configuration of nature's "single sacred community" became yoked under humankind's indomitable will through the progressive transition toward the now-hegemonic dualist worldview (Berry, 1999: 22–23).

## Dualistic Religion versus Monistic Science

Tyler's *Primitive Culture* affirmed the dualistic dichotomy between humans and nonhumans the same year as Charles Darwin's *Descent of Man* showed that "the difference in mind between man and the higher animals . . . is certainly one of degree and not of kind" (Darwin, 1871: 105). Tylor's theory of religion thus traveled in one direction at the very moment when science started to move in the opposite one. This scientific redirection toward a monist view was reinforced a century later when Jane Goodall's 1971 work, *In the Shadow of Man*, documented that humans were not the only animals to use tools. Calvo's *Planta Sapiens* makes the case for the difference between plants and animals also being a matter of degree. From the book's outset, where it is demonstrated that plants can be anesthetized in the same way as animals, he emphasizes this continuity, noting that plants and animals share "the same ancestry, springing from the same single-celled progenitor that lived billions of years ago" (Calvo, 2022: 218).

The question, then, is not whether plants are sentient and sapient but why we would assume they are not. Calvo writes that "plants exploit coordinated physiological activities [. . .] to deal with demanding environments. In a dangerous and constantly shifting world organisms must be able to respond to negative events. These events must be represented with some kind of internal state or feeling in order to *motivate* a response, which figures as [. . .] awareness" (Calvo, 2022: 188–89). Sarah Abbott also contends, without emphasizing plants' imperative of responding to threatening events, that trees, in particular, should be understood as conative entities, "deeply embedded in their own life force, purpose, and interconnections with the environment(s) they interact with as home and community" (Abbott, 2020: 224).

Having explored the erstwhile and newfound understanding of tree sentience, we now consider whether recognizing sentience will help us to rediscover trees' sacredness. To explore this further, we touch on the work of Suzanne Simard and Peter Wohlleben (who popularized Simard's research) and then circle back to Calvo's contribution.

## Simard's *Wood-Wide-Web*

Simard is a professor of forest ecology at the University of British Columbia and the author of *Finding the Mother Tree* (2021). Her earlier *Nature* publication reported the pathbreaking finding that nutrients are exchanged between Douglas fir and birch trees through fungal networks (Simard et al., 1997). Via what is now known as the *wood wide web*, "fungi extract sugars from the tree roots that they can't produce on their own, and in return, the fungi ferry water and nutrients to the tree roots, and [. . .] from tree to tree" (Banks, 2022: 18).

Simard's research moved from one revelation to another, each deepening her understanding of forest dynamics, culminating in her poetic depiction: "The old trees were the mothers of the forest. The hubs were *Mother Trees* [. . .] This Mother Tree was the central hub that the saplings and seedlings nested around, with threads of different fungal species [. . .] linking them, layer upon layer, in a strong complex web" (Simard, 2021: 228). Indeed, she explicitly confronted and overturned the dogma that competition was the only interplant interaction in forests, leading her to urge that we embrace "[a] philosophy of treating the world's creatures, its gifts, as of equal importance to us. This begins by recognizing that trees and plants have agency. They perceive, relate and communicate [. . .] They co-operate, make decisions, learn, and remember—qualities we normally ascribe to sentience, wisdom, intelligence. By noting how trees, animals and even fungi—any and all nonhuman species—have this agency, we can acknowledge that they deserve as much regard as we accord ourselves" (Simard, 2021: 294). Among the follow-ups to her work is the Mother Tree Project, involving nine experimental forests that retain their mother trees in order to investigate "which combinations of harvesting and planting will be most resilient to the stresses our planet is facing, [and] how the healthiest connections can thrive alongside our needs to use resources from the forest" (Simard, 2021: 304).

## Farming in All but Name

We must now reflect carefully on the limitations of what this leading proponent of plant sentience is telling us. The "Mother Tree" trope is apposite as mother trees recognize their offspring and nurture and care for them. But then Simard, perhaps unable to overcome the industry mindset in which she had grown up and progressed in her career, forsook her metaphor. She illuminated previously unseen intricacies of subterranean forest life and their myriad of relationships but dimmed the lights when it came to harvesting mother tree *children*.

Wohlleben practices what Simard teaches in his management of 3,000 acres of German woodland, by selectively felling trees and extracting them using horses rather than heavy machinery. So that "old trees can fulfil their destinies," 5 to 10 percent of forest areas are completely protected, which implies that 90 percent or more of trees can presumably be legitimately harvested or at least be in the harvesting zone (Wohlleben, 2016: 243). Wohlleben regards trees as making friends and communicating with one another, learning, and screaming in drought conditions. He repeatedly refers to trees feeling pain. Given all of this evidence, the question that for us shouts from the pages of *The Hidden Life of Trees* is this: rather than treating trees better but still *killing* them (Wohlleben's term), should we be killing them at all?

Considerable emphasis should rightly be placed on halting clear-cutting and protecting old-growth forests, which Simard strongly advocates. These recommendations, however, on their own, are not commensurate with the severity of the crisis afflicting the world's forests. These researchers dared us to think the unthinkable, that plants are sentient beings; but with this revolutionary thought, they conclude that while we should treat plants well, we can still utilize them for human benefit in ways that entail their deaths. Calvo agreed, indicating that plants should be treated ethically—taking his cue, oddly, from the procurement policies for meat, dairy, and eggs of an airline that he flew with in 2016 (Calvo, 2022). Simard, Wohlleben, and Calvo all advocate the equivalent of free-range animal agriculture over factory farming, thereby retaining the dualistic ideology that extols human entitlement over the rest of the natural world. Is this because of the intractable quandary? We need to consume plants—there is no alternative! The ethical challenge, however, remains: "what we do with what we know, and how we act" (Bekoff, 2023: 324).

This brings us back to those cardinal reasons in which the fate of forests is inextricably linked to our treatment of animals and our understanding of their sentience, and we earlier alluded to a third connection to reflect upon. We suggest that it is these authors' *phytocentric* predilections that preclude them from reaching conclusions consistent with their science. Calvo bemoaned the zoocentric bias we all grow up with, but had he begun thinking about sentience through the lens of animal suffering, perhaps he (as well as Simard and Wohlleben) would have recommended more fundamental changes in our relationship with plants other than to treat them better yet still farm them (Calvo, 2022). It appears, instead, that they gave little thought to animal suffering; Calvo's reliance on the policy of an airline he happened to be traveling on seems a somewhat flimsy approach to the whole issue, one especially incongruous in a book asking searching questions about plant sentience and the implications that this has for our relations with plants. Our starting point when thinking about sentience, in contrast, is animals, with a zoocentric bias perhaps. Yet in so doing we concur with Bekoff that "it's not enough to say that animals think and feel. This knowledge should affect our actions" (Bekoff, 2014: 2–3).

The arc of moral consideration has now widened to include plants, and our specific focus here—trees. The position our three plant sentience authors take would be inconceivable for Bekoff, as it is for us. However difficult or "absurd" our position, as Calvo put it, that is the inescapable quandary that faces us. What, then, is to be done? How must we change in response?

## Ancient Ways for Modern Living

It is not a leap to conclude that the bottomless hunger visited upon Erysichthon is mirrored in our perpetual drive for economic growth, which, if unchecked in what E. O. Wilson termed its "extensive" form, will inexorably lead to the extirpation of forests as we know them, not simply through felling but also human-driven pestilence, disease, fire, drought, and defaunation, with incalculable consequences for all Earth's inhabitants (Wilson, 2016). Slowing the spread and intensity of forest fires depends on humanity's willingness to switch to predominantly plant-based diets, while simultaneously adopting other measures to combat greenhouse gas emissions. It is wholly consistent to suggest that eating more plants is a way of aiding Earth's trees (Hall, 2011). A global transition to plant-based diets could reduce the amount of land needed to grow food by more than 75 percent, helping to preserve existing forests and treescapes, and to reforest and afforest on a scale proportionate with the climate and extinction crises. Eliminating animal agriculture completely would release an area of land the equivalent in size to Africa, some three billion hectares, providing enough land to return forests from the current four billion to their preindustrial level of six billion hectares (Poore and Nemecek, 2018).

The question, however, then becomes whether this necessary transition would simply substitute the suffering of animals for the suffering of plant beings. Indigenous epistemologies recognize "ancient ways of knowing" across different cultures and continents, Western and non-Western traditions, and proffer a new way of being with plants that speaks to the quandary we are addressing (Abbott, 2021). The 2,500-year-old Jain religion implicitly acknowledges the sentience of plants, eschewing the consumption of root and similar vegetables; the spiritual stance of the Jains is echoed by the Plant Initiative (founded in 2020), which advocates a diet focusing on fruits and seeds rather than whole plants (see https://

plantinitiative.org/act). Diet is central to the Jain principle of *ahimsa*, a philosophy of nonviolence, and demonstrates that the bulk of our plant consumption—the food we eat—need not entail harming plants or animals. What's more, analogue materials, such as non-wood-based paper, is already marketed. The Japanese form of forestry, *Daisugi*, and European traditions of coppicing (harvesting branches at ground level for wood fuel or construction materials) and pollarding (cutting branches above browsing height) can extend tree lives by centuries rather than killing them. The "intractability" of the quandary, therefore, is not one of principle but rather of process and scale.

## Restoring the Sacred to Forest Groves

Western thought's trajectory, from ancient philosophers desacralizing groves to the displacement of animist cultures with human–nature dualism, succeeded in converting nature "from a subject to be revered to an object to be used" (Simkins, 2017: 222). The human chauvinism inherent in the dualistic division between humankind and nature began to be unraveled by Darwin, and has been further deconstructed by ethologists such as Bekoff and Goodall (Kopnina, 2016). Disappointingly, the pioneering plant scientists discussed, though demonstrating plant sentience and more—in some respects with animal sentience being their benchmark—ultimately uphold human–nonhuman "radical discontinuity." They refuse to abandon the utilitarian value of nonhuman beings, seemingly unable to break away from the human supremacist paradigm.

Trees have been—and, in part, continue to be—revered as the abodes for, or embodiments of, incorporeal entities. We wonder whether the basis of this belief is that the architecture of an old-growth forest carries the aura of a numinous presence, just as ancient temples did. At the same time, there is the tantalizing thought that our forebears' cognizance of tree sentience was given expression through their belief in dryads within a pagan cultural landscape. However, learning that trees are sentient in the modern scientific sense—that they are not "senseless bio-mechanical matter"—changes everything. From a mere collection of alive statuesque objects, trees come to form a congress of persons, and, as such, become sacred. We revere what we hold sacred, and reverence, at its heart, recognizes value beyond utility.

Life's diminishment, as exemplified by the depletion of forests and burgeoning forest fires across the globe, can be couched in terms of a long-standing conflict, wherein an objectified nature forms the "footholds" for one dominant species climbing ever onward alone, bereft of companionship, ultimately destroying itself alongside the myriad of lifeforms falling prey to its rapacious appetite. Let us, instead, embark on a holy quest alongside our earthly relations, all of us belonging to the same sacred family, to live in accordance with what Albert Schweitzer called "reverence for life" (Berry, 1999). Implementing this ethic, as Schweitzer recognized, is not immune from practical challenges, but demolishes the "hierarchy that place[d] humanity at the top of a pyramid of descending moral worth" (Barsam, 2005: 1493). Overturning the dualistic ideology central to human supremacy, therefore, and replacing it with an ecocentric ethic of unity, is key to recognizing what the intractable quandary *really* is: namely, an excuse for avoiding difficult questions and not embracing necessary change.

In closing, the corollaries to our argument are clear. First and foremost, we believe, there is a need for a mass switch to predominantly plant-based diets, in order to eliminate the suffering that animal agriculture causes, but, importantly, to also reduce greenhouse gas emissions and free up land for reforestation. Second, landscapes dedicated to the return of the forest should, in line with the true principles of rewilding, be set aside and left to age naturally, unmanaged (Leadbeater et al., 2023). Among the reasons for this are that old trees embedded within wild nature sequester carbon most effectively (Crane, 2020). Together these two measures will help ameliorate the climate crisis *and* create more habitat. Third, traditional forms of product harvesting, such as coppicing in place of clear-felling, need to be revived, perhaps adjacent to, but separate from, newly created forest landscapes and preserved old ones. Fourth, a move toward consuming more of the *fruiting* components of plants to reduce plant suffering and mortality should, we feel, be the next step. These changes will only ever be implemented earnestly and at the necessary scale, however, if the dualistic resource paradigm is "dethroned," if an ethic of unity is restored, and if reverence returns. Upon this, all of Earth's life is ultimately contingent.[1]

## Notes

1. Dedication: We dedicate this chapter to Professor Marc Bekoff, whose eclectic curiosity began with pioneering ethological research and now encompasses plant sentience and sapience. His inspiration over many years provides the golden thread guiding our chapter's invocation for a future predicated on reverence for

all life. We must not only learn about the rich lives of animals and plants but also act upon our discoveries. As Marc writes in his revised and updated *The Emotional Lives of Animals* (2024, "It is painful to acknowledge when we've caused harm, but the only solution is change" (Bekoff, 2024: 5).

Acknowledgments: The authors would like to thank Dr. Sarah Abbott, whose writings and online conversations have provided much of the background underpinning this chapter, and Paul Moss of the Plant Initiative, for commenting on an early draft.

# References

Abbot, S. (2020). Filming with nonhumans. In P. Vannini (Ed.), *The Routledge International Handbook of Ethnographic Film and Video* (pp. 224–33). Routledge.

Abbott, S. (2021). Approaching nonhuman ontologies: Trees, communication, and qualitative inquiry. *Qualitative Enquiry, 27*, 1059–71. https://doi.org/10.1177/1077800421994954

Banks, K. (2022). The "wood-wide-web" explained. *National Geographic*, May, 18.

Barsam, A. (2005). Schweitzer, Albert (1875–1965). In B. Taylor (Ed.), *The Encyclopedia of Religion and Nature*. Thoemmes Continuum.

Bekoff, M. (2014). *Rewilding Our Hearts: Building Pathways of Compassion and Coexistence*. New World Library.

Bekoff, M. (2023). Rewilding from the inside out: A personal commitment to other animals and their homes during the anthropause and afterwards. In S. Hawkins, I. Convery, S. Carver, & R. Beyers (Eds.), *Routledge Handbook of Rewilding* (pp. 320–26). Routledge. https://doi.org/10.4324/9781003097822

Bekoff, M. (2024). *The Emotional Lives of Animals: A Leading Scientist Explores Animal Joy, Sorrow, and Empathy—And Why They Matter* (Rev. ed.). New World Library.

Berry, T. (1999). *The Great Work: Our Way into the Future*. Bell Tower.

Brindley, D. (2022). Forests, for life. *National Geographic*, May, 4–5.

Calvo, P. (2022). *Planta Sapiens: Unmasking Plant Intelligence*. Bridge Street Press.

Carver, S. (2022). Personal communication, December 2.

Carver, S. (2023). Mapping wildness and opportunities for rewilding. In S. Hawkins, I. Convery, S. Carver, & R. Beyers (Eds.), *Routledge Handbook of Rewilding* (pp. 92–102). Routledge. https://doi.org/10.4324/9781003097822

Chidester, D. (1987). *Patterns of Action: Religion and Ethics in a Comparative Perspective*. Wadsworth.

Crane, E. (2020). *Woodlands for Climate and Nature: A Review of Woodland Planting and Management Approaches in the UK for Climate Change Mitigation and Biodiversity Conservation*. Royal Society for the Protection of Birds.

Curry, P. (2011). *Ecological Ethics: An Introduction*. Polity Press.

Cusack, C. (1998). Sacred groves and holy trees. In M. Griffith & J. Tulip (Eds.), *Spirit of Place: Source of the Sacred?* (pp. 252–61). Centre for Studies in Religion, Literature and the Arts.

Darwin, C. R. (1871). *The Descent of Man, and Selection in Relation to Sex*. John Murray.

Fauna & Flora International (2022). Tree amigos. *&FFI*, 4, 34–38.

Frazer, J. G. (1926). *The Golden Bough: A Study in Magic and Religion* (Part 1). Macmillan.

Graves, R. (1952). *The White Goddess: A Historical Grammar of Poetic Myth*. Faber and Faber.

Goodall, J. (1971). *In the Shadow of Man*. Weidenfeld and Nicolson.

Goodall, J. (2022). Personal communication, July 15.

Greenberg, J. H. (2013). Avatar and Artemis: Indigenous narratives as neo-romantic environmental ethics. In B. Taylor (Ed.), *Avatar and Nature Spirituality* (pp. 201–19). Wilfrid Laurier University Press.

Greenberg, J. H. (2015). From sacred grove to dark wood to re-enchanted forest (part I): The evolution of arborphilia as neo-romantic environmental ethics. *Journal for the Study of Religion, Nature and Culture*, 9, 376–413. https://doi.org/10.1558/jsrnc.v9i4.28905

Haberman, D. L. (2013). *People Trees: Worship of Trees in Northern India*. Oxford University Press.

Hall, M. (2011). *Plants as Persons: A Philosophical Botany*. State University of New York Press.

Harnad, S. (2019). Personal communication, April 27.

Harwatt, H., & Hayek, M. N. (2019). *Eating Away at Climate Change with Negative Emissions*. Harvard Law School. https://animal.law.harvard.edu/wp-content/uploads/Eating-Away-at-Climate-Change-with-Negative-Emissions--Harwatt-Hayek.pdf

Kirby, K. (2021, June 18). *A Long Relationship: Humans and Oaks in Britain* [Online presentation].

Kopnina, H. (2016). Nobody likes dichotomies (but sometimes you need them). *Anthropological Forum*, 26, 415–29. https://doi.org/10.1080/00664677.2016.1243515

Leadbeater, S., Kopnina, H., & Cryer, P. (2023). Knepp wildland: The ethos and efficacy of Britain's first private rewilding project. In S. Hawkins, I. Convery, S. Carver, & R. Beyers (Eds.), *Routledge Handbook of Rewilding* (pp. 362–73). Routledge. https://doi.org/10.4324/9781003097822

Poore, J., & Nemecek, T. (2018). Reducing food's environmental impacts through producers and consumers. *Science*, 360, 987–92. https://www.science.org/doi/10.1126/science.aaq0216

Richter, J., MacCarthy, J., Weisse, M., & Tyukavina, S. (2022, August 17). Two decades of fire-driven loss in unprecedented detail. *Global Forest*

*Watch*. https://www.globalforestwatch.org/blog/data-and-research/trends-tree-loss-from-fires-unprecedented-detail/

Simard, S. (2021). *Finding the Mother Tree: Uncovering the Wisdom and Intelligence of the Forest*. Allen Lane.

Simard, S. W. (2022). Lives depend on forests. *National Geographic*, May, 15–20.

Simard, S. W., Perry, D. A., Jones, M. D., et al. (1997). Net transfer of carbon between ectomycorrhizal tree species in the field. *Nature, 388*, 579–82. https://doi.org/10.1038/41557

Simkins, R. A. (2017). The Bible, religion, and the environment. In H. Kopnina & E. Shoreman-Ouimet (Eds.), *Routledge Handbook of Environmental Anthropology* (pp. 222–35). Routledge. https://doi.org/10.4324/9781315768946

Tudge, C. (2005). *The Secret Life of Trees: How They Live and Why They Matter*. Allen Lane

Tylor, E. (1871). *Primitive Culture*. John Murray.

Vestin, P., Mölder, M., Kljun, N., et al. (2020). Impacts of clear-cutting of a boreal forest on carbon dioxide, methane and nitrous oxide fluxes. *Forests, 11*, 961. https://doi.org/10.3390/f11090961

Welch, C. (2022). The future of forests. *National Geographic*, May, 34–73.

White, L. T. (1967). The historical roots of our ecological crisis. *Science, 155*, 1203–7. https://doi.org/10.1126/science.155.3767.1203

Wilson, E. O. (2016). *Half-Earth: Our Planet's Fight for Life*. Liveright.

Wohlleben, P. (2016). *The Hidden Life of Trees: What They Feel, How They Communicate—Discoveries from a Secret World*. Greystone Books.

Wohlleben, P. (2021, July 21). Plants feel pain and might even see: It's time to retire the hierarchical classification of living things. *Nautilus*. https://nautil.us/plants-feel-pain-and-might-even-see-9869/

World Economic Forum (2022). Here's how the earth's forests have changed since the last ice age. https://www.weforum.org/agenda/2022/04/forests-ice-age/

# 16

# Seeking Ecosocial Cultural Change

## Boldly Going beyond Nature Deficit Disorder

SEAN BLENKINSOP

As much as I would like to be able to present in this chapter a comprehensive vision for how society can work to counter nature deficit disorder (NDD), I don't believe that we yet know what this "new" society might look like, nor do we have enough depth of understanding on why NDD exists. What I can offer instead, however, is a series of vignettes drawn from years of trying to "ecologize" public education on the west coast of what is now called Canada. I have chosen vignettes as a way into the discussion for a series of reasons.

First, as stories, they are inviting for the reader and take us into the work at the level of grounded shared experiences. In so doing, the vignettes open space for a wider range of interpretations and let the complexities, paradoxes, and blurry complications exist in a fullness and unresolvedness that more traditional systematic argumentation, particularly that which seeks resolution—the definitive answer—does not. Second, although I don't have answers, I do, in a hermeneutical sense, have moments of provocation and intellectual disturbance of which I can't let go. The persistence and shared commonality of these stories that recycle and reappear in my thinking suggest there is something here of importance that deserves attention and serious consideration. And third, given that this chapter is intended not to present a solution but to be provocative and at least a touch hopeful, it makes sense to place real stories of the possible and of the incomplete—in the *muddle* of it all—at its heart.

I invite you, then, to join this journey as we provoke and possibly inspire a field, education, and an environmental conversation, NDD and cultural change, to reexamine the "solutions" that have been arrived at (and, quite possibly, become too easily relied upon). This provocation seeks to challenge educators, parents, caregivers, and the larger community to step into a set of problems, with regard to the modern Western cultural relationship with the natural world, that are more complex than we have been led to expect. At the same time—to reinforce a point made above—I aim to open discussions through real examples from real schools that are hopeful, that encourage the desire to respond, and that come with a sense of possibility for change. This change, which exists within the realm of achievability, is one that aims for a more ecosocially just and flourishing world.

Since it first appeared in the general lexicon, Louv's concept of nature deficit disorder (2008) has been bandied usefully about. It has challenged and encouraged educators, parents, and caregivers alike to get their charges outside more often in the hopes of moving them toward deeper, more committed, and caring relationships with the more-than-human world. And yet, after almost fifteen years, we might be hard-pressed to say that things have really changed for the better. Now, an argument can be made that without this work (and the years of environmental education, natural history projects, stewardship and conversation work, and simple close-to-the-land living that have happened before and alongside) things could have been much worse. But it is a hard argument to make convincingly, and even if it is convincing, that doesn't really help the planet today. At least, I suppose, we can say that we are burning up and slipping beneath the waters while still fighting.

What, however, if the challenge to overcoming NDD is more than just rectifying the "deficit" of nature connection between singular human individuals and their burbling, twittering, pacing, and budding locales and locals? What if the separation is in fact merely a small piece of a very wicked problem? What if the disorder that Louv is pointing to is baked into a cultural way of being in the world? And what if it is not even seen as a disorder by some? What if we take this problem of cultural-level NDD seriously? What might public educators and education writ large do in response? And how does education become part of the solution rather than a furtherance of the problem?

All this is too much to argue for, to respond to, and to cogently shape into a discussion in the space of this chapter—even if we knew with clarity where we needed to be heading—but I can begin, in the aforementioned vignettes, to offer some hints at useful paths to explore. The stories are real, and together they form the principal narrative arc for this chapter. This is an arc that opens well, that runs into potentially ruinous challenges, and that ends not quite *happily ever after* but at least with an indication that there might be *hopeful possibilities ever after*. Each vignette offers an unexpected gift: nature as coteacher; nature as colonized; and nature as supporting the cultural change we need along the road. The stories also open a discussion into three important domains for considering cultural change: the relational, the critical, and the existential. It is certainly a worthy aim to extend discussion of NDD into the realm of cultural change and to think about the potential of educators as activists, advocates, and allies in the work of achieving ecosocial justice.

## Nature as Coteacher

Here is the first of the vignettes that I shall present, drawing on our research:

> *Almost thirteen years ago a little group of us, teachers and researchers, gathered to discuss what we might do in response to a deep sense that public education wasn't working in British Columbia, Canada (and with likely parallels in other places). It wasn't working for the students, the teachers, or their communities, and it definitely wasn't working for the natural world. Our sense was that school had adopted the alienated, individualized, speciesist motifs that Louv outlines. In fact, education was immersed in the consumptive, colonial, capitalist culture that was dangerously unjust both socially and ecologically. To put it bluntly, public education was implicitly anti-environment, furthering the separation between humans and "all-our-relations" (Laduke, 2008), because the culture out of which education arises and the one that it seeks to prepare the young for is the same. Thus, the project was to try to create a public elementary school where we might critique, and hopefully change, education all the way down. The result was the Maple Ridge Environmental School.*[1] *This story comes from there.*

*An important component from the get-go of this K–7 school (one for children, typically, up to the age of 12 or 13 years) was to have no school building at all. Our theory was that the physical structure of the school shaped expectations and enforced limits to change. Further, if being outside is crucial for change, then why not. During the first two years there were researchers present every day, gathering data, helping with teaching and safety, and just being part of this dynamic community and culture. And it wasn't long before encounters between students and the natural world began to unfold that we felt were positive and deeply interesting. Below is a slice of conversation between one of the researchers and a nine-year-old student who chose the nature name "Raven."*

*Raven is asked what it is like to listen to the natural world after she mentions that she feels like she can talk to plants . . .*

*Researcher: So do you hear the plant?*

*Raven: Yeah, but you have to hear it through your heart.*

*Researcher: I was going to ask where you hear it . . . do you hear it in your heart?*

*Raven: Little words curl into your mind. You have to know that you're not thinking.*

*Another day the researcher asks Raven again what the process of listening to the natural world is like for her . . .*

*Raven: This sounds funny, you're focused on something but you're not actually thinking about it. If you're thinking then you're not really listening. See, I can't do it now when I'm talking.*

*Researcher: Do you feel like you have "conversations" with the natural world?*

*Raven: It's not exactly like that, it's not "speaking," it's more like energy or signals. You don't hear it out loud. It's something that your mind, and only your mind, can understand because nature is that open to any language. So, if you were just thinking, not even in your language, just showing pictures, it would still work.*

*Researcher: The conversation you mean?*

*Raven: Yes, it doesn't have to be "speaking."*

*Researcher: So you mentioned "energies" and "signals." What did you mean by that?*

> *Raven: Well, see, you speak your way, they speak different ways, like thousands of different ways. Billions. It's like the birds with those signals, like when you see a bird flapping up in the sky and a flock of birds, how they all move at the same time, it's because they tell each other like through mental speaking.*[2]

This understanding of the natural world as having agency, as being able to communicate, and as having intrinsic worth was not an unusual phenomenon in our early work, and it was one that not only inspired us but filled us with awe. Bear in mind that this was a nine-year-old, who was quite aware that she was describing something culturally unusual, and who was doing her best to describe a difficult-to-enunciate literal encounter. This was not a metaphorical description of time spent in the forest. This also suggested to us that Raven was immersed in a deeply educational relationship, that the natural world was teaching her and offering gifts that "curled" into her mind.

Witnessing and interviewing students like Raven pushed us, as educators and researchers, toward two important further considerations. The first was framed as nature as coteacher (Blenkinsop & Beeman, 2010; Jickling et al., 2018). Raven's experiences made clear that the natural world was more than simply a backdrop for rich educational experiences. Rather, it was full of myriad agential communicating beings. Furthermore, if given mental space and careful listening, these beings were able to be teachers. To draw on the work of Robin Wall Kimmerer (2013), we can see Salmon and Cedar, say, as holders and sharers of knowledge who gift insights to human learners in "thousands of different ways." For the students, this learning from nonhuman beings was more than a simple experiential encounter with "hot" sun and "cold" water. It was a way of knowing that arose organically in the shared space between the human mind and the interlocutor with which they were in relation at the time (Sheridan & Longboat, 2006).

Intriguingly for educational theorists and environmental philosophers, this discussion points in several ecologically important directions. There is the decentering of the human teacher, who loses their status as the holder of all knowledge, the designer of all curricula, or the producer of all outcomes. This is a push against the problem of anthropocentrism and an epistemological challenge that questions human elitism. For knowledge understood in this way becomes shared, dispersed beyond human holding, and ever incomplete. There are too many knowers, from too many positions, for any single being, or species even, to "know it all."

A second important consideration, which several students, including Raven, made us aware of, was the pressure of culture and community beyond the school. They were being pressed to not know, to cease listening, and to stop opening themselves up to the natural world. Students found themselves being talked down to and being positioned as weird or quaint. They were told "The natural world can't speak" and "You will grow out of this." They were also being asked, in both subtle and not so subtle ways, to choose between belonging to the mainstream and staying connected with the more authentic, kin-filled relationality that they were experiencing. As we reflected on this cultural push in our own lives, and in the adult lives of our admittedly nature-loving friends, we recognized the effects of this same force on us. In many ways students like Raven were leading the way for us in terms of thinking about and experiencing relationality. We were in equal parts envious and disbelieving of these students, and this opened the desire to consider and seek out practices that might bridge the kind of separation that is fostered and maintained by our settler culture, while finding ways of being more eco-relationally able adults in this antiecological climate. We went as far as thinking about the need to recover an ecological birthright drummed out of us by a colonial, violent, and destructive worldly orientation. And it is to the darkness of this cultural pressure that our story now turns.

## Nature as Colonized

The narrative continues with this second vignette:

> *One of the first things we did with the curriculum at the Maple Ridge Environmental School followed Sobel's work on the need of children to have free play and the opportunity to build dens, huts, and even communities (Sobel, 2001). We thus allowed the students time every day in a particular place in the forest (for remember: this was education without buildings, where the students were outside all the time, whatever the weather), and during this time they could create their village and immerse themselves in rich, extendable, and ongoing imaginative place-based play.*

*They were experimenting with how to be in the world, cultivating deep connections to place and nonhuman others.*

*A lot of things happened over the course of the first few months: we saw incredible skills being developed, we involved ourselves when particular areas began to be denuded of natural materials, and we helped negotiate space for other ideas to emerge. For the most part, though, the children were left, immersed in the forest, to their own devices. We assumed—somewhat naively upon reflection—that this process would allow relationships to build, that the natural world would be heard and would do some teaching, and that maybe Louv's deficit would be overcome or at least lessened. However, we saw something different begin to appear.*

*By about four months, the village had begun to organize itself along autocratic lines. One of the older boys (a student aged 12) had appointed himself ruler and gathered a posse of other boys as enforcers of that leadership. Three prisons were created (there were only 88 children at this point, so that is a lot of incarceration), a casino was opened, and a whole economic system arose that was built on scarcity and hoarding (rope and wood became the tender, for it is hard to build anything without either). Children were forced into this play or incarcerated, and a clear and quite ruthlessly protected hierarchy was formed. At this point we actively intervened and began the process of opening space for other ideas, for other ways of being and playing in this village, and for other means of governing, caring for, and involving the natural world. But the experience struck us deeply as researchers, educators, and cultural beings.*

Our sense of this experience is that the children were, quite logically, using the tools of their experienced culture as the imaginative building blocks of their play. The voice of the natural world was, for the most part, drowned out. It simply wasn't present enough to change the narrative of the village. And, as we worked with the students, it became apparent that we too had to do a lot of mental work if we were going to rethink culture, even at an imaginative level. A key point here is that overcoming NDD was, in our example, much more complex than just allowing children to spend more time in the natural world and trying to facilitate relationship-building exercises. We had to engage ourselves in the project of seeing the limitations of our cultural imagination and then find ways to go beyond these (Jickling & Blenkinsop, 2020). As a result of that experience—and with much thinking, experimenting, teaching, and struggling—we came to a realization that there is a series of stubborn blockages that need considering if we are truly going to support a shift of modern Western culture and its children, through the domain of education, away from instrumental, anthropocentric, and alienated relationship with the larger world. In our experience, the process of recognizing and seeking to respond to these blockages has opened rich and hopeful avenues for change; in other words, all is not lost. One of the challenges that we identified was the deep-seated colonial orientation to the world, human and natural. And in naming nature as colonized we found partners in critical race theory, gender studies, activism, and other theories and practices focused on deep change. This actually made it easier for us to think about ideas, such as human-teachers as activists, which I explore a little later, and then find ways to act (Blenkinsop et al., 2021).

Following a careful reading of Albert Memmi's classic anticolonial text *The Colonizer and the Colonized* (1991)—and drawing on previous work (Blenkinsop et al., 2017a; Blenkinsop et al., 2017b)—we identified key themes and compared them to modern Western cultural relations in, with, and to the natural world. Even that framing of the "natural world" is a troublesome colonial move, as Memmi points out. Memmi was from Tunisia, and, in Africa, the colonizers tended to place all the peoples of the continent in a single category—Africans—thereby actively ignoring the diversity and particularity that exists. This allowed the colonizers to "manufacture" the other, positioning them in whatever ways worked best for the colonial project, freezing the colonized in historical time, ignoring their voice, and appointing the colonizer as the expert. In this way they could write a marginalizing, degrading, and manipulative narrative for the continent while positioning themselves, the colonizers, as the civilizing, advanced, caring, and superior overseers of everyone and everything. And one would be hard-pressed to deny just how forcibly that has been applied, in parallel, to the diverse, changeable, self-governing, polyvocal mystery of those burbling, buzzing, bleating, and bouncing beings beyond the human.

In our work we named five key characteristics identified by Memmi as being part of the weaponry of the colonizer's practice. For our purposes here, two will be enough. The first, as discussed above, is the manufacture of the colonial other, which involves the construction, by the colonizer alone, of "self-sustaining and syncretic systems, be they economic, political, or judicial, that support and constantly reaffirm a colonial relation" (Blenkinsop et al., 2017a: 354). This puts control into the hands of the colonizer and also works as a kind of twisted justification for the colonization. The second characteristic is alienation. Here Memmi points toward a two-step approach, which involves exceptionality and then centering. The colonizer focuses on particular attributes (e.g., the arts, science, or the rule of law) that are deemed to be important and in the possession of the colonizer but "lacking" in the colonized.

These attributes position the colonizer, without consultation, as exceptional in relation to the colonized, which is often then used as a justification for the centering of all the colonial ways of being. Thus, the colonized are made voiceless and removed from history (for they are not allowed to either rebut or change the colonizer's writings), and they are positioned as being on the margins and of a lesser status. In turn, these manufactured false descriptions of the colonized are made "true" by the colonizer, with no room for critique. This process of normalization then becomes the justification for ongoing colonization in a kind of sick closed loop. Again, this seems quite apparent in some cultural orientations to the natural world, as has been well critiqued. For this is the anthropocentrism, human elitism, and alienation that so many see as problematic. Nature is made voiceless, singular, and monolithic, and rendered *lesser than*; and understanding it is within the purview of humans alone (Plumwood, 2002). Gaining knowledge of any part of nature can happen through whatever means is deemed permissible, be it extractive, manipulative, or violent.

Making this move—naming the natural world as colonized—had a cascade of results. First, it challenged us as educators and researchers to see ourselves as activists and advocates. No longer "protected" by the myth of neutrality, we were challenged to be more critical of our own educative practices and assumptions and those of education as an endeavor. Second, we were pressed to position ourselves and our work as being explicitly oriented to justice, both social and ecological. Third, we had to recognize that just placing learners into the natural world, even for long stretches of time, was not enough. There were cultural and imaginational limits that needed to be overcome. Learners, and by extension teachers and caregivers, were challenged, through rethinking the norms of something like the children's village play, to begin the work of imagining, and even living, a different role for humans in the world. Intriguingly, changes began to happen after certain small interventions:

naming the governance challenges, facilitating a more consensual model of interaction, teaching toward different forms of economics, expanding the presence of gratitude, and encouraging students to listen to *all* our relations. Governance became more diverse, quieter voices—human and beyond—began to appear, different and varied strands of play flourished, scarcity and incarceration decreased, and allowable possibilities for being in the village expanded.

## Nature as Supporting Cultural Change

The narrative takes another turn, with the third vignette:

> *It is leaning into fall here on the west coast of Canada, and although the cliché tends to have the world preparing for sleep, there is also a fecundity of activity and possibility that belies this prospect of a quiet, cozy winter. Mushrooms are popping up everywhere, pine siskins are flitting to and fro, and, of course, there is the water.*
>
> *Creeks are speaking in their loudest voices of the year. The forest, after the season of dry discomfort, is drinking in its fill. And the nearby ocean has been turned upside down as its gifts rain down on all and sundry. But it is Salmon, or the lack thereof, that is the teacher today. Two students, who have grown up in this school without walls and now reached the age of 11, are anxiously scanning the river for that first splash or silvered flash of a returning Coho. Over the past seven cycles of fall they have fished for, watched, pondered, dissected, admired, and connected to Salmon. It is not school without them, and the sense of sadness is palpable among the students as they discuss the disappearance. One student notes that this loss of Salmon is not just for them (i.e., Salmon and children) but for the place itself. In fact, another child responds, "Without Salmon, Orca can no longer be Orca, and Kwantlen [one of the local Indigenous First Nations] can't be Kwantlen."*
>
> *In that moment, 10 years into this challenging school creation project, a crucial development appears. Ecosocial justice, interconnectedness, rights, and identity are all part of the fabric of our lives. For to understand how Water, Salmon, Orca, and*

> Kwantlen are connected is to enact the direction in which this
> school thinks our culture must go. This is certainly a moment
> worth noting.³

Change, and maybe hope, comes slowly and subtly. It is partially visible in learner experiences, in the health and well-being of the school community, and also in what and how things are being said and done. In this encounter we hear the experience of Salmon's slow return described in ways that might, by the standards of mainstream culture, be considered unusual. I am not certain yet, but this might be an example of NDD being overcome and of an ontological shift occurring, with these Canadian students at the very least understanding a humanness embedded in the wider world, as opposed to the current norm of autonomous and independent being. For not only are the students aware of and concerned for Salmon as meaningful others, but they are understanding the world as interconnected. And they are feeling the repercussions of the absence of Salmon not only for modern human culture, but for the Kwantlen First Nation, for Orca, and for Salmon themselves. They are grasping the existential crisis that the disappearance of Salmon causes. Salmon, as brothers and sisters, are at the heart of the cosmology of the Kwantlen First Nation. No Salmon equals no Kwantlen—not in terms of survival, for there are other foods, but in terms of a distinct way of being in the world. And so, after more than a decade of work with students being outdoors every day, all day, in deeply relational and actively critical ways—change, I repeat, is slow—we are seeing and hearing shifts in language used, in metaphors employed, and even in the positioning of humans in the world. This project is a response to the nature deficit identified by Louv, but one that seeks to overcome the challenge at a more complex and culturally inclusive level. Here, powerful glimpses of possibility exist, as we saw when another school joined the work:

> It is late fall and the class of six- and seven-year-olds at a new
> school started by one of the former Maple Ridge researchers
> is gathering for a gratitude circle. In the mind of the human
> teacher, the "plan was to send thanks to the Salmon by sharing
> words in a circle." The school has been spending a lot of time
> with Salmon at the River's edge, and there has been a desire
> expressed by adults—one inspired by their readings and by the
> Indigenous Elders who are helping—to make reciprocity and

*gratitude much more a part of the school's life. However, for this teacher, the gratitude event "became completely student led."*

*Student one: I think singing a song would be a better way of thanking the Salmon teachers.*
*—All students agreed.*
*Student one: Let's sing the Salmon song*[4] *so they know we are appreciating them.*
*Student two: After that I want to sing the Water song because the Water is so important to the Salmon.*
*—Totally unprovoked by the human-teacher, the students sing two songs to the Salmon . . . and then . . .*
*Student three: [Gets upset.] I feel like we weren't singing to the Salmon since we were looking at each other. I want to face the Salmon.*
*—Everyone agrees and faces towards the creek bed.*
*Student four: I think we should sing "The Water Is Flowing" next.*

In this moment we see the deepening of relation as the humans literally turn toward their teachers, River and Salmon. We see a human-teacher humbly, and with criticality, decentering themselves and seeking to undo some of the norms of public schooling in terms of who is in charge and where knowledge is located. An imaginative release of control has allowed a different way of being student and human to come to the fore, at least for the majority of these settler-culture learners. And we see a much more ecosocially inclusive and just orientation to the world. This is an educational scene, enacted in a way that offers restraint, shows respect, and holds deep reverence.

## Conclusion

In our work it has been important to name tools—nature as coteacher, nature as colonized, and nature as supporting cultural change—and to take them seriously. It has also been useful to see the project of overcoming NDD as being cultural in nature. From these vignettes, it is hopefully clear that in order to overcome nature deficit, even at the level of the individual, the educator must think at the broader level of community and culture. Happily, this is not impossible. Substantial changes to the mode of schooling, as described in the vignettes above, has made space for students to discover and respond to the cultural limits of imaginative play. It has allowed human-teachers to create the kind of environment in which the occurrence of children talking to trees is not shunned or seen as "weird." And it has given us the time to learn from nature in a deeply embodied way. This work has gone beyond just getting kids outside into careful considerations of how we *be* outdoors, how we engage and interact with all our relations, and how all of this can be shaped, framed, and even modeled for learners. This has also meant challenging adults to reconsider their own relational practices and ways of being, for it is apparent not only that mainstream Western culture actively discourages many of the forms that this relationality might take but that this has probably affected adults more than children.

Positioning the challenge as cultural has also encouraged us to be more critical in orientation toward the accepted norms of public education, and other larger systems. We have named the antiecological language and premises that permeate the conversation while leaning into the work that seeks change. This criticality has also opened new ways of being outside in both urban and nonurban locales and changed the frameworks that are being employed in encountering, interpreting, and relating to these beings and places.

The process of transformation is difficult and often frustratingly slow, and yet at the same time hopeful, for we can, after more than a decade, see the kinds of significant restorative responses to NDD that we have been seeking for a long time. And finally, considering the work to be existential in nature—to be about finding ways to be human differently—has had repercussions for how we think about teacher training, for where we draw our ontological inspirations, and for how we speak, listen, orient ourselves, and act in this agential, vibrant, living world.

## Notes

1. See https://es.sd42.ca/.
2. See Blenkinsop & Piersol (2013).
3. See Blenkinsop et al. (2023).
4. Gifted to the school and its students by the local Indigenous community.

## References

Blenkinsop, S., & Beeman, C. (2010). The world as co-teacher: Learning to work with a peerless colleague. *Trumpeter, 26*(3), 26–39.

Blenkinsop, S., & Piersol, L. (2013). Listening to the literal: Orientations towards how nature communicates. *Phenomenology and Practice, 7*(1), 41–60. https://doi.org/10.29173/pandpr21167

Blenkinsop, S., Affifi, R., Piersol, L., & Derby, M. (2017a). Shut-up and listen: Implications and possibilities of Albert Memmi's characteristics of colonization upon the "natural world." *Studies in Philosophy and Education, 36*(3), 348–65. https://doi.org/10.1007/s11217-016-9557-9

Blenkinsop, S., Piersol, L., Sitka-Sage, M., & Ho, Y. C. (2017b). The natural world as colonized other(s): Educational implications. *Canadian Journal of Environmental Education, 21*(1), 198–218.

Blenkinsop, S., Fettes, M., Cole, L., et al. (2021). *Living within the Earth's Carrying Capacity: Towards an Education for Eco-social-cultural Change.* SSHRC-funded knowledge synthesis project.

Blenkinsop, S., MacQuarrie, J., & Maitland, C. (2023). The Maple Ridge Environmental School, a case study: Ten years as an outdoor public elementary school and what we think we know now. In J. Činčera, B. Johnson, D. Goldman, et al. (Eds.), *Outdoor Environmental Education in the Contemporary World* (pp. 229–41). Springer. https://doi.org/10.1007/978-3-031-29257-6

Jickling, B., Blenkinsop, S., Timmerman, N., & Sitka-Sage, M. (2018). *Wild Pedagogies: Touchstones for Re-negotiating Education and the Environment in the Anthropocene.* Palgrave-MacMillan.

Jickling, B., & Blenkinsop, S. (2020). Wild Pedagogies and the promise of a different education: Challenges to change. In D. Wright & S. Hill (Eds.), *Social Ecology and Education: Transforming Worldviews and Practices* (pp. 55–64). Routledge. https://doi.org/10.1007/978-3-030-90980-2_2

Kimmerer, R. W. (2013). *Braiding Sweetgrass: Indigenous Wisdom, Scientific Knowledge and the Teachings of Plants.* Milkweed Editions.

Laduke, W. (2008). *All Our Relations: Native Struggles for Land and Life.* South End Press.

Louv, R. (2008). *Last Child in the Woods: Saving Our Children from Nature-Deficit Disorder.* Algonquin Books.

Memmi, A. (1991). *The Colonizer and the Colonized* (transl. H. Greenfeld). Beacon Press.

Plumwood, V. (2002). *Environmental Culture: The Ecological Crisis of Reason.* Routledge.

Sheridan, J., & Longboat, D. (2006). The Haudenosaunee imagination and the ecology of the sacred. *Space and Culture, 9*(4), 365–81. https://doi.org/10.1177/1206331206292503

Sobel, D. (2001). *Children's Special Places: Exploring the Role of Forts, Dens, and Bush Houses in Middle Childhood*. Wayne State University Press.

17

# Gratitude Is a Way of Life

KATHLEEN DEAN MOORE

The Earth bestows gift after gift—life and the living of it, light and the return of it, the growing things, the roaring things, fire and dreams, falling water and the wisdom of friends. Forgiveness. Time and the kelp-tongued tides. What do gifts as great as these tell us about how we might live lives worthy of all the world grants us?

—Moore and Haverluck (2022: 105)

The cove in front of my Alaskan cabin is a world of intersecting circles. The narrow blades of sedges bend with the wind, drawing compass roses on the sand. Every drop of water that slips from an overhanging branch raises a ring on the silver cove. Offshore, a cormorant perches on a derelict piling, her drenched and bedraggled wings outstretched to accept the warmth of a weak sun. So often does she perch there that her droppings have created soil where wild plants grow—huckleberries and blueberries that feed the ravens—and this is a kind of circle too, an ongoing cycle of giving, receiving, and giving in turn. In a ring around the massive trunk of a Sitka spruce, bears have placed decaying salmon on the moss, as carefully as if they had set the table for a pine marten's picnic. The bodies lie there, hooked jaw to frayed tail, shimmering with the movement of maggots under their skin. The salmon's nutrients will nourish the moss, the seedlings, and the blackflies that will in due course feed the fingerlings.

This is another circle, and what I want to say is that these cycles of giving and taking and giving in turn are what make the world go around. Without them, the life-supporting systems of the world would unreel and lie in broken coils. No less than the salmon and the maggots, humanity is part of a global ontology of giving and receiving that spirals through the limestone caves and clear water to the saltwater cove, where starfish feed on mussels and feed the gulls, who lift their beaks and announce the feast to rainclouds that fatten potatoes in the gardens. The gifts of life and death spiral endlessly, and people join in the circle dance, receiving gifts that fall, as the rain falls, undeserved and unearned, but generous and essential.

The implications for how we ought to live are staggering. Here's a summary of what I believe (Moore, 2010: 107):

> The gifts of the Earth (what economists might call "natural resources" or "ecosystem services") are freely given—rain, sun, fresh air, rich soil, all the abundance that nourishes the planet's lives and spirits. I don't know why; let that remain a mystery. What is important is that they are given. We do not earn these gifts. We have no claim on them. If they were taken away, there is little we could do to get them back. At the same time, our lives are utterly dependent on them.
>
> By receiving these gifts, we enter into a community of mutual sharing, caring, and celebration. It is a community that is both ecological and ethical, imposing role-responsibilities that are both material and moral. We may understand these to be responsibilities of reciprocity, following the language given us by Potawatomi elder Robin Kimmerer.
>
> Earth's gifts call us fundamentally to gratitude, a glad appreciation of the worth and generosity of the gifts. Furthermore, they call us to give our own gifts in turn. Like the cormorant, like the salmon, like the yammering gulls, we reciprocate when we use our gifts well for the benefit of Earth and the inhabitants who depend on it. In this way, gratitude for our abundant gifts is the root of our moral obligations to the past, for the gifts it has protected and passed on to us, and our duties to the future, to keep the circles spinning, to avert the coming environmental calamities, and to leave a world as rich in possibilities as the world that has been given to us.

## What Is a Gift?

A gift is a thing of value that is freely given or acquired without effort or asking. A knitted mitten could be a gift. So might be advice from an old fisherman. Sunlight is a gift, pouring down life-giving energy.

A gift is not fungible; it cannot be interchanged with something of equal value. If money or some other thing of value is given in exchange for a gift, it becomes a commodity. Moreover, because a gift is freely given, it cannot be earned. It is not a payment or a wage, a salary, a debt paid. For the same reason, no one is entitled to a gift. No one deserves a gift, as one might deserve a raise. No one can claim it, as one might claim luggage at the airport. One can't collect on a gift, the way one might collect a debt. One can't ask or demand it as one's due. So gift giving is outside the brittle *transactional economy* that constrains, hopelessly complicates, and sours contemporary life.

The community of mutual sharing, caring, and thriving that a gift-based worldview offers might be called a *gift economy*, if *economy* is understood in its original sense, as household management. Ecological principles explain life systems as interconnective, interdependent, cyclic streams of energy from past to future—a kind of gift economy. Many Indigenous ontologies describe a familial gift economy, where gifts are bestowed by Pachamama, Mother Earth. Religious traditions of many varieties describe a divine giver of gifts of life and transformation—again, a gift economy. In our time, we begin to see what I want to call a Great Convergence, in which the wisdom traditions of Earth are converging on a common ethos—a vision of a world shaped and empowered by the free sharing of life-giving gifts and the responsibilities that come with participation in that mutuality of thriving.

Whether described as material or spiritual or somehow both, in all its gifts freely bestowed, the world is generous. *Generous*, from the same roots as *generate* or *genesis*, a beginning, a sudden outpouring, *and there was light*. Gifts pour down. So we who receive Earth's gifts are like cormorants, spreading our miserable wings and accepting the sun—which owes us nothing but shines on us nonetheless. We are like the alpine meadows, soaking up the snowmelt. We are like the cove, accepting the creek. "The season of rain is coming," wrote the young poet Greta Wrolstad in 2005. "Hold out your hand."[1]

The world's generosity calls us to gratitude and joy. As the Persian poet Hafez is said to have written,

Even
After
All this time
The sun never says to the earth,
"You owe
Me."
Look
What happens
With a love like that,
It lights the
Whole
Sky.

## What Does a Gift Ask of Us?

There is a time in November when the first winter storm advances up the inlet where our cabin sits. Purple clouds pour through mountain passes and smash onto the sea. With rain in its teeth and foam on its lips, the sea writhes and groans under the lash of the wind, throwing logs into the forest and ripping at the kelp. In the cove, powerful surf tears rockweeds loose from their holdfasts and heaves the stipes and blades into windrows on the beach.

The storm may last for days. But when it finally moves through, the sun sheds watery light on suddenly silver water. That's when the heaps of rockweed deposited on the beaches glow like polished bronze. Rockweed, a kind of brown algae with gelatinous leaves and knobby swellings, is a great gift that the storm gathers and lays at the feet of the gardeners in my little boardwalk town.

At low tide the next morning, people bring pitchforks and wheelbarrows to gather what the storm has brought to them. Up the beach to the community garden, they trundle wheelbarrows of algae and heap it high on the sleeping soil. Warm under the rain, the piles decompose all winter long. When gardeners spade up the steaming black humus in the spring, it smells of pine duff and clams and the sharp brine of the sea. This is what the gardeners breathe as they bury the eyes of potatoes in the fertile dark.

Come fall, before the winter storms begin, an old man called Sky Blue Henry digs the potatoes in the community garden. He piles them into all the baskets on his bike and toils down the trail, stopping to leave sacks of potatoes for his neighbors. That is why, on this foggy autumn day, I will have potatoes in my chowder, and who would have thought that, like the salmon, the potatoes come to me as a gift from the sea?

What is a response worthy of these gifts? Humility, I would say, restraint, and gratitude, which itself is made of attentiveness and gladness, wonder, and reciprocity. This is "mostly standing still and learning to be astonished," writes the poet Mary Oliver. "Which is mostly rejoicing, since all the ingredients are here, which is gratitude, to be given a mind and a heart and these body-clothes, a mouth with which to give shouts of joy to the moth and the wren, to the sleepy dug-up clam" (Oliver, 2007: 1).

## Humility

Potatoes, sunlight, rain, salmon, clams, fresh air—these are what the people in my town are made of. Powhatan-Renape poet Jack Forbes explained how we are constituted by nature's gifts when he said, "Take away my eyes, and I will still live. Take away my ears, and I will still live. Take away my arms, my feet, and I will still live. But take away the sun, and I will die. So why do I think my eyes are more a part of me than the sun?" (Forbes, 2006). We are one with the sunlight and rain that make us. We have no control over them and no claim to them. So the appropriate response to such gifts is humility, awareness that we are no higher than, no better than, no more powerful than the givers of the gifts that constitute us.

Courtney Campbell, a Christian scholar, made this case: "Awareness of the biological reality that our very existence is contingent on Earth, soil, water, air, and so on, should cultivate moral dispositions of humility, gratitude, and solidarity [. . .] I must be consciously aware that I am, as one sacred text puts it, a 'beggar before God,'" (Campbell, 2010: 146).

## Restraint

When Earth bestows its gifts, we should take no more than is offered. Grasping, seizing, or "hoarding the gift," as Robin Kimmerer wrote, "we become constipated with wealth, bloated with possessions, too heavy to join the dance" (Kimmerer, 2010: 142). If Earth were merely an endless market-basket of commodities, there might be few constraints in the taking. Consider the international banker who sees the great Alaskan forests not as green and living beings nourished by the sun but as a line on a balance sheet, something that can be traded for dollars. Unrestrained by the ethos of gift giving, he takes all he can cut from Earth and will not stop until he leaves the land denuded, poisoned, scraped, and—most importantly—used up and empty.

What if he understood instead that the forest, indeed all the planet, is astonishing, contingent, beautiful, unique and irreplaceable, beyond value, beyond human understanding, and generous to life? If the good English word for this combination of characteristics is *sacred*, then we should not be afraid to use this word. Then the riches of Earth are not commodities but the sacred body of a planet spun from the stars, and the timber industry's limitless taking is a *sacrilege*, literally the stealing of sacred things, *sacralegium*, from *sacer* (sacred) + *legere* (take possession of). Here are the sacred hermit thrushes with earthmovers in their vision and lesions on their eyes. Here is the bulldozed and broken aspen tree, the sacred leaves that once danced in silver light now buried in mud. Here is a sacred young father, with broken limbs and frightened eyes, pinned under a clear-felled Douglas fir.

As the clearcut hillsides amply show, the gift-giving cycles of the planet become broken when essential pieces are destroyed. No longer do the forests shelter streams, nourish trout, raise the young of the songbirds, offer deer and mushrooms to the families. Unlike a full cycle of gifts, a plundered planet cannot continue to provide. So Kimmerer goes on to point out that the ethos of gift giving and receiving requires the restraint of an "Honorable Harvest." Here are its principles (Kimmerer, 2015):

> Ask permission of the ones whose lives you seek. Abide by the answer.
> Never take the first. Never take the last.
> Harvest in a way that minimizes harm.
> Take only what you need and leave some for others.
> Use everything that you take.
> Take only that which is given to you.
> Share it, as the Earth has shared with you.
> Be grateful.
> Reciprocate the gift.
> Sustain the ones who sustain you, and the Earth will last forever.

## Gratitude

A gift calls also for gratitude, the quality of being thankful for the gifts one has received. And what is it to be thankful? To pay attention to the gift, to be glad for it, to wonder at it, and to reciprocate.

*Attentiveness:* At its etymological roots, *thank* is closely related to *think*, to hold in the mind, as one would hold a mental image of what is given. Accordingly, gratitude is being thankful, *think-full*. Hold the gift in mind. Attend to it. Notice it. Turn it this way, wonder at it, turn it that way, pay attention.

The opposite, of course, is disregard, failure to notice the gift. Taking it "for granted" is literally that, as simply granted, unworthy of particular attention. Failing to notice a gift dishonors it and deflects the generosity of the giver. That's what's wrong with living a careless life, storing up sorrow, waking up resentful, walking unaware. But to turn the gift of life in your hands—to say, this is wonderful, this is a great gift—these honor the gift and the granting of it. Be astonished by it. Be glad for it, care about it. Keep it in mind.

In our self-centered and self-complacent lives, how often do we greet the rising stars with astonishment and song? How often do we notice that it is air, not ourselves, that makes the music in the flute? When we feel ourselves stagger, are we glad to be embraced by the planet's perfectly balanced forces? Do we feel the strong arms of gravity holding us to Earth's fiery heart? Maybe we don't stop to notice the pearly astonishment of clams. Or the scented solace of shade. It may be possible to go through life unaware, taking and taking, but what a lonely, precarious, and ultimately destructive life that would be.

*Gladness:* Paying attention to what sustains our lives is the beginning of appreciation, respect, and even wonder. "I would maintain that thanks are the highest form of thought; and that gratitude is happiness doubled by wonder," said Christian writer G. K. Chesterton (1917: 463). Appreciation: to appraise, to value highly, to hold in high esteem, to be glad for. It focuses our attention on what we have, rather than what we do not have.

This is why I imagine it is impossible to be grateful and sorrowful at the same time. I am not sure of this. But here's what I say now. Pay attention to the present moment; every moment we are wondering at the path of wind across the water or smiling to see a dog rest in the sun, we are not rehearsing our misfortunes. Breathe: sea wind, kelp brine, woodsmoke, ice. Notice: fireweed, otter tracks, foxglove, fog, music in firelight.

The opposite of gladness is dissatisfaction. To want more, rather than be glad to have enough. Worse, to claim more as a privilege based on some presumed superiority of wealth or race or gender. Pride, gluttony, envy, and avarice are all deadly sins in Christian theology. Why? Because they overlook or deny the constitutive generosity of the universe and so speak of a willful separation from the sources of our lives and strength.

Robin Kimmerer says a prayer of thanksgiving every morning and at the beginning of every meeting. "As is the custom in my culture and in many others, let us begin with gratitude, for we are showered daily with the gifts of Mother Earth—food to eat, sweet air to breathe, and the preciousness of water. Gratitude for each other as people, for the privilege of our shared work" (Kimmerer, 2021: 249).

When I heard this prayer, I was ashamed of the prayer I said every night as a child. With folded hands, I knelt by my bed, bare-legged on the hardwood floor: "God bless mommy and daddy and Nancy and Sally and Pixie the Dog, and make Kathy a good girl, Amen." Never did I say, thank you for a good-enough dog and for parents who love me and sisters who tolerate my existence. Never did I say, thank you for not making me more wicked than I already am. I was too busy asking for more blessings to say thank you for the ample blessings I had already received. That is a failure of gratitude. Meister Eckhart could have told me, "If the only prayer you say in your entire life is thank you, it will be enough."

*Reciprocity:* Gratitude calls us to give gifts forward, turn the circle of thanksgiving, create a continuance of support that benefits everyone mutually. In this way, we honor our responsibilities for all we have been given. In gratitude for nourishing food, we replenish the soil. In gratitude for birdsong, we protect the forest. In gratitude for a child's love, we keep the child safe. In gratitude for life, we make ourselves, as we can, worthy bearers of that great gift. In gratitude for Earth and our place in its cycles, we honor it and protect its thriving through careful and joyful use. In these ways, by these great circle dances, we assure that flourishing can continue. Kimmerer explained: "We are bound by a covenant of reciprocity, a pact of mutual responsibility to sustain those that sustain us. Plant breath for animal breath, winter and summer, predator and prey, grass and fire, night and day, living and dying. Water knows this, clouds know this. Soil and rocks know they are dancing in a continuous give-away of making, unmaking, and making again Earth. We live in a moral landscape [. . .] Earth is a gift that we must pass on, just as it comes to us" (Kimmerer, 2010: 144).

Thus, although the *re-* prefix might suggest differently, reciprocity is not giving a gift in return for one that has been received; it is not a trade or a payback or a debt paid. Rather reciprocity is recognition of a gift through full participation in the cycles of sharing that sustain life. When one is given a great gift, the question is not, how can I repay you? But, how can I pay this forward, and so celebrate and fulfill my role in the conveyance of gifts from the past into a future of mutual sustenance and joy?

Because we recognize our radical dependence on and interdependence with the rest of the world, we participate in an ethos of mutual aid and accountability that manifests in overlapping circles of reciprocity. This, one might say, is what makes the world go around.

## How Can Gratitude Become a Way of Life?

Psychologists debate whether gratitude is a character trait or a mood or an emotion. If it is a character trait, is it a virtue? Cicero took a strong stand on the issue: "Gratitude is not only the greatest of virtues, but the parent of all others" (Cicero, 1891: section 80). If gratitude is a virtue, can it, by practice, become a way of life? And if so, what exactly might one practice? What habits of thought must first be broken?

It is important to acknowledge the challenges to be overcome, in order to live a fully grateful life. Enlightenment philosophers have mapped out a miserable, lonely world for us to live in. For three, four hundred years, we children of the Enlightenment strode alone and gimlet-eyed through a world of nothing but mute commodities, the only spirit in a universe of matter and mechanical animal-clocks, the only shining eyes on a planet stripped of mystery, diminished by human avarice, desperately endangered by the endless quest for human convenience. In the mirror of the dominant Western culture, we see ourselves as selfish, grasping kings of the stony mountain we call Earth. Where is the place for gratitude in such a world?

Taking the United States as an example, "the third Thursday in November" is an obvious answer, when many Americans demonstrate their gratitude for the fecundity of Earth by eating as much of it as possible. Or "December 21st," when we set as much as possible on fire, struggling to light even the ice cream. Clearly, the practice of gratitude calls for the redefinition of these old traditions, the creation of new rituals of celebration and thanksgiving, and the rediscovery of old celebrations that restore us to the circles of life. More than this, it calls us to lives that foreswear the careless destruction of what is given and embrace a full, conscious participation in the life-renewing processes of Earth.

*Rituals of thanksgiving:* In an effort to reimagine Thanksgiving, the young members of my family walk out into the dark to make themselves again a part of the night. This past Thanksgiving, they decided to walk the beach from our cabin to the navigational buoy at the end of the inlet. Understand: At 8pm, the night was raven black. Wind north at 35 knots. Rain sheeting sideways. Beach? Mud-slicked cobbles threatened by a rising tide. Surf thunderous and invisible. They geared up. Slickers, headlamps, knee boots.

Darting anxious beams from their headlamps onto the rising tide, they stumbled on, steering a course toward the buoy that drew a red path along the wrinkled swash. They gave thanks for the hibernation of grizzly bears, for the predictable tides, for wool hats, and for the buoy itself. It was a navigational buoy, marking the channel into the harbor. Red Right Return, it signaled mariners: if you keep the light to starboard, you will find safe passage home. That is what I thought about the next morning, as sun lit the frost-rimmed cobbles, coffee offered its burnt-dirt smell, and the children slept safely, piled in the back bedroom. Even when the nights are dark and the wind is against us, if we lift our faces to the rain, we will find a signal that leads us to where we belong. Gratitude offers moral guidance. It is a kind of wayfinding, a path. It is a way of life.

What if each day, you and I walked out into the generous morning, frightened of the wind or glad under the sun, with this determination: to notice, to be glad, to give thanks? That would be a beginning, but by no means enough. In a world desperately damaged by human avarice and exceptionalism, gratitude also requires acts that heal the life-giving circles. That is how we pay the gift forward.

*Acts of healing:* It is important to notice that these thoughts about gratitude and reciprocity come at a dangerous time in Earth's history. I don't know if the work of healing the damage we have done to the Holocene and all its improbable gifts—the lovely, welcoming, life-graced world that humans evolved in—is a lost cause. No one can say. But science warns that we may have already crossed too many thresholds, set in motion too many feedback loops, cut too many arteries, waited too long to stanch the flow of brutal, endless extraction. Earth will continue to exist, but the life we know and love—the piney forests and wild whales—may be bleeding out. I'm sorry, but somebody's got to say it.

In this context, the duties to defend and heal Earth's life-supporting systems, the gifts that come to us unbidden, are unconditional. There are many reasons why we have a moral obligation to protect Earth's imperiled power to grant and sustain lives, as Michael P. Nelson and I outlined in *Moral Ground*: For the survival of humankind and for the sake of all forms of life on the planet. For the stewardship of God's creation. To keep our promises to the children. To acknowledge our debt to the past and honor our obligations to the future. Because compassion requires it. Because justice requires it. Because the world is beautiful. Because we love the world. Because our moral integrity requires us to do what is right. And this above all, to honor our duties of gratitude and reciprocity for the gifts that come to us, unasked, from the sea of the stars (Moore and Nelson, 2010).

As we undertake this work, it is important to say also that the projected passing of the Holocene is not an all-or-nothing thing. Climate change is like a leak in a boat; there are degrees of danger, and to some extent, these are under human control. By kicking on the bilge pumps or planking over a hole in a boat's hull, deckhands can probably keep her afloat until they limp into port or find a place to beach her, although they will be working hard and the outcome is uncertain. But if they do nothing, the boat will surely sink. In much the same way, a moderate rise in Earth's temperature is probably survivable for many species, including our own; a large rise may not be. It makes no sense to give up the struggle because you can't be confident of success. It makes no sense to do nothing for the lovely, reeling planet because you can't do everything.

So along this coast, people push stranded whales back into the sea, although the whales often return to die. They wipe bunker oil from cormorant wings, although the birds seldom survive the toxins. With kayaks, they block a barge carrying oil-drilling equipment to the Arctic, although the barge will eventually make its way north. There is gratitude in the trying and virtue in shared work. Regardless of its outcomes, the work is beautiful in itself, out in the wind and seagull wings. It is perfectly aligned with the life-urgency of the gleaming planet, the cleansing rhythms of waves and tides, the creative energy of devoted people (Moore and Haverluck, 2022).

Canadian theologian-artist Bob Haverluck says that we should give up "the foolish notion that we should act to oppose the wounding only if we can win. Maybe we act," he suggests, "because it is a way of giving thanks for the gift of a ride on this ball of fire wrapped in water, stone, and morning air" (Moore and Haverluck, 2022: 85).

Yes, we can work for Earth simply as a way to give thanks. Give thanks for the ball of fire—the center of Earth that is hot enough to melt iron. Give thanks for the water that wraps the rock—a light-shot wave that rolls along the beach, revealing the silhouette of a harbor seal. Give thanks for the stone—the black basaltic rocks, polished for a billion years to a high gloss, sheltering orange sea stars and barnacles blue as twilight. Give thanks for the morning air—on thin, cold light comes the scent of woodsmoke and the song of a flute from the garden.

## Note

1. After the tragic death of the young poet Greta Wrolstad, her words were inscribed on a bench at the top of Marys Peak in Corvallis, Oregon.

## References

Campbell, C. (2010). From the mountain, a covenant. In K. D. Moore & M. P. Nelson (Eds.), *Moral Ground: Ethical Action for a Planet in Peril* (pp. 146–53). Trinity University Press.

Chesterton, G. K. (1917). *Collected Works of G. K. Chesterton*. Ignatius Press.

Cicero, M. T. (1891). *In Defense of Planicus: The Orations of Marcus Tullius Cicero* (transl. C. C. Yonge). George Bell and Sons.

Forbes, J. (2006). Presentation to Native American studies class at Oregon State University. N.p.

Kimmerer, R. (2010). The giveaway. In K. D. Moore & M. P. Nelson (Eds.), *Moral Ground: Ethical Action for a Planet in Peril* (pp. 141–45). Trinity University Press.

Kimmerer, R. (2015, November 26). The "Honorable Harvest": Lessons from an Indigenous tradition of giving thanks. *Yes!* https://www.yesmagazine.org/issue/good-health/2015/11/26/the-honorable-harvest-lessons-from-an-indigenous-tradition-of-giving-thanks

Kimmerer, R. (2021). The giveaway. In T. A. Kerns & K. D. Moore (Eds.), *Bearing Witness: The Human Rights Case against Fracking and Climate Change* (pp. 249–50). Oregon State University Press.

Moore, K. D. (2010). Yes, to honor our duties of gratitude and reciprocity. In K. D. Moore & M. P. Nelson (Eds.), *Moral Ground: Ethical Action for a Planet in Peril* (pp. 131–32). Trinity University Press.

Moore, K. D., & Nelson, M. P. (Eds.) (2010). *Moral Ground: Ethical Action for a Planet in Peril*. Trinity University Press.

Moore, K. D., & Haverluck, B. (2022). *Take Heart: Encouragement for Earth's Weary Lovers*. Oregon State University Press.

Oliver, M. (2007). *Messenger*. Beacon Press.

# Contributors

## Coeditors

**Joe Gray** is a writer, editor, and natural historian based in Great Britain. He holds a BA and MA in zoology from the University of Cambridge and an MSc in forestry from the University of Bangor. Writing on a variety of issues in conservation and ecology, he has authored or coauthored dozens of articles, including academic papers and pieces aimed at broader audiences. Joe has a particular interest in, and fondness for, insect life. He is a founding editor of the *Ecological Citizen*. For more information, see https://deepgreen.earth/.

**Eileen Crist** is associate professor emerita in the Department of Science, Technology, and Society at Virginia Tech. She holds a PhD in sociology from Boston University, and a BA, also in sociology, from Haverford College. Her work focuses on the ecological crisis and its root causes as well as pathways toward creating an ecological civilization. She is the author of numerous academic papers and writings for general audience readers. Her most recent book, *Abundant Earth: Toward an Ecological Civilization*, was published in 2019. Eileen is also an associate editor of the *Ecological Citizen*. For more information, see https://eileencrist.com/.

## Contributors

**Samuel Alexander** is academic director of Sustainability and Environmental Action with the School for International Training. He's also director of the Simplicity Institute. Previously he was a lecturer and researcher with the University of Melbourne, Australia. His books include *Beyond Capitalist Realism: The Politics, Energetics, and Aesthetics of Degrowth* (2021), *Degrowth in the Suburbs: A Radical Urban Imaginary* (2019, coauthored with Brendan Gleeson), *Prosperous Descent: Crisis as Opportunity in an Age of Limits* (2015), and *Entropia: Life beyond Industrial Civilisation* (2013). His writing can be found at https://samuelalexander.info/.

**Ryan D. Andrews** is currently an assistant professor of nutrition at Regis College. He completed his education and training at the University of Northern Colorado, Kent State University, Johns Hopkins Medicine, and Columbia University. Ryan has experience in nutritional counseling, school lunch programs, farming, and trauma-informed yoga, and he has worked with Precision Nutrition, Equinox, Insider, Allergic to Salad, Silver Hill Hospital, and Purchase College.

**Nandita Bajaj** is the executive director of Population Balance, a US nonprofit that works to inspire narrative, behavioral, and system change toward substantially downscaling human impact to enable natural ecosystems, nonhuman animals, and humanity to flourish together. She is a senior lecturer at the Institute for Humane Education at Antioch University, where she teaches about the combined impacts of pronatalism and human expansionism on reproductive, ecological, and intergenerational justice. In addition to a number of peer-reviewed papers and forthcoming book chapters, her work has appeared in major news outlets such as Canadian Broadcasting Corporation, the *Washington Post*, the *Guardian*, *Newsweek*, *Ms. Magazine*, the *Globe and Mail*, and *National Post*. She has an MEd (humane education) from Antioch University, a BEng (aerospace engineering) from Toronto Metropolitan University, and a BEd from University of Toronto.

**Chelsea Batavia** is a daughter, sister, friend, and companion. She studied theology as an undergraduate student in Washington, DC, before becoming certified in classic French pastry in New York City. As it became apparent that beautiful yet foolish dreams of owning a bakery were not to be, she fell into professional limbo and spent a few years doing nothing particularly interesting before finally making her way back to graduate school. She completed her graduate studies at the Oregon State University College of Forestry, where she concentrated on interdisciplinary social sciences and environmental ethics. She currently works for the state of Washington, where she attempts to contribute to efforts in service of environmental justice.

**Sean Blenkinsop** is a professor in the faculty of education at Simon Fraser University, Vancouver, Canada. His current research explores place-, nature-, and land-based teacher education, ecosocial cultural change, nature as coteacher, and the challenges of justice in a rapidly changing world. Sean has also been, and still is, involved in creating and researching three (soon to be five) innovative public elementary schools in British Columbia that are focused on being much more community-, place-, and nature-based in both pedagogy and curriculum. His most recent books are *Wild Pedagogies: Touchstones for Re-Negotiating Education and the Environment in the Anthropocene* (2018), *Ecoportraiture: The Art of Research When Nature Matters* (2022), and *Education as Practice of Eco-social-cultural Change* (2023).

**Tarik Bodasing** is a landscape ecologist and naturalist who has spent most of his adult life working in African wildlife conservation. He is currently working for the RSPB in West Africa as a technical advisor on wildlife and forest crime and is supporting local government agencies to improve protection and conservation of indigenous fauna and flora and to build an appreciation and respect for nature among rural communities.

**Matthew Calarco** is professor of philosophy at California State University, Fullerton, where he teaches courses in Continental philosophy, history of philosophy, animal studies, and environmental philosophy. He is author most recently of *The Three Ethologies* (2024), *The Boundaries of Human Nature* (2021), and *Beyond the Anthropological Difference* (2020).

**Patrick Curry** is a Canadian-born writer and scholar who has lived in London for over forty years. He holds a PhD in the history and philosophy of science from University College London, has been a lecturer at the University of Kent and Bath Spa University, and is a staff member in the Sophia Centre for the Study of Cosmology in Culture at the University of Wales Trinity Saint David. He is the author of (among other books) *Defending Middle-Earth: Tolkien, Myth, and Modernity and Ecological Ethics: An Introduction*, as well as many papers in journals and collections. Most of them can be found on his website: http://www.patrickcurry.co.uk/. He is also editor in chief of the *Ecological Citizen*.

**John Michael Greer**, best known as a leading figure in today's nature spirituality movement, is an independent scholar, author, and blogger. He has also published eleven books on the future of industrial society, focusing on the failure of the ideology of progress and the need to retool society for sharply reduced access to energy and nonrenewable resources. He served for twelve years as Grand Archdruid of the Ancient Order of Druids in America. He lives in Rhode Island.

**Helen Kopnina** (PhD, Cambridge University, 2002) is employed at Northumbria University and is the author or coauthor of over two hundred peer-reviewed articles and is the author, editor, or coeditor of seventeen books covering the interrelated topics of environmental sustainability, the circular economy, biological conservation, environmental ethics, animal ethics, and environmental education.

**Simon Leadbeater**. After a career in local government and the third sector living a conventional life in an ordinary house, Simon and his wife, Toni, find themselves living off-grid on the edge of a Hertfordshire wood in southern England with their wolfdogs. Simon now divides his time acting as a small business advisor, caring for the woodland, running a small farm animal sanctuary, and, when time allows, writing on the themes of rewilding and environmental ethics. Simon tweets as @OurSacredGrove.

**Freya Mathews** is emeritus professor of environmental philosophy at Latrobe University, Australia. She is the author of over a hundred books, articles, and essays in the area of ecological philosophy, including the 1991 classic *The Ecological Self* (reissued in the Routledge Classics Series in 2021). Her latest book, *The Dao of Civilization: A Letter to China*, appeared in 2023. In addition to her research activities, she comanages a private conservation estate in northern Victoria. She is a fellow of the Australian Academy of the Humanities.

**Stephanie Mills.** Longtime bioregionalist Stephanie Mills is the author of *Whatever Happened to Ecology?* (1989), *In Service of the Wild: Restoring and Reinhabiting Damaged Land* (1995), and *Epicurean Simplicity* (2002), among other books. For more information, visit her website: https://smillswriter.com/.

**Kathleen Dean Moore**, PhD, works at the nexus of moral philosophy, environmental advocacy, and the literary arts. Responding to the terrible urgency of the climate and extinction crises, she left her position as distinguished professor of philosophy at Oregon State University for a new life as a public philosopher, writing and speaking out about why, exactly, it's wrong to wreck the world. Among her dozen books, her best-known are *Moral Ground: Ethical Action for a Planet in Peril* and *Earth's Wild Music: Celebrating and Defending the Songs of the Natural World*. A multiple-award-winning writer, she collaborates with musicians, scientists, creative artists, and filmmakers to carry the call to action.

**Reed F. Noss** is a writer, lecturer, photographer, and consultant in ecology and conservation. He served as editor in chief of *Conservation Biology*, the flagship journal of this field, and as president of the Society for Conservation Biology. He is an elected fellow of the American Association for the Advancement of Science and has current faculty appointments with University of Florida and University of Central Florida. His most recently published books are *Forgotten Grasslands of the South: Natural History and Conservation* (2013) and *Fire Ecology of Florida and the Southeastern Coastal Plain* (2018).

**Luke Philip Plotica** is an adjunct professor of political science at Virginia Tech, Blacksburg, Virginia. His teaching and research focus upon political and legal theory, with special interests in individual agency, ethical responsibility, and political and legal institutions. He is the author of *Michael Oakeshott and the Conversation of Modern Political Thought* (2015) and *Nineteenth-Century Individualism and the Market Economy: Individualist Themes in Emerson, Thoreau, and Sumner* (2018) as well as numerous articles on modern political thought, democratic theory, ecological ethics, time, and American constitutional law. An ethical vegan and organic gardener, he enjoys experiencing wonder in daily encounters with the nonhuman world.

**Clive L. Spash** is an economist and chair of Public Policy and Governance at WU Vienna University of Economics and Business and was formerly editor in chief of *Environmental Values and President of the European Society for Ecological Economics*. His work on conservation and biodiversity relating to economic value and ethical issues has extended over thirty years. He has published extensively and his books include *Foundations of Social Ecological Economics* (2024), *Routledge Handbook of Ecological Economics: Nature and Society* (2017), *Ecological Economics: Critical Concepts in the Environment* (four volumes; 2009), and *Greenhouse*

*Economics: Value and Ethics* (2002). More information can be found at https://www.clivespash.org/.

**Kirsten Stade** is communications manager with the nonprofit Population Balance, where she manages social and traditional media engagement. She is a writer and advocate who has worked for over two decades with nonprofit organizations focused on conserving wildlife, challenging extractive industries on public lands, and defending the integrity of regulatory science. She holds a master's degree in conservation biology from Columbia University and a bachelor's in earth systems from Stanford University, and has published work on topics ranging from reproductive autonomy and ecological overshoot to the impacts of livestock grazing on ecosystem health in the American West to conflicts of interest within the US federal advisory committee system.

**Ian Whyte** is an amateur field naturalist, and has been for many decades. Over these years he has developed a strong ecocentric sense and philosophy that acknowledges that all life has agency and fully qualifies for deep respect. Ian is an associate editor of the *Ecological Citizen*.

# Index

Abbott, Sarah, 242
Abernethy National Nature Reserve, 201
Aboriginal Australia, Indigenous Law in, 107
Abram, David, 7
absolute deprivation, relative deprivation compared to, 40–41
accommodation, and least resistance, 104–105
Adams, Carol, 224
aesthetic state, 85
aesthetics
   animal issues addressed with, 222, 225–227
   of degrowth, 87
   of existence, 230–232
   *homo aestheticus*, 84, 91
   inhumanist, 14, 226–227, 231–232
   meaning engaged through, 82–84, 85, 90
   in SMPLCTY, 91–92
Africa, 11–12
   colonization in, 258–259
   conservation in, 129–131, 133–134, 138
   illegal wildlife trade in, 132–133
   lions in, 130, 131, 132, 134
   predator species in, 129, 130–138
   rewilding in, 135–136
   sub-Saharan, 135, 136
   trophy hunting in, 131–132
African American peoples, slavery of, 164, 189n5
African Parks Network, 130, 135
African wild dogs, 135
agency
   moral, 187–188
   in wilderness, 184
aging crisis, 27
agroecology, 168–171
*ahimsa* (nonviolence), 246
Alagona, Peter, 197–198, 201
Alaska, US, 267–268
Alexander, Samuel, 9–10
Amazon, Brazil, 236
Americas, early modern era fish population depletion in, 149–150
Andrews, Ryan, 12–13
animal ethics, 223, 224
animal issues
   aesthetics addressing, 222, 225–227
   Singer, Peter, on, 222–223
animal products, consumption of, 166, 167
animal subjectivity, 227–230
animals, 173n1. *See also* fish populations; lions; predator species; species conservation
   African wild dogs, 135

animals *(continued)*
    Aristotle on, 228–229, 232n2
    bears, 198
    cheetahs, 133, 134
    deer, 202
    Donaldson and Kymlicka on, 224–225
    ecological catastrophes impacting, 221
    human–animal relations, 223, 224–225, 226, 231
    keystone species, 103
    leopards, 132, 133, 137
    octopus, 154
    outdoor recreation impacting, 194
    prey species of, 105
    proanimal discourse on, 227
    respect for, 167
    salmon, 154, 260–262
    sea turtles, 146, 154
    seabirds, 151
    shrimp, 154
    in Yosemite Valley, 193
*animism*, 240
Anthropocene, 2–4, 5, 6, 16
anthropocentrism, 123, 137, 259
antibiotics, for livestock, 164, 166
apex predators, 103, 108
apocalypse, 177, 188
appropriate technology movement, of 1970s, 59
Archimedean point, 186
Arendt, Hannah, 45, 186
Aristotle, 210, 228–229, 232n2
art
    history, 91
    meaning engaged through, 82–84, 85, 90
    in SMPLCTY, 91–92
Artemis (Greek goddess), 239, 240
artful descent, 87, 89, 91. *See also* simplification, voluntary

artistic geniuses, 84, 91
artists, 83
attentiveness, 273
Australia
    Aboriginal, 107
    New South Wales, 69
Australian Green Party, 73

Bacon, Francis, 4
Bajaj, Nandita, 8
Batavia, Chelsea, 13
Bateson, Gregory, 212
Baudrillard, Jean, 40
bears, 198
Behrens, W. W. III, 49
Bekoff, Marc, 238, 246, 247n1
Berry, Thomas, 240, 241
*Better Growth Better Climate* (Global Commission on the Economy and Climate), 66–67
bicycle, technological suite of, 56
Big Tech, 36
biobanking, 69
biodiversity, 5, 6, 104, 109n3
    biological minimum of, 100–101
    civilization harmony with, 50
    conservation of, 100–102
    financial impacts of, 68–69
    industrial agriculture impacting, 164
    of marine life, 148, 155, 156
    predator species influence on, 129
    of seamounts, 152–153
biological clock, 25
biomass, technosphere mass compared to, 3
biosphere, 3, 4, 7
biosynergy
    Indigenous Law intimated by, 106–107
    normative logic of, 105–106
bird flu, 165
Black, Christine, 107

Blenkinsop, Sean, 15
Bodasing, Tarik, 11–12
Branson, Richard, 71
*Brave New World* (Huxley), 81
Brazil, Amazon, 236
British Columbia, Canada, 15
Brown, Bob, 73
Brundtland Report (World Commission on Environment and Development), 63, 109n3
bycatch, 144, 153, 155, 156

CAFOs. *See* confined animal feeding operations
Cairo, Egypt, 23, 25–26
Calarco, Matthew, 14–15
Caledonian pine forest, 201
California, Sacramento, 177
Calvo, Paco, 237, 242, 244
Campbell, Courtney, 271
Camus, Albert, 82
Canada
　British Columbia, 15
　ecosystem conservation in, 118
　education in, 15, 251, 253–256
　salmon in, 260–262
canal systems, 56
　in Great Britain, 55, 60
　technological suite of, 57–58
cap and trade, 65. *See also* emissions trading system
Cape Cod, 145
capitalism
　socialism compared to, 42
　stakeholder, 70
capitalist market, reforms of, 9
carbon storage, through regenerative agriculture, 169
carbon tax, ETS compared to, 67
Caribbean, marine life depletion in, 146
carnivores. *See* predator species

carrying capacity, 21
Carson, Rachel, 143
Cartesianism, 211
Carver, S., 121, 122
Challenger, Melanie, 147
cheetahs, 133, 134
Chesterton, G. K., 214, 273
Chidester, David, 238
China
　ancient, 106
　industrial fishing of, 150
　one-child policy of, 27
Chipko movement, 240
Christianity, 211, 241, 274
circumstance, 178
civilizations
　biodiversity harmony with, 50
　collapse of, 90, 92
　complexification of, 87–88
　of poet-farmers, 86–92
　SMPLCTY in, 87–88, 91
Clean Development Mechanism, of Kyoto Protocol, 65–66
climate change, 277
　growth benefiting from, 64–67
　livestock farming impacting, 238, 247
　marine life impacted by, 146
　science, 73
　Stern on, 64–65
colonization
　in Africa, 258–259
　of nature, 256–260
*The Colonizer and the Colonized* (Memmi), 258
colonizers
　deforestation instigated by, 240
　othering of, 258–259
Comer, P. J., 115
Committee for the Study of Plant and Animal Communities, of ESA, 116

290 | Index

Committee on the Preservation of Natural Conditions, of ESA, 115
complexification, of civilizations, 87–88
conativity, 104
confined animal feeding operations (CAFOs), 164, 166
Conscious Impact Living, 13, 198–199
conservation, 11, 179. *See also* ecosystem conservation
  in Africa, 129–131, 133–134, 138
  anthropocentrism impacting, 137
  of biodiversity, 100–102
  categories of, 97–98
  decolonization of, 183–184
  Deep Law dictating, 108, 109
  defensive, 129–131, 138
  energy, 59
  Gray and Noss on, 196
  Indigenous peoples erasure in, 99
  of marine life, 12, 156, 158
  of predator species, 130–131, 133, 134, 135, 138
  of species, 113–115, 180
  of wilderness, 98–100
conservationists
  nature-led rewilding compared to, 103
  oppression dismantled by, 13
consumer culture, 38, 45, 79–82, 230
consumer societies, imaginaries of, 72, 73
consumerism, 40, 83
  green, 42, 43
  postconsumerism, 87
consumers, 37
consumption
  of animal products, 166, 167
  conscious, 29, 39
  individual, 41–42, 43
  institutional, 42, 43
  of livestock, 22–23
  production relationship with, 35–36, 38
  restraint in, 8–9, 10, 35–46
  wants relationship with, 38, 40, 45
continental shelves, 146
coral reefs, 2, 150–151
corporate capture, of ENGOs, 70–71
corporate green strategy, 70–72
corporate polluters, of GHGs, 67
coteacher, nature as, 253–256
COVID-19 pandemic, GHGs impacted by, 66
craftsmanship, 44
*Cratylus* (Plato), 211
Crist, Eileen, 12, 123
crops, regenerative agriculture initiatives for, 168–169
cultural capital, 68
cultural change
  through education, 262–263
  around nature deficit disorder, 253, 262, 263
  nature supporting, 260–262
Curry, Patrick, 14, 238

*Daisugi* (Japanese forestry), 246
Dao, 106
*Daodejing*, 106
Daoism, 106
Darwin, Charles, 241, 246
Davos 2020, 66, 69, 70
decolonization, of conservation, 183–184
deer, 202
defaunation, 237
defensive conservation, 129–131, 138
deforestation, 238, 240
Demeter (Greek goddess), 235
*Demystifying Materiality* (UN Environment Programme Finance Initiative), 68
Dennis, Roy, 200

Descartes, René, 211, 214, 241
*Descent of Man* (Darwin), 241
Despret, Vinciane, 35
Deutsche Bank, 68
developed countries, food waste in, 172
developing countries, food waste in, 172
Devi, Amrita, 239–240
diet
   animal product consumption in, 166, 167
   Foer on, 171
   plant-based, 165–166, 245, 247
   seafood avoidance for, 157
Dinerstein, Eric, 118
disenchantment, 214
dog walking, 199–200, 201
domesticated animals, 224, 225
Donaldson, Sue, 224–225
Donovan, Josephine, 224
Dr. Seuss, 152
dualism, human–nature, 178, 186, 188n1, 189n6, 246
   *Homo dualismus*, 181–182, 183, 185
   human supremacy within, 179, 180
   monism compared to, 240, 241

Earle, Sylvia, 154
early modern era
   in Americas, 149–150
   in East Asia, 50
Earth, 210, 277
   ecosystem conservation percentages of, 117–118, 123
   gifts of, 267, 268–275
   gratitude for, 278
   sacred, 272
East Asia
   China, 27, 106, 150
   in early modern era, 50
Eastern Cape Parks, 135
EAT-Lancet Commission, 165
ecocentrism, 30, 123, 203–204, 247

ecocide, 210, 217
ecological custodianship, of Indigenous peoples, 99, 184
Ecological Society of America (ESA)
   Committee for the Study of Plant and Animal Communities of, 116
   Committee on the Preservation of Natural Conditions of, 115
ecologists, economic language adopted by, 64
Ecologists' Union, 116
The Economics of Ecosystems and Biodiversity project, 68
economy
   climate change relationship with, 64–65
   environmental activists on, 69
   food system decentralization benefiting, 170
   gift, 269
   global, 23
   green, 67
   pronatalist calls on, 26–27
   social ecological transformation of, 72–74
ecosocial justice, 260, 262
ecosystem conservation, 113
   Earth percentages of, 117–118, 123
   IUCN categories of, 117
   Jenkins on, 114
   predator species inclusion in, 116, 122
   Red List of Ecosystems on, 115
   through restoration, 119–121
   through rewilding, 121–123
ecosystems, 119
   functionality of, 103–104, 105
   keystone species engineering, 103
   restoration of, 184
   rewilding of, 102–104
ecotechnics, Greer on, 157

education. *See also* Maple Ridge Environmental School
  in Canada, 15, 251, 253–256
  cultural change through, 262–263
  nature deficit disorder response of, 252
egoism, 86–87
Egypt, Cairo, 23, 25–26
electric grids, 51
electricity
  consumption, 37
  entropy, 51
Eliot, T. S., 92
Ellis, John, 50
*The Embers and the Stars* (Kohák), 7
emissions trading system (ETS), 66
  for GHGs, 65
  in Paris Agreement, 67
*The Emotional Lives of Animals* (Bekoff), 247n1
enchantment
  humans experiencing, 216
  with more-than-human world, 14, 45, 209, 214, 215–218
*Enchantment without Supernaturalism* (Griffin), 212
endangered species credits, 68
energy
  concentration, 52
  conservation, 59
  technology, 52–53
ENGOs. *See* environmental NGOs
Enlightenment, 275
environmental activists
  on economy, 69
  targeting of, 71–72
Environmental Defense Fund, 67
environmental injustice, 63
environmental NGOs (ENGOs), 63, 64, 67, 70–71
environmentalism, 63
  environmental pragmatism of, 64
  revisionist, 183–184, 185

environmentalists
  messaging of, 64
  political awareness of, 73–74
Eriksen, Marcus, 157
ESA. *See* Ecological Society of America
etherealization, 88
ethics
  animal, 223, 224
  assumptions within, 178
ETS. *See* emissions trading system
EU. *See* European Union
eugenics movement, 23, 27
Europe, fish population depletion in, 149
European Commission, Green Deal of, 70
European Union (EU), 65
Ewaso Lions, 135
existential crisis, 80
expansionist way of life, 16
extinction
  African predator species facing, 129
  biodiversity conservation relationship with, 100–101
  crisis, 1–2
  Sixth Mass Extinction, 5
Extinction Rebellion, 69
Ezemvelo KZN Wildlife, 135

family, pronatalism pressure from, 24
family planning, 23–24, 25–26, 28
faux leopard skin, 133
fences, for conservation, 129–131
fertility
  industry, 25
  rates, 27–28
fertilizers, synthetic, 168, 169, 171
Figueres, Christiana, 71
financial crisis, 2008, 66
financialization, 72
*Finding the Mother Tree* (Simard), 242
fire exclusion, from grasslands, 120

fire-maintained pine savannas, 120
fish populations
  historical, 145–146, 149–150
  industrial fishing impacting, 144, 146, 149–150, 155
  seafood, 151, 152, 153, 154, 157–158
  tuna, 154
fisheries management, 155
fishing, artisanal, 150, 156–157
fishing gear, marine life impacted by, 144
Fletcher, Colin, 193, 196
Foer, Jonathan Safran
  on dietary changes, 171
  on fish population deaths, 157
food systems, 12–13
  decentralization of, 169–170, 171
  environmental impacts of, 164
  GHGs produced by, 163, 171, 172
  human health impacts of, 165, 166
  middle class burdening, 22
  technological suites for, 57, 58
food waste, 164, 171–172
food web, of marine life, 146–147
Forbes, Jack, 149, 271
forests, 15, 245
  Amazon, 236
  Caledonian pine, 201
  deforestation of, 238, 240
  management of, 243
  sacred, 238–239, 246–247
fossil fuel, 51
  era, 9
  industry, 67
  1970s energy crisis, 59
Foster, Craig, 154
Foucault, Michel, 231
Frazer, James, 239
freedom, 81, 82
freshwater withdrawals, from food system, 164
Freud, Sigmund, 83

FridaysForFuture, 69
Furs for Life, 133
fusion power research, 54–55

Gagarin, Yuri, 143
Galbraith, John Kenneth, 38, 40
garbage, marine life impacted by, 148
GDP. *See* gross national product
G8+7, 68
geotagging, 199
German Federal Government, 68
Germany, 239, 241, 243
GHGs. *See* greenhouse gas emissions
gifts
  of Earth, 267, 268–275
  economy of, 269
  gratitude for, 273–275
  humility for, 271
  restraint for, 271–272
gladness, 273
Global Commission on the Economy and Climate, *Better Growth Better Climate* by, 66–67
Global Green New Deal, by UN Conference on Trade and Development, 70
Global North, 35, 37, 40
Global South, 40, 56
glyphosate, 5
Gnosticism, 210
God's-eye view, 186
*The Golden Bough* (Frazer), 239
Goldman Sachs, 71
Goodall, Jane, 237, 242, 246
Goodnow, J., 202
*Gorgias* (Plato), 211
Gorongosa National Park, Mozambique, 135
government subsidies, for industrial fishing, 151
Grand Canyon, 193
grasslands, restoration of, 119–120

294 | Index

gratitude, 15
  for gifts, 273–275
  prayers of, 274
  for salmon, 261–262
  as way of life, 275–278
Graves, Robert, 235
Gray, Joe, 13, 196
Great Britain, 55, 60, 201
Great Convergence, 269
Great Simplification, 89
Green Deal, of European Commission, 70
greenhouse gas emissions (GHGs)
  corporate polluters of, 67
  ETS for, 65
  food systems contributing to, 163, 171, 172
  Net Zero Asset alliance claims about, 71
  offsets, 65, 66
  regenerative agriculture offsetting, 169
greenwashing, 42
Greer, John Michael, 9, 89, 157
Greta effect, 66
grief, 177
Griffin, David Ray, 212
gross national product (GDP), 64
grouper, 154

Haberman, David
  on dualism and monism, 240
  on Tylor, 241
habitat protection, 116, 201
Hadot, Pierre, 14, 229
Hafez, 269–270
happiness, 81, 82
Haraway, D. J., 44
Harris, Jean, 151
Haverluck, Bob, 267, 277–278
HEAL Food Alliance, 163
healing, acts of, 276–277

Hegel, Georg Wilhelm Friedrich, 212
Heidegger, Martin, 39
Henning, Brian, 227
Hennings, Lori, 200
Heraclitus, 228–229
*Hidden Life of Trees* (Wohlleben), 237, 244
Holocene, 6, 276, 277
*homo aestheticus*, 84, 91
*Homo dualismus*, 181–182, 183, 185
*homo economicus*, 91
*Homo sapiens*, *Homo dualismus* compared to, 182
H1N1, 165
Honorable Harvest, Kimmerer on, 272
hope, 177, 188
Houge Mackenzie, S., 202
human capital, 68
human health, food systems impacting, 165, 166
human supremacy, 4, 5, 6, 30, 136, 149, 222, 246
  carrying capacity overlooked by, 21
  within human–nature dualism, 179, 180
  Schweitzer on, 247
human–animal relations, 223, 226
  aesthetics of existence for, 231
  Donaldson and Kymlicka on, 224–225
humanization, 2–4, 5, 6, 16
humans, 182, 186–187, 189n4
  enchantment experienced by, 216
  health of, 165, 166
  predator species conflict with, 133–135, 137
  teachers, 255, 258, 259, 261–262
  wilderness agency of, 184
humility, for gifts, 271
Husserl, Edmund, 39
Huxley, Aldous, 81

I humbly receive (Itadakimasu), 173
ICPD. See International Conference on Population and Development
ideology of progress, 50, 55, 57, 58
illegal wildlife trade, of predator species, 132–133
imaginaries, of consumer societies, 72, 73
imagineers, 86
*In the Shadow of Man* (Goodall), 242
India
  commercial tree exploitation in, 240
  Rahasthan, 137
Indigenous Law, biosynergy intimating, 106–107
Indigenous peoples, 7, 10, 149, 225
  ecological custodianship of, 99, 184
  Kwantlen, 260–261
individual consumption, 41, 42, 43
individualism, 86
Indra's net, 6–7
industrial agriculture, 157
  soil health impacted by, 168
  water pollution from, 164
  zoonotic diseases from, 165
industrial development, biodiversity impacted by, 101
industrial fishing, 12
  of China, 150
  fish populations impacted by, 144, 146, 149–150, 155
  government subsidies for, 151
  moratorium on, 155–156
  trawlers, 152–153
infertility, 24–25
InfluenceMap, 71
inhumanist aesthetics, more-than-human world perceived through, 14, 226–227, 231–232
innovation, 53, 56
  of sustainable technologies, 54–55
  of technology, 88

institutional consumption, individual consumption compared to, 42, 43
insurers, catastrophe profits of, 72
International Conference on Population and Development (ICPD), 23, 25–26
International Union for Conservation of Nature (IUCN), 114
  ecosystem conservation categories of, 117
  Red List of Ecosystems of, 115
intractable quandary, 237–238, 244, 247
invasive species, 180
inverted quarantine, 39, 43
irrigation water, 171
*Itadakimasu* (I humbly receive), 173
IUCN. See International Union for Conservation of Nature

Jackson, Jeremy, 154, 158
Jain religion, 245–246
Japan, in early modern era, 50
Japanese forestry *(Daisugi)*, 246
Jeffers, Robinson, 14, 226, 230
Jenkins, Robert E., 114
*Journal of Outdoor Recreation and Tourism*, 199

Kakabadse, Yolanda, 71
*kalocentric* approach, 227
Kant, Immanuel, 211–212
Kareiva, Peter, 71
Kendeigh, S. C., 116
Kenya, Africa, 135
Keohane, Nat, 67
keystone species, 103
Kimmerer, Robin Wall, 255, 268, 271
  gratitude prayer of, 274
  on Honorable Harvest, 272
  on reciprocity, 274–275
kin, making, 44, 45

Kirby, Keith, 239
Kohák, Erazim, 7
Kopina, Helen, 15, 239
krill, sustainable fishing of, 151
Kwantlen, salmon relationship with, 260–261
Kymlicka, Will, 224–225
Kyoto Protocol, Clean Development Mechanism of, 65–66

labor, division of, 44
Lai, Bun, 163
land ethic, of Leopold, 123
land use, for livestock farming, 166, 245
Law, Deep
  conservation dictated by, 108, 109
  rewilding protocol of, 107–109
law of diminishing returns, innovation impacted by, 54
Law of Progressive Simplification, 88
Leadbeater, Simon, 15, 200
least resistance (and accommodation), 104–105
Leave No Trace, 13, 196–198, 199
leopards
  in illegal wildlife trade, 132
  in India, 137
  Panthera's Furs for Life program for, 133
Leopold, Aldo, 11, 123
von der Leyen, Ursula, 70
liberation, 185
libraries, public, 58
liminal animals, 224, 225
*Limits to Growth* (Meadows, Randers and Behrens), 49
Lion Guardians, 135
lions
  in Africa, 130, 131, 132, 134
  extinction facing, 129
  fencing for, 130
  in illegal wildlife trade, 132
  in Namibian conservancies, 134
  trophy hunting of, 131
livestock, 4–5, 167–168
  CAFOs for, 164, 166
  middle class consumption of, 22–23
livestock farming, 221
  climate change impacted by, 238, 247
  compensatory mechanisms for, 135
  and human–predator species conflict, 133–135
  land use for, 166, 245
lobsters, 154
logging, restoration through, 120
logic of oppression, 181–182, 185
Louv, Richard, 252, 257, 261
Luke, Timothy, 41–42

Maathai, Wangari, 1
Madrid negotiations, UN, 67
Malawi, 130, 135
managed wildfire, 120
mangroves, shrimp aquaculture impacting, 154
Maple Ridge Environmental School
  nature colonization at, 256–260
  nature coteaching at, 253–255, 256
  play at, 256–257, 259–260
  students at, 254–255, 256–257, 259–260
marine life
  biodiversity of, 148, 155, 156
  climate change impacting, 146
  conservation of, 12, 156, 158
  depletion of, 143–148
  fishing gear impacting, 144
  food web of, 146–147
  plastic impacting, 148, 157, 170
  terrestrial life relationship with, 148–149
  trawlers impacting, 152–153

Marx, Karl, 212
material affluence, 85
Mather, Cotton, 240
Mathews, Freya, 10
Maxwell, Sean, 1–2
Meadows, Donella, 49
meaning
  art and aesthetic creative engagement with, 82–84, 85, 90
  in midlife, 25
  politics and poetics of, 84–86
  utopian society questioning, 79–82
meat alternatives, 167
media
  on pronatalism, 24, 29
  social, 133
Memmi, Albert, 258–259
middle class, livestock consumption of, 22–23
Middle East, illegal cheetah trading in, 133
midlife, meaning in, 25
militarism, 6
Miller, A. B., 202
Miller, Vince, 177
mining, deep-sea, 153
monism, human–nature dualism compared to, 240, 241
de Montaigne, Michel, 214
Moore, Kathleen Dean, 15, 267, 277
*Moral Ground* (Nelson and Moore), 277
moral residue, 187–188
more-than-human world, 4–5, 188n2. *See also* nonhuman nature
  enchantment with, 14, 45, 209, 214, 215–218
  inhumanist aesthetics perception of, 14, 226–227, 231–232
  restraint toward, 8, 44
Moskowitz, David, 197, 198–199, 201, 204

Mother Trees, 243
Mozambique (Africa)
  Gorongosa National Park in, 135
  illegal wildlife trade in, 132
Muir, John, 193, 196, 198

Namibia, Africa, 134, 135
national parks, 195
National Wildlife Federation, 70–71
native species, 180
*natura naturans* (nature doing what nature does), 121
natural capital, 22, 68, 71, 213
natural heritage program network, 114
Natural Resources Defense Council, 71
nature
  colonization of, 256–260
  conflict and competition in, 105
  conservation of, 98
  as coteacher, 253–256
  cultural change supported by, 260–262
  nonhuman nature and, 179–180
  philosophy of death on, 213
  rewilding led by, 103
  Romantic era significance of, 98–99
  student encounter with, 254–255
*Nature*, 3
*Nature* (Simard), 242
The Nature Conservancy, 71, 114, 116
nature deficit disorder (NDD), 15, 251, 257–258
  cultural change around, 253, 262, 263
  education response to, 252
nature doing what nature does (*natura naturans*), 121
NDD. *See* nature deficit disorder
Nelson, Michael P., 277

Net Zero Asset alliance, WWF and UN Environment Programme Finance Initiative launching, 71
net zero emissions, 65, 66
New Deal for Nature, of UN Environment Programme, 70
New England, US, 240
New South Wales, Australia, 69
Nietzsche, Friedrich, 84, 213
1970s
  appropriate technology movement of, 59
  wilderness conservation in, 98, 99
no action (wu wei), 107, 108
"no take" marine areas, 156
nonhuman nature, 188n2, 230. *See also* more-than-human world
  nature and, 179–180
  respect for, 199–204
nonviolence *(ahimsa)*, 246
normative logic of life, 104–106
North American Coastal Plain, 120
Noss, Reed, 11
  on conservation, 196
  on rewilding, 121–122

Oceana, 157
oceans. *See also* marine life
  exploitation of, 145
  pollution of, 157
  rewilding of, 158
octopus, 154
Odum, E. P., 117
Odum, H. T., 117
OECMs. *See* other effective area-based conservation measures
oil companies, green rebranding of, 71
Oliver, Mary, 271
one-child policy, of China, 27
ontology, 268
oppression, 13, 181–182, 185, 186, 188

Oregon, US, 188
other effective area-based conservation measures (OECMs), 117
othering, 181, 182, 258–259
Ottey, Darcy, 197, 198–199, 201, 204
Ought, 106, 107, 109
*Our Common Future* (World Commission on Environment and Development), 63. *See also* Brundtland Report
outdoor recreation, 13
  animals impacted by, 194
  codes for, 196–199
  ecocentric questions on, 203–204
  nonhuman nature relationship with, 199–204
  resource footprint of, 201–202
  restraint in, 200–201
  wilderness impacted by, 194–195
overfishing, fish populations impacted by, 144, 146, 149–150, 155
overpopulation, 8
  pronatalism and, 24–28
  in sub-Saharan Africa, 136
overshoot, 21, 23, 30
  overpopulation and, 28
  vulnerable populations impacted by, 22
oyster beds, 150–151

Packham, Chris, 201
paganism, Christianity overthrowing, 241
Panthera, 133
Panthera's Furs for Life, 133
Paris Agreement, 72
  ETS in, 67
  oil company green rebranding after, 71
Parmenides, 210
Paul (Saint), 211

Pauly, Daniel, 154, 155
*People's Manifesto for Wildlife* (Packham), 201
perpetual motion machines, 54
pesticides, synthetic, 169
petroleum, energy concentration of, 52
*Phaedo* (Plato), 211
philosophy, utilitarian, 81, 137
philosophy of death, 14, 217
   hierarchy of, 212
   on nature, 213
   Plato on, 211
   Plutarch on, 210
photovoltaic cells (PV), 53
Plant Initiative, 245
plant sentience, 15, 236
   Calvo on, 242
   intractable quandary from, 237–238, 244, 247
   Simard on, 243
*Planta Sapiens* (Calvo), 237, 242
plant-based foods, 167–168
   diet foundation of, 165–166, 245, 247
   Jain religion on, 245–246
plastics
   marine life impacted by, 148, 157, 170
   single-use, 170
Plato, 211, 214, 240
Platonism, 210–211
play, at Maple Ridge Environmental School, 256–257, 259–260
Plotica, Luke Philip, 8–9
Plumwood, Val, 181, 213
Plutarch, 210
poet-farmers
   ecological civilization of, 86–92
   SMPLCTY citizens of, 91
policies, pronatalist, 26, 27
political action, 42, 43, 73

political activism, 73, 74
pollution
   from industrial agriculture, 164
   ocean, 157
   plastic, 148, 157, 170
population denialism, 23–24
Population Media Center, 29
postconsumerism, 87
prayers, of gratitude, 274
predator species, 105
   in Africa, 129, 130–138
   apex, 103, 108
   cheetahs, 133, 134
   conservation of, 130–131, 133, 134, 135, 138
   ecosystem conservation including, 116, 122
   human conflict with, 133–135, 137
   illegal wildlife trade of, 132–133
   trophy hunting of, 131–132
Pressey, R. L., 118
prey species, 105
*Primitive Culture* (Tylor), 240–241
proanimal discourse, 227
production
   consumption relationship with, 35–36, 38
   technological optimism of, 37
Project Drawdown, 168
projects of oppression, 181–182
pronatalism
   bias, 8
   media on, 24, 29
   overpopulation and, 24–28
   policies promoting, 26, 27
   religious leaders promoting, 25–26
public relations firms, 70
PV. *See* photovoltaic cells

Rahasthan, India, 137
Randers, J., 49
rattlesnakes, 193

reciprocity, 268
　of gifts, 274–275
　interspecies, 103, 105
recreation ecology, 194, 204
recyclable materials, 170
Red List of Ecosystems, of IUCN, 115
Regan, Tom, 222, 223
regenerative agriculture, 168–169, 170–171
regulation
　of illegal wildlife trade, 133
　of trophy hunting, 131
relative deprivation, absolute deprivation compared to, 40–41
religion, 91
religious leaders, pronatalism promoted by, 25–26
renewable resources, 51
reparations
　ecosystem restoration, 184
　slavery, 164, 189n5
reproductive autonomy, 28–30
reproductive responsibility, 28–30
reproductive rights violations, 23
*Republic* (Plato), 211
resource consumption, 22
resource footprint
　of outdoor recreation, 201–202
　of solar power, 53
　thermodynamic limit of, 52–53
respect, 10, 12
　for animals, 167
　through conservation, 11
　for nonhuman nature, 199–204
　in outdoor recreation, 13
restoration
　ecosystem conservation through, 119–121
　of ecosystems, 184
　of grasslands, 119–120
restraint, 21
　in consumption, 8–9, 10, 35–46
　for gifts, 271–272
　toward more-than-human world, 8, 44
　in outdoor recreation, 200–201
　of reproductive responsibility, 30
　in technology, 9
retrovation, 53–56
reverence, 218
　enchantment rediscovered through, 14
　through gratitude, 15
revisionist environmentalism
　conservation decolonization of, 183–184
　on sustainability, 185
　wilderness preservation and restoration of, 184
rewilding, 116
　of African predator species, 135–136
　Deep Law protocol of, 107–109
　ecosystem conservation through, 121–123
　of ecosystems, 102–104
　of oceans, 158
　Soulé and Noss on, 121–122
Richter, Jessica, 236–237
Ripple, W. J., 136
Roberts, Callum
　on fish population depletion, 144, 145, 150, 152
　*The Unnatural History of the Seas* by, 145
rockweed, 270
*Rolling Stone*, Thunberg interviewed in, 70
Romantic era, nature's significance in, 98–99
Rosa, Hartmut, 38
Rousseau, Jean-Jacques, 45
Royal Society for the Protection of Birds, 201
Rwanda, 130, 135

Sacramento, California, 177
salmon, 154
   gratitude for, 261–262
   student interactions with, 260–262
savannas, 119, 120
Schopenhauer, Arthur, 212
Schweitzer, Albert, 247
science
   climate change, 73
   environmental, 178
Scientific Revolution, 211
Scotland
   Abernethy National Nature Reserve in, 201
   deer browsing reduction in, 202
   outdoor recreation codes in, 197
sea turtles, 146, 154
seabed, trawlers impacting, 152
seabird population decline, 151
seafood, 151, 152, 154, 158
   consumer ignorance about, 153
   dietary avoidance of, 157
seamounts, trawlers impacting, 152–153
*The Secret Life of Trees* (Tudge), 238
Seife, Charles, 55
shark finning operations, 151
Shelford, Victor E.
   ESA leadership of, 115, 116
   on rewilding, 121, 122
Shembe Church, 132
Shoushan National Nature Park, Taiwan, 197
shrimp, 154
Sierra Club, 71
Simard, Susan, 242–243, 244
Simon, Gregory, 197–198, 201
simplification, voluntary, 87, 89, 91
   industrial civilization collapse without, 90
   technological innovation and dematerialization within, 88

Singer, Isaac Bashevis, 213
Singer, Peter, 222–223
Sisyphus, 82
Sixth Mass Extinction, 5
slavery, in US, 164, 189n5
Smith, Adam, 35, 36, 37, 44
SMPLCTY, 86, 89–90
   art and aesthetics in, 91–92
   in civilizations, 87–88, 91
   poet-farmer citizens in, 91
Sobel, D., 256
social acceleration, 38
social capital, 68
social ecological economies, 72–74
*The Social History of the Machine Gun* (Ellis), 50
social media platforms, illegal wildlife trade regulated on, 133
socialism, capitalism compared to, 42
sociopsychological malaise, 16
soil health
   industrial agriculture impacting, 168
   regenerative agriculture crop initiatives benefiting, 169
solar power, 51
   resource footprint of, 53
   sustainable uses of, 52
solar water heating, 53
Somaliland, 133
Soulé, Michael, 121–122
South Africa, 132, 135
Southeastern Grasslands Institute, 119
Soviet Union, GHG emissions impacted by, 66
Spash, Clive, 9
species conservation, 113
   coarse filter for, 114, 115
   fine filter for, 114
   of native species, 180
speciesism, 222
*Spell of the Sensuous* (Abram), 7

Spinoza, Baruch, 104
Stade, Kirsten, 8
stakeholder capitalism, 70
Stanford University, natural capital project of, 71
sterilization, voluntary, 25
Stern, Nicholas
  *Better Growth Better Climate* lead by, 66–67
  on climate change and economic growth, 64–65
students
  at Maple Ridge Environmental School, 254–255, 256–257, 259–260
  nature encounter of, 254–255
  salmon interactions of, 260–262
sub-Saharan Africa, 135, 136
Sukhdev, Pavan, 68, 71
sunlight, energy concentration of, 52
superfoods, 165
supply chain, of solar water heating, 53
sustainability, 68, 185
sustainable development, 63, 101
sustainable finance, 72
sustainable fishing, 151, 155
sustainable technological suites
  adoption strategies for, 59–60
  regional and national basis for, 59
sustainable technologies
  development pitfalls of, 54–55
  unsustainable technologies compared to, 58
synergy, of interspecies reciprocity, 105
Szasz, Andrew, 39, 42

Taiwan, Leave No Trace in, 197
Tanzania (Africa)
  illegal wildlife trade in, 132
  trophy hunting in, 131
taxonomic expansionism, 144, 153, 154
teachers, human, 255, 258, 259, 261–262
technological optimism, 36, 37, 39, 54–55
technological suites
  for food systems, 57, 58
  substitutions in, 56–57
  sustainable, 59–60
technology, 50–51, 60
  appropriate technology movement, 59
  energy, 52–53
  innovation of, 88
  restraint in, 9
  retrovation, 53–56
technosphere, humanization driven by, 2–4
Tercek, Mark, 71
terrestrial life, marine life relationship with, 148–149
Tessman, Lisa, 187–188
Thanksgiving, 275–276
thanksgiving, rituals of, 276
thermodynamic limits, 51
  of energy concentration, 52
  of resource footprint, 52–53
Thoreau, Henry David, 46
  on affluence and meaning, 83
  on division of labor, 44
  on wilderness, 102
throwaway societies, 38
Thunberg, Greta, 66
  FridaysForFuture fronted by, 69
  *Rolling Stone* interview with, 70
Tolkein, J. R. R., 216
Tolstoy, Leo, 167
Toynbee, Arnold, 88
Trade Records Analysis of Flora and Fauna in Commerce (TRAFFIC), 132

transhumanism, 213, 217
trawlers
  seabed impacted by, 152
  seamounts impacted by, 152–153
Tread Lightly!, 197
tree sentience, 236, 237, 242, 243, 246
trees, 235–236
  harvesting from, 246, 247
  human–nature dualism and monism informing, 240
  Mother Trees, 243
  Wohlleben on, 243–244
trophy hunting, 131–132
Tudge, Colin, 238
tuna, 154
Tunisia, Africa, 258
Tylor, Edward, 240–241

*Übermensch*, 84
UN. *See* United Nations
UN Conference on Trade and Development, Global Green New Deal by, 70
UN Environment Programme, New Deal for Nature of, 70
UN Environment Programme Finance Initiative
  *Demystifying Materiality* by, 68
  Net Zero Asset alliance launched by, 71
UN Framework Convention on Climate Change, 71
United Nations (UN)
  Madrid negotiations, 67
  plastic pollution planetary crisis declaration of, 170
United States (US)
  Alaska, 267–268
  electricity generation entropy in, 51
  ENGOs in, 70
  environmental cultural divide in, 60
  food waste in, 171–172
  grassland loss in, 119
  New England, 240
  Oregon wildfires in, 188
  Sacramento, 177
  slavery in, 164, 189n5
  Thanksgiving in, 275–276
  US Wilderness Act, 99
  victory gardens in, 170
  wetland banking in, 68–69
*The Unnatural History of the Seas* (Roberts), 145
Unuigbe, Ngozi, 7
US. *See* United States
utilitarian philosophy, 81, 137
utopian society, 79–82, 84

Vatican, 25–26
victory gardens, in US, 170
Vincent, Amanda, 151
Virgin Group, 71

waste, 4
water, irrigation, 171
water heating, solar, 53
water pollution, from industrial agriculture, 164
Watson, Paul, 155
Weber, Max, 214, 215
Western modernity, 209, 216
wet markets, illegal wildlife trade at, 132
wetland banking, 68–69
whalers, 147
whales, population depletion of, 147–148, 151
whaling, 147–148
White, Lynn, Jr., 240, 241
Whitehead, Alfred North, 212
Whyte, Ian, 13
wild animals, 224, 225
*Wild Earth*, 121

wilderness
  biodiversity compared to, 100, 101
  conservation of, 98–100
  movement, 109
  outdoor recreation impacting, 194–195
  revisionist environmentalism approach to, 184
  valorization of, 101–102
Wilderness Act, US (1964), 99
wildfires, 120, 188, 236–237, 245
Will to Art, 91, 92
Wittgenstein, Ludwig, 212, 215
Wohlleben, Peter, 237, 243–244
Wolf, C., 136
*wood-wide-web*, 242–243
Working Group on Statistics for Sustainable Development, 68

World Commission on Environment and Development, Brundtland Report by, 63, 109n3
World Economic Forum, 69
World Wildlife Fund (WWF), 64, 71
Worm, Boris, 144
Wrolstad, Greta, 269, 278n1
wu wei (no action), 107, 108, 110n6
WWF. *See* World Wildlife Fund
Wyoming, Yellowstone, 237

Yellowstone, Wyoming, 237
yin-yang polarity, 106
Yosemite Valley, animal life in, 193

Zambia, Africa, 130, 135
Zimbabwe, Africa, 131
zoonotic diseases, 165
*Zoopolis* (Donaldson and Kymlicka), 224

www.ingramcontent.com/pod-product-compliance
Lightning Source LLC
Chambersburg PA
CBHW020638230426
43665CB00008B/221